T0394104

A New Era in Democratic Taiwan

In January 2016, Taiwan's former authoritarian ruler, the KMT, the Nationalist Party of China, lost control of both the presidency and the legislature. Having led the democratization process in Taiwan during the 1980s, it had maintained a winning coalition among big business, the public sector, green-collar workers and local factions. Until now.

A New Era in Democratic Taiwan identifies past, present and future trajectories in party politics and state-society relations in Taiwan. Providing a comprehensive examination of public opinion data, it sheds light on significant changes in the composition of political attitudes among the electorate. Through theoretical and empirical analyses, this book also demonstrates the emergence of a 'new' Taiwanese identity during the transition to democracy and shows how a diffusion of interests in society has led to an opening for niche political organizations. The result, it argues, is a long-term challenge to the ruling parties.

As the first book to evaluate Taiwan's domestic and international circumstances after Tsai's election in 2016, this book will be useful for students and scholars of Taiwan Studies and cross-Strait relations, as well as Asian politics more generally.

Jonathan Sullivan is Associate Professor in the School of Politics and International Relations (SPIR) at the University of Nottingham, UK, where he is also Director of the China Policy Institute and the China Soccer Observatory.

Chun-Yi Lee is Associate Professor in the School of Politics and International Relations (SPIR) at the University of Nottingham, UK, where she is also Director of the Taiwan Studies Programme.

Routledge Research on Taiwan Series

Series Editor: Dafydd Fell

SOAS, UK

The *Routledge Research on Taiwan Series* seeks to publish quality research on all aspects of Taiwan studies. Taking an interdisciplinary approach, the books will cover topics such as politics, economic development, culture, society, anthropology and history.

This new book series will include the best possible scholarship from the social sciences and the humanities and welcomes submissions from established authors in the field as well as from younger authors. In addition to research monographs and edited volumes, general works or textbooks with a broader appeal will be considered.

The Series is advised by an international Editorial Board and edited by *Dafydd Fell* of the Centre of Taiwan Studies at the School of Oriental and African Studies, London.

For more information about this series, please visit: www.routledge.com/asian studies/series/RRTAIWAN

A New Era in Democratic Taiwan

Trajectories and Turning Points in Politics and Cross-Strait Relations

Edited by Jonathan Sullivan and Chun-Yi Lee

Routledge
Taylor & Francis Group

LONDON AND NEW YORK

First published 2018
by Routledge
2 Park Square, Milton Park, Abingdon, Oxon OX14 4RN

and by Routledge
711 Third Avenue, New York, NY 10017

Routledge is an imprint of the Taylor & Francis Group, an informa business

British Library Cataloguing-in-Publication Data
A catalogue record for this book is available from the British Library

Library of Congress Cataloging-in-Publication Data
Names: Sullivan, Jonathan, editor. | Lee, Chun-Yi, editor.
Title: A new era in democratic Taiwan : trajectories and turning points in politics and cross-strait relations / edited by Jonathan Sullivan and Chun-yi Lee.
Description: New York : Routledge, [2018] | Series: Routledge research on Taiwan series | Includes bibliographical references and index.
Identifiers: LCCN 2018004348| ISBN 9781138062429 (hardback) | ISBN 9781315161648 (ebook)
Subjects: LCSH: Political culture–Taiwan. | Political parties–Taiwan. | Democracy–Taiwan. | National characteristics, Taiwan–Political aspects. | Taiwan–Politics and government–2000- | Taiwan–Foreign relations–China. | China–Foreign relations–Taiwan.
Classification: LCC JQ1536 .N49 2018 | DDC 320.951249–dc23
LC record available at https://lccn.loc.gov/2018004348

ISBN: 978-1-138-06242-9 (hbk)
ISBN: 978-1-315-16164-8 (ebk)

Typeset in Times New Roman
by Wearset Ltd, Boldon, Tyne and Wear

Contents

Figures

Tables

Contributors

Nathan F. Batto is an Associate Research Fellow at the Institute of Political Science, Academia Sinica, Taiwan, and he holds a joint appointment at the Election Study Center, National Chengchi University, Taiwan. Dr Batto specializes in electoral systems and legislative studies and has published in journals such as *Electoral Studies, Legislative Studies Quarterly*, and *Women, Politics, & Policy*. His recent book is *Mixed-Member Electoral Systems in Constitutional Context: Taiwan, Japan, and Beyond* (co-edited with Chi Huang, Alexander C. Tan, and Gary W. Cox, 2016).

Dafydd Fell is Reader in Comparative Politics with special reference to Taiwan in the Department of Political and International Studies of the School of Oriental and African Studies (SOAS), University of London, UK. He is also the Director of the SOAS Centre of Taiwan Studies. He has published numerous articles on political parties and electioneering in Taiwan. He is also the book series editor for the Routledge Research on Taiwan Series.

Chien-san Feng is Professor in the Department of Journalism at National Chengchi University, Taiwan. As a political economist of communication, he has published seven books in Chinese, including *Media Publicness and the Market* (2012). Moreover, he has (co-)translated 16 books from English into Chinese, including John Roemer's *For a Future of Socialism*, Edwin Baker's *Media Markets and Democracy*, Dan Schiller's *Theorizing Communication: A History*, and James Curran *et al.*'s *Misunderstanding the Internet*.

Edward Friedman is Emeritus Professor in the Department of Political Science, College of Letters and Science at the University of Wisconsin, USA. Professor Friedman's research interests are China, democratization, globalization, human rights, political economy, post communism, revolution. He has long been involved with the politics of democracy in an autonomous Taiwan threatened by the CCP state. Starting as a graduate student first in Taiwan in 1964, 1965 and 1966, then as a participant in 1969 in the discussion on China–Taiwan relations for the Kissinger National Security Council, and then as the China–Taiwan staff person for Congressman Steve Solarz in 1981, 1982 and 1983 working on protecting the Kaohsiung prisoners and promoting democracy on Taiwan. He was the chief editor and organizer for the 2012 translation and publication of Yang Jisheng's study of the worst famine in human history, *Tombstone*.

Ming-sho Ho is Professor in the Department of Sociology at the National Taiwan University, Taiwan. He researches social movements, labor and environmental issues. His recent publications include *Working Class Formation in Taiwan* (New York, 2014) and *Challenging Beijing's Mandate from Heaven: Taiwan's Sunflower Movement and Hong Kong's Umbrella Movement* (Temple University Press, 2019).

Saša Istenič is Assistant Professor in the Department of Asian Studies at the University of Ljubljana, Slovenia, and Director of the Taiwan Study Center in Slovenia. She is also an Executive Board Member of the Slovene East Asia Resource Library (EARL), an Associate Board Member of the *International Journal of Taiwan Studies* (IJTS) and a former Executive Board Member of the European Association of Taiwan Studies (EATS).

Chun-Yi Lee is Associate Professor in the School of Politics and International Relations (SPIR) at the University of Nottingham, UK. Her current research project is 'Chinese Investment in Taiwan: Opportunities or Challenges to Taiwan's Industrial Development?' Dr Lee is the Director of the Taiwan Studies Programme at Nottingham University.

Frank Muyard is Assistant Professor, National Central University, Taiwan, and Head of the Ecole Française d'Extrême-Orient's Taipei Center (EFEO, French School of Asian Studies). He was previously Taiwan Fellowship Scholar at the Research Center for Humanities and Social Sciences, Academia Sinica, and Director of the French Center for Research on Contemporary China (CEFC) Taipei Office. His research focuses on political, cultural, and historical sociology, in particular on the issues of modernity and nationalism. He is currently researching the history of Taiwanese archaeology and its interactions with nationalism and indigenous peoples. Recent publications include 'Taiwan Archaeology and Indigenous Peoples' in L. Hung ed., *Archaeology, History and Indigenous Peoples* (Taipei: Shung Ye Museum, 2016); 'Voting Shift in the November 2014 Local Elections in Taiwan', *China Perspectives*, 2015/1; 'Comparativism and Taiwan Studies', in S. Shih and P. Liao eds, *Comparatizing Taiwan* (London: Routledge, 2015).

Ming-yeh T. Rawnsley is a Research Associate in the Centre of Taiwan Studies, School of Oriental and African Studies (SOAS), University of London, UK and Non-Resident Senior Fellow, Taiwan Studies Programme, University of Nottingham, UK. She was also Secretary-General, European Association of Taiwan Studies (2012–2018) and Editor-in-Chief of the *International Journal of Taiwan Studies* (IJTS, 2017–present). She has published widely in both English and Chinese on the subjects of Taiwan media, cinema and culture. Her most recent book is *Taiwan Cinema: International Reception and Social Change* (edited with Kuei-fen Chiu and Gary Rawnsley, 2017).

Shelley Rigger is Brown Professor and Assistant Dean for Educational Policy in the Political Science Department at Davidson College, North Carolina, USA. She is the author of *Why Taiwan Matters: Small Island, Global Powerhouse* (2011) as well as two books on Taiwan's domestic politics, *Politics in Taiwan: Voting for Democracy* (Routledge, 1999) and *From Opposition to Power: Taiwan's Democratic Progressive Party* (2001). She has also published articles on Taiwan's domestic politics, the national identity issue in Taiwan–China relations and related topics. Her monograph, *Taiwan's Rising Rationalism: Generations, Politics, and 'Taiwan Nationalism'* was published by the East West Center in Washington, DC. Her current research studies the effects of cross-Strait economic interactions on Taiwan people's perceptions of mainland China.

James Smyth is a Master in Public Affairs candidate in the International Relations field at Princeton University's Woodrow Wilson School of Public and International Affairs, USA, as well as a 2018 U.S. government Presidential Management Fellows Finalist. He has previously worked as an editor and translator for the Republic of China (Taiwan) Executive Yuan, as an Assistant Language Teacher in the Japan Exchange and Teaching Programme, and as a research intern at the Institute of Energy Economics, Japan. He earned his bachelor's degree at Duke University, NC, USA, graduating cum laude with a major in Philosophy and minors in Mathematics and Spanish.

Jonathan Sullivan is Associate Professor in the School of Politics and International Relations (SPIR) at the University of Nottingham, UK, a China specialist, political scientist, and Director of the China Policy Institute at the University of Nottingham, UK. Dr Sullivan is interested in most aspects of Chinese life, from his specialist research on political behaviour and political communications to distinctly amateur interests in Chinese literature, movies, music, and, naturally, food.

1 Introduction

Jonathan Sullivan and Chun-Yi Lee

On 16 January 2016, President Tsai Ing-wen was elected 14th President of the Republic of China (ROC). Her party, the Democratic Progressive Party (DPP), also returned a majority of seats in the Legislative Yuan. The 2016 elections were the sixth time the ROC president has been elected by popular vote and the eighth general election of all representatives to the Legislative Yuan. They also represent the third turnover of party-in-power, and the first time that the Democratic Progressive Party (DPP) has won simultaneous control of the presidency and the legislature. These are practical changes in the composition of political power in Taiwan. But Tsai's victory is also symbolically important. First, Tsai is the ROC's first female president, and the only elected female leader of a Chinese-heritage polity. That gender hardly featured as an issue in her election is indicative of a society in Taiwan where "tradition" is becoming less of a barrier to political participation. Second, Tsai is a descendant of both Hakka and aboriginal ethnic groups. Within three months of her inauguration, on 1 August 2016, she formally apologized to Taiwan's indigenous peoples for past injustices and unequal conditions imposed upon them under successive ROC governments (Ramzy, 2016). Tsai's apology suggests an opportunity for Taiwan to embrace its minority peoples and redress the unfair treatment they have received in Taiwanese society. Third, the election of legislators representing small parties with social movement roots was a symbol of continuing support for diverse and progressive causes, and a demonstration that such causes can lead to political success.

For all these signs that Taiwan's democracy is in rude health, Tsai Ing-wen faces substantial challenges. In terms of China, an existential threat and predominant economic partner, she inherits a relationship that is more intense and multifaceted than any of her predecessors faced. The vast scale of economic interactions across the Taiwan Strait has implications for virtually every policy sector in Taiwan, touching on the most basic elements of Taiwanese life, from education and housing to employment opportunities and the cost of living. Positions and processes initiated by outgoing President Ma Ying-jeou constrain Tsai's policy alternatives. Acceptance of the "1992 Consensus" of "one China, respective interpretations", for instance, has solidified as a necessary condition for cooperation with China. Tsai, consistent with many Taiwanese, rejects the notion that an ad hoc agreement between the Chinese Communist Party (CCP) and a then-unelected KMT (Chinese Nationalist Party) should dictate democratic Taiwan's options. Yet, Tsai's refusal to acknowledge the "1992 Consensus" quickly soured cross-Strait relations, with Beijing breaking off governmental communications, imposing limits on Chinese tourist visits and wooing Taiwan's diplomatic allies. As China's economic and military capabilities, and global influence, continue to grow, Tsai must balance domestic constraints with the reality of China's preferences and power. She has consistently evinced a moderate position on cross-Strait relations, insisting that she will uphold the "status quo", recognizing the diplomatic and economic constraints that Taiwan faces. However, Beijing views her with great suspicion, including her ability to control the factions within the DPP that support "Taiwan independence".

Despite the justified domestic opposition to Ma's China policy, he successfully oversaw the management of the cross-Strait relationship, a challenge that Tsai Ing-wen and the DPP have found difficult. From the missile crisis during Lee's tenure to the formal gridlock, the unseemly "dollar diplomacy" and international isolation characteristic of the Chen era, cross-Strait relations had never been as outwardly warm as they were under Ma. Apart from the early breakthroughs made during Lee's time as unelected President, the institutionalization of cross-Strait interactions fostered by Ma's China policy were by far the most impressive. Ma oversaw a substantial increase in trade and the economic value of cross-Strait interactions. On the other hand, Taiwanese society became more unequal, with a greater sense of widespread relative deprivation than ever before. Taiwan's dependence on and exposure to the Chinese economy are now greater than at any point in history, with concomitant vulnerabilities for Taiwan's national security. The underlying militarization of the Strait, embodied by approximately 1,800 Chinese missiles stationed across the Strait in Fujian Province, remains unchanged by Ma's China-friendly orientation. China's military posture represents an undiminished threat to Taiwan's national security. The passage of the PRC's Anti-Secession Law, China's growing military capacity and rapid modernization, the changing military balance in the Taiwan Strait, broad popular nationalism and the undiminished pressures of "hawks" within the CCP leadership (including the People's Liberation Army), threaten Taiwan's security environment.

While there are significant divisions in Taiwanese politics, and a lot of noise, there is a high degree of consensus in society and convergence between the major parties. Fundamentally, both major parties have limited room for manoeuvre when it comes to China policy: public opinion does not support extreme moves in either direction and the range of policy options is limited by Beijing's position and the reality of cross-Strait economic interdependence driven by market forces. Thus, the fact that the DPP controls both branches of government does not mean radical changes in China policy. Tsai is more pragmatic than former President Chen Shui-bian and she has inherited a complex set of foreign policy and socio-economic dynamics that require careful judgement. Tsai has pledged to recalibrate the Taiwanese economy, with a greater focus on distribution and addressing ongoing livelihood issues, such as increasing provision of affordable social housing and raising graduate salaries. While this reorientation is welcomed by many Taiwanese, there are obstacles outside her control that come with being closely tied to a turbulent global economy. The DPP has aspirations to internationalize Taiwan's economy, reducing reliance on China and integrating Taiwan into regional and pan-regional projects, and reanimating Lee Teng-hui's Southbound policy. But the lure of the Chinese market exerts a substantial pull over Taiwanese capital. Meanwhile Taiwan's participation in international society depends on PRC goodwill or acquiescence, qualities Beijing has not demonstrated since Tsai's election. As Xi Jinping has taken personal leadership of the PRC's Taiwan policy decision-making, marginalizing the Taiwan Affairs Office, Beijing's position on acceptance of "one China", even in the guise of "one China, respective interpretations", has hardened. Absent conciliatory gestures from Tsai that Beijing deems to be "sincere", Taiwan's remaining diplomatic allies will come under pressure to switch allegiances.

Tsai had emerged as leader of the DPP from the wreckage of Chen's second term, and successfully resuscitated the party. Unlike many DPP politicians, Tsai had little factional or ideological baggage and proved capable in balancing competing factions within the party. There were high hopes for Tsai's agenda as she entered office. But Taiwan has been here before. On assuming the presidency in 2008, similarly with a comfortable margin of victory and a substantial legislative majority for his party, Ma Ying-jeou's aims were to stabilize cross-Strait relations after a period of instability and deadlock during his predecessor Chen Shui-bian's tenure, to revive Taiwan's economic fortunes through closer integration with the Chinese economy, to balance the imperative of economic incentives with the maintenance of "national dignity", and to roll back the "de-Sinicization" elements of Chen's "Taiwanization" programme by emphasizing Taiwan's Chinese cultural heritage and situating Taiwan within the framework of the greater Chinese nation. But the optimism that greeted Ma's election quickly subsided, as the economic and social implications of his policies, and his disdain for Taiwan's democratic institutions, emerged over eight years.

Taiwan's famously even distribution of wealth became a thing of the past and social mobility was no longer something that Taiwanese could take for granted. Education was no longer the passport to mobility it once had been, with an increasing proportion of graduates earning a desultory NT$22,000 starting monthly salary (US$650). While widespread feelings of economic dissatisfaction took hold, corporations and individuals with political connections profited from opening up Taiwan's economy to China. Squandering a long-held reputation as stewards of the "Economic Miracle" in the 1960s and 1970s, the KMT came to represent the privileged and well connected. Taiwanese companies swapped investment in Taiwan for China (61 per cent of Taiwanese investments since 1991 have been in China), moving out R&D operations and depressing the domestic job market. Chinese investment in real estate caused bubbles and made housing unaffordable for ordinary Taiwanese. As in Hong Kong, an influx of

Chinese tourists exacerbated the sense of difference and antipathy towards people from the PRC. And Ma's espousal of Taiwan's commitment to being part of the imagined Chinese nation created resentment at perceived attempts to lock Taiwan into a narrowing range of future options.

With its "old guard" and "princelings", the KMT lost touch with the electorate, neglecting its changing demographics and preoccupations. The extent of this estrangement should have been clear in the spring of 2014, when two years of large-scale popular protests over various issues culminated in students occupying the Legislature for three weeks. Inexplicably, the KMT, which had long proved so skilful in adapting from authoritarian rule to the conditions of democratic competition, failed to heed the warnings. Instead their campaign strategies relied on using vastly superior financial resources to attack opponents via negative advertising and by leveraging long-nurtured factional networks, while the Party came under the sway of an unpopular pro-China faction. In the post-Sunflower era, these tactics failed to connect with voters, particularly the younger generation and their lived reality of stagnant wages, poor job prospects and little hope of getting onto the property ladder.

The emergence of a generational shift is a significant development in Taiwanese society. The notion that wise elders should take care of decision-making, in the family and in politics, has long been deeply embedded in Taiwan's political culture, underpinning and propagated by four decades of KMT one-party rule. Taiwan's transition to flourishing democracy is a rebuttal to the self-serving narratives of conservative, change-resistant elites. Taiwanese have proven that there is nothing inherent in Chinese or Confucian cultural heritage that disqualifies them from having a fully functioning democracy. Yet, the legacy of one-party rule and instrumental quasi-Confucian notions did not expire with the coming of elections. Political elites retained their sense, and carefully framed a narrative, about knowing what was best for the people. And many citizens, conditioned by decades of priming through the media and education systems, continued to have a narrow understanding of what democracy meant, sometimes complaining to pollsters that democracy was too messy and divisive. There is no democratic tradition in Chinese culture, and the late political scientist Tianjian Shi argued that many Taiwanese came to understand democracy via the idea of *minben* (民本), a restricted form of government by benevolent elites that he called "guardianship democracy" (Shi, 2015). More recent research shows that the attitudes towards authority that underpin support for this form of government are not widespread among young Taiwanese. The 19–35 cohort is more supportive of democracy as a political system, and accepting of the noise and contention that accompany it. And while they are more likely to call themselves Taiwanese, it is identification with democracy that is a crucial part of this trend. The cohort that has grown up under a democratic system takes for granted liberal democratic norms such as freedom of speech, accountability and transparency to a much greater extent than their elders, who had to "learn" them. This attitude change represents a significant challenge to the foundations of "guardian democracy", which is magnified by the popularization of digital and social media. Unlike their parents, younger cohorts have grown up with the norms associated with internet culture, where there is little deference to authority and obvious scepticism and mistrust of government. Befitting the generation that has rejected the notion of "guardian democracy", Taiwanese young people are politically active on a greater scale than their forebears, and their demand for accountability and transparency is something that will affect the contours of political competition for years to come.

Taiwan's transition to democracy was a process rather than a single event. However, the 1996 presidential election, the first direct election of that office, is the milestone from which Taiwan's democratic system can be traced. Taiwan has thus experienced more than two decades of democratically elected leadership, which provides a comparative context across time by which to evaluate the consolidation and direction of travel of Taiwan's democracy. This distance and perspective allow the contributors to this volume to evaluate the significance of the 2016 elections, situate longer-term developments and make an assessment about whether the election results and the societal trends that facilitated them signal a qualitative change, a new era in Taiwan's democracy.

Structure of the book

In Chapter 2, Batto's analysis of public opinion data identifies trends in the electorate that suggest significant changes in the composition of political attitudes. In short, Batto's data pour cold water on KMT supporters' hope that the election results could be laid at the feet of departing President Ma. In fact, despite Ma's personal shortcomings, his character was not responsible for the KMT's defeat, and thus this is not as easily remediable as removing Ma from the scene. Batto does find evidence for dissatisfaction focused on Ma's performance in the economy and providing for people's livelihood issues, but more significantly he argues that the 2016 election marked a transformative shift in Taiwan's political landscape. Large numbers of voters who had previously supported the KMT switched sides, throwing their weight behind the DPP. They did so because they discovered themselves at odds with the KMT on basic policy issues such as national identity, Taiwan's future status, and cross-Strait policy, the core issues in Taiwan's politics. Batto argues that this large cohort of switch voters have finally chosen the correct party, i.e. the one with policy preferences that most closely matches their own. The 2016 elections thus represent a re-alignment in which voters have finally got it right. If this realization lasts, and the KMT fails to reorient its own issue positions, the electoral landscape will have fundamentally altered, with the DPP set to be the dominant party for the foreseeable future.

Although the 2016 campaigns were fought predominantly on economic issues, national identity remains the core issue and the major cleavage in Taiwanese politics. It is, however, anything but static, as Muyard demonstrates in Chapter 3, in his rich theoretical and empirical analysis of the emergence of a 'new' Taiwanese identity during Taiwan's democratization processes. Marshalling longitudinal opinion data, Muyard shows how attitudes towards Taiwanese identity vary substantially by demographics. In short, there is substantially higher support for Taiwanese identity and independence among the younger cohorts educated during the transition and consolidation of democracy. Older generations express more support for dual and Chinese identity, the status quo and unification, emblematic of the "generation gap" that is fast becoming a major force in Taiwanese society. Muyard's sophisticated theoretical case explains why younger generations are more cohesive and less diverse in political views about the Taiwanese nation than older generations. His conclusion is portentous for proponents of unification. A new Taiwanese national identity defined by civic nationalism and multiculturalism has emerged in the past two decades and become pre-eminent, especially among the younger generations. Observed longitudinal trends in public opinion, which are unequivocally moving towards identification with Taiwan and disfavouring unification, will thus continue to colour electoral competition and restrict the range of policy options available to Taiwanese parties. Echoing Batto's analysis, Muyard's argument suggests that the DPP is best placed to dominate political competition, absent unforeseen changes in the KMT's core policy position.

Muyard's study also provides an explanation for another observation about the younger generations, their political activism. Internalizing expectations of transparency and procedural justice as fundamental features of democracy, young Taiwanese were responsible for the upsurge in social activism examined in Chapters 4 and 5 by Fell and Ho, respectively. The two chapters approach social movement mobilization in Taiwan in different ways. For Fell, the development of social movements has transformed the Taiwanese political terrain, rendering it more diverse and allowing causes to be fought outside of national identity politics. The emergence of small parties has given organizational forms to activist movements, and the successful entrance of the New Power Party (NPP), which emerged out of the Sunflower Movement, into electoral competition, has demonstrated a pathway for social movement activism into politics. After almost continuous mobilization during Ma's second term, social activists have not disappeared with Tsai's election, suggesting that popular discontent has become normalized as a mode of political participation. Activism and popular protest have already taken on the cause of pension cuts, the rising cost of utilities and most controversially, changes to the working week. Ho's deep analysis of the societal trends that reached a crescendo, but did not end, with the Sunflower Movement, shows that social activism has become a major political force that will continue to condition the behaviour of major political parties. Even though the DPP is closer in political alignment to the grassroots activists and non-governmental organizations (NGOs), the frequency of protests during Tsai's administration remains high. Both Ho and Fell's analyses suggest that the diffusion of interests in Taiwanese society has become untethered from the concerns of the major parties, opening space for niche political organizations but resulting in a longer-term challenge to ruling parties.

As Ho shows, while the advent and popularization of digital media communications are not responsible for social movements, they have changed their mobilization and communication strategies. As Sullivan *et al.*'s Chapter 6 on the evolution of Taiwan's media-sphere demonstrates, digital media have had a transformative effect on the information environment. Digital media have challenged the operating structures and norms of legacy media, and complicated the media's role and contribution to Taiwan's democracy. The authors' analysis of successive waves of media reform show how Taiwan has struggled to find a balance between regulation and market forces. For political and economic reasons, Taiwan has not found a solution to cultivating quality independent media, resulting in a polarized and politicized media-sphere. Unlike the one-party era, the problem of the media in Taiwan today is not control by the authoritarian regime, but dependence on capital which is unavoidably affiliated to political interests. As the chapter shows, this includes Chinese capital and the cultivation of Chinese interests, which are actively targeting Taiwanese media as a means to achieving political influence.

In Chapter 7, Friedman's analysis of Taiwan's position in the thinking of China's past and current leadership, and comprehensive review of the cross-Strait relationship, helps situate Tsai Ing-wen and Taiwan's situation and options within a historical-ideological framework. Friedman's analysis suggests China's intractable and hardening position on Taiwan is a relatively recent development, but that may be cold comfort for the Tsai administration facing a narrow range of options. Following Friedman's chapter on China's policy towards Taiwan, it is appropriate that Rigger asks in Chapter 8 whether that policy has failed. Rigger argues that China's Taiwan policies have succeeded in terms of preventing the worst-case scenario – a declaration of independence. Furthermore, the combination of military threats, economic incentives and international diplomatic pressure has effectively removed independence from Taipei's range of possible alternatives. This is a significant achievement. That said, Beijing has not made progress towards its best-case scenario, unification. The trends in Taiwanese politics and popular opinion are not promising, as Batto and Muyard's analyses unequivocally show. While the pro-China wing of the KMT threatens to marginalize the Party still further from the electorate, the DPP has found it is comfortable working in the framework of the ROC's existing "independence". Public opinion meanwhile has moved monotonically in the direction of an exclusive Taiwanese identity. In terms of encouraging Taiwanese to choose unification as a desired future choice for Taiwan, Chinese policy has failed to deliver results. One of the strategies that China has employed, with success, is to restrict Taiwan's ability to participate in international society. However, Istenič's Chapter 9 charting the waxing and waning of Taiwan's fortunes on the international stage, demonstrates that Taipei has been able to avoid isolation through a clever use of informal diplomacy and economic connections.

The symbolism and practical significance of Tsai and the DPP's election victories are considerable. However, in isolation, the current configuration of political power in Taiwan is an insufficient basis on which to argue that Taiwan's democracy has entered a "new era". Multiple changes in the ruling party since free and fair elections were introduced for all political offices strongly suggest that it would be unwise to predict the long-term dominance, or decline, or particular parties. As the experience of Chen Shui-bian and Ma Ying-jeou demonstrated, governing a changing, complex and diverse polity, one that is simultaneously subject to external influences in the form of integration into the global economy and an active threat from across the Strait, is difficult. It is a political cliché that governing is harder than winning the election. Thus, our characterization of a 'new democratic era' must be based on something more concrete than a single election. The contributions to this volume allow us to do just that, situating the socio-political trends that facilitated Tsai and the DPP's victory in a longer timeframe to identify continuities and change.

First, the continuities. Taiwan's relationship with China remains the major preoccupation, threat and vulnerability. While the DPP has made peace with the ROC framework, and, like the majority of the population, is content to maintain the "status quo" of functional autonomy or "*de facto* independence", Beijing is not. Having witnessed the difficulties its preferred Taiwanese political partner, the KMT, encountered in trying to press for greater economic integration, and observing the trends in self-identification, Beijing has to acknowledge that its repertoire of "carrots and sticks" has not delivered. But as its economic, military and diplomatic power surges globally, marshalled by a leader emboldened by his own consolidation of power, China has turned to other means, including strategic investments in the Taiwanese economy and cultivation of links with Taiwanese business and political elites and grassroots. It has successfully constrained Taiwan's participation in international society and its relations with the rest of the world. Consequently, Taiwan's international role is incommensurate with a major world economy and successful liberal democratic society. With significant anniversaries on the horizon in China, including centennials for the CCP and the PRC, pressure on Taipei will continue to define the parameters of Taiwan's options and behaviours. Despite the "new Southbound policy", Taiwan's economy continues to rely heavily on China, and economic interests served by cross-Strait business retain a significant influence in Taiwanese politics, where the two major parties also remain predominant. Although the emergence of smaller parties was a feature of the 2016 campaigns, the institutional architecture in Taiwan makes the two-party-dominant system hard to budge.

Given these fundamental continuities, in what sense is Taiwan entering a new era? While the fundamental parameters of Taiwanese politics externally and domestically remain intact, changing social attitudes demand that political actors in government, parties, the media, business and civil society recalibrate their positions. Generational change has changed expectations and behaviours, as more cohorts of young people are born into a democratic political system and society. As they become numerically dominant, these cohorts which have internalized liberal democratic norms and are willing to fight for them, not just online but on the streets, add a new component to political actors' decision-making calculus. The emergence of a "precariat" among young people where education is no longer a ticket to a job, housing is unaffordable and social mobility is not guaranteed, has turned young people into a political force, increasing the spread of issue and identity politics and giving rise to multiple pockets of single-issue activism and protest. This heterogeneity of interests complicates governance and electoral competition, but it is ameliorated by the consolidation of Taiwanese identity as a mainstream societal norm. While Taiwan's future status remains a question on which there are multiple viewpoints, consensus on what Taiwan is now is driven by Taiwanese identity and democratic norms.

References

Ramzy, A. (2016). "Taiwan's President Apologizes to Aborigines for Centuries of Injustice", *New York Times*, 1 August. Available at: www.nytimes.com/2016/08/02/world/asia/taiwan-aborigines-tsai-apology.html. (accessed 20 August 2017).

Shi, T. (2015). *The Cultural Logic of Politics in Mainland China and Taiwan*. New York: Cambridge University Press.

2 The KMT coalition unravels

The 2016 elections and Taiwan's new political landscape

Nathan F. Batto

The January 2016 presidential and legislative elections in Taiwan saw a disastrous meltdown for the long-time ruling Kuomintang (KMT) and swept the Democratic Progressive Party (DPP) into power with an unprecedented level of support. Tsai Ing-wen won the presidential election with 56.1 percent, the second highest percentage of votes for any candidate in the six elections since 1996. Though 2016 was not the first time the DPP had won the presidency, it was the first time that the DPP had won a majority in the legislature. During President Chen's eight years in office, a KMT-led coalition maintained a majority in the legislature and continually stymied Chen's ambitions. In 2016, the DPP secured 60.2 percent of the seats in the legislature and a firm grip on both executive and legislative power. The DPP's 2016 triumph followed its tidal wave in the November 2014 local elections, in which the DPP and its allies won control of 14 of the 22 local governments, including all but one of the six direct municipalities. Following the 2016 elections, the KMT had been reduced to 35 seats (31.0 percent) in the legislature, control of the New Taipei City government, and not much else. After seven decades, the KMT had been resoundingly booted out of power.[1]

In the aftermath of this momentous election, there are two fundamental questions. What happened? And will these changes be ephemeral or will they persist? The two questions are intimately related. If the election result represented short-term and relatively superficial impulses, the political balance of power might soon revert to the old pattern of KMT superiority. However, if the shift to the DPP reflected more basic shifts in some of the fundamental identities and issues defining Taiwanese politics, there is a good chance that the new political landscape will persist.

In this chapter, we argue that superficial factors, such as mobilization and dissatisfaction with President Ma's style, cannot account for the massive shift of voters away from the KMT. Instead, the election turned on more fundamental shifts related to the continuing growth of Taiwan identity. Ma managed to hold the old KMT majority coalition together one last time in 2012, but this coalition fractured during his second term. Large numbers of erstwhile Ma supporters shifted sides. Some turned to James Soong and the People's First Party (PFP). In the identity cleavage that defines Taiwanese politics, the PFP and KMT are on the same side vying for leadership of the Chinese nationalist camp. Since the two parties differ mainly on secondary issues, there is a reasonable chance that the KMT will be able to win these voters back in the future. However, defections to the PFP were not the KMT's main problem. Nearly twice as many erstwhile Ma supporters turned to the DPP as to the PFP. More importantly, the data suggest that these people switched sides for reasons related to the identity cleavage. If that is the case, it will be much harder for the KMT to win them back. Doing so would require them to either change their minds about their identities or the KMT to make basic and painful revisions to its core principles. More likely, these voters have permanently shifted sides and will be part of the DPP's coalition in the future.

Until now, the KMT has enjoyed a structural advantage in the electorate. The DPP might win if it had a particularly appealing candidate or if the electoral context were especially favorable. However, it was always fighting uphill. The tectonic shifts over the past few years have reversed those roles. Barring another dramatic and fundamental change, the KMT will be fighting uphill for the foreseeable future.

A cursory summary of President Ma's second term

President Ma's second term featured a relentless stream of bad news. Between repeated food scandals, military abuses, corruption cases, vicious KMT party infighting, massive street protests, constant agitation by social activists, legislative stalemates, terrible economic news, and a government that seemed tone-deaf to public opinion, there was almost no escape from the unending flow of bad news. By the time the 2016 elections arrived, it seemed as if everyone in Taiwan, including people from every corner of the political spectrum, was furious at the KMT and President Ma's administration. A blow-by-blow account of all the significant happenings during Ma's second term is beyond the scope of this chapter, though many of the more prominent events are briefly summarized in Table 2.1.

Perhaps the quickest way to summarize Ma's second term is to consider his three most important goals: (1) opening the fourth nuclear power plant; (2) passing the Services Trade Agreement; and (3) arranging a personal meeting with Chinese leader Xi Jinping. The first two ended in complete failure. The nuclear power plant was shuttered in the face of overwhelming popular opposition, and the Sunflower Movement ensured that the Services Trade Agreement would never pass the legislature. Ma did eventually secure a meeting with Xi. However, since the summit was held in the heat of a presidential campaign that everyone expected Ma's KMT to lose, the meeting was less of a triumph than it might have been had it been held earlier in his tenure. Domestically, the summit had very little impact on public opinion. Overall, the highlights of Ma's second term were rare and not that high while the lowlights were commonplace and very low. It was in the context of this terrible record in office that the KMT was swamped in the 2016 elections.

Table 2.1 Major events during President Ma's second term

Date	Event
January 2012	Ma wins re-election.
April–May 2012	The cabinet approves steep price increases in oil and electricity prices.
May 2012	Ma's second term begins.
March–July 2012	The cabinet promotes a capital gains tax as a way to raise revenue and redistribute wealth. The bill that finally passes is heavily watered down and widely panned.
June 2012	DPP legislators protest the cabinet's efforts to open the market to American beef.
June 2012	KMT Secretary General Lin Yi-shih arrested in a sensational corruption scandal.
2012	According to DGBAS, the economy grew 2.06% in 2012.
February 2013	Premier Sean Chen resigns due to low approval ratings. He is replaced by Jiang Yi-huah, a close ally of President Ma.
February 2013	Facing public opposition, Ma and Jiang do a turn-round and agree to hold a referendum on the fate of the fourth nuclear power plant. This decision backfires when polls show that opposition to nuclear power soars even higher. KMT legislators refuse to introduce the cabinet's unpopular referendum proposal.
June 2013	Taiwan and China sign the Services Trade Agreement (STA).
July 2013	Taipei city councillor Lai Su-ju is indicted for corruption. Lai had served in the KMT's Central Standing Committee and as spokesperson for Ma's 2012 campaign.
July 2013	Corporal. Hung Chung-chiu dies while being disciplined during his military service. Massive protests are organized by the internet-based group Citizen 1985 to protest military abuses.
September 2013	Frustrated with stalemate in the legislature, Ma attempts to purge Speaker Wang by accusing him of influence peddling and stripping his KMT Party membership. This would automatically cost Wang his seat on the party list and, thus, his position as speaker. The gambit fails when a judge orders a last-minute injunction.
September 2013	Ma's approval rating hits a new low of 9.2% in a media survey.
October 2013	In his national day address, Ma states that "the cross-Strait relationship is not an international relationship."
2013	According to DGBAS, the economy grew 2.20% in 2013.

Table 2.1 Continued

Date	Event
March–April 2014	On March 18, the STA passes a legislative committee review via questionable procedures. That evening a group of students break into the legislature and repulse efforts to dislodge them. Word spreads on social media and soon thousands of students gather around the legislature in support. The Sunflower Movement occupies the legislature for the next three weeks. On March 23, students break into the nearby Executive Yuan building. Using water cannons, police forcefully remove all protesters before dawn. Premier Jiang and the police are heavily criticized for what many consider an excessive use of force. On March 30, a massive demonstration is held outside the legislature in support of the students. The students vacate the legislature on April 10, after Speaker Wang agrees not to review the STA until an oversight mechanism is first passed. This effectively kills the STA.
April 2014	Former DPP chair Lin Yi-hsiung holds a hunger strike to protest the fourth nuclear power plant. Under intense public pressure, Premier Jiang agrees to stop construction and not to proceed with further testing, effectively killing the project.
July 31, 2014	A gas explosion in Kaohsiung kills 31 and injures over 300 people. Rather than releasing emergency funds, the cabinet orders the DPP mayor to use city funds to repair the damages and compensate the victims.
September 2014	Cooking oil made from recycled waste oil is found on the market. Ting Hsin, a company with close ties to the KMT, is rocked by widespread condemnation and boycotts. This is one of many food safety scandals in Taiwan in recent years.
December 2014	The KMT suffers unprecedented losses in the mayoral elections. Premier Jiang resigns, and Ma resigns as KMT chair.
2014	According to DGBAS, the economy grew 3.92% in 2014.
January 2015	New Taipei City mayor Eric Chu is elected KMT chair.
May 2015	Only two candidates register for the KMT's presidential nomination including legislative deputy speaker Hung Hsiu-chu, who is regarded as a hardliner. All of the top-tier possibilities decline to run.
June 2015	After Hung passes the polling primary threshold, the KMT formally nominates her for president.
June 2015	An explosion at an amusement park in New Taipei City results in 12 deaths and nearly 500 burn injuries. The cabinet immediately authorizes emergency funds. Critics contrast this response with the inaction in the earlier Kaohsiung explosion.
July–August 2015	Students occupy the Ministry of Education for two weeks to protest textbook revisions they believe are hastily implemented and excessively Sino-centric.

continued

Table 2.1 Continued

Date	Event
August 2015	James Soong announces he will run for president under the PFP banner. He soon overtakes Hung in the polls.
October 2015	The KMT dumps Hung as nominee, and replaces her with KMT chair and New Taipei mayor Eric Chu. His poll numbers are only slightly better than hers.
November 2015	Mr. Ma Ying-jeou and Mr. Xi Jinping hold a summit in Singapore.
November 2015	The capital gains tax is repealed.
2015	According to DGBAS, the economy grew 0.65% in 2015.
January 2016	The DPP wins the presidential and legislative elections.
May 2016	Ma's second term ends.

Sources: Compiled from newspaper reports and the Directorate-General of Budget, Accounting, and Statistics website www.dgbas.gov.tw/point.asp?index=1.

Is the sky really falling?

Almost immediately after the votes were counted, voices appeared arguing that Tsai Ing-wen's victory did not reflect any basic changes in the political structure. The clearest statement came in a column evocatively entitled, "Blue Is Still Blue, Green Is Still Green, The Political Map Has Not Shifted,"[2] in the *United Daily News* by political scientist Hung Yung-tai. Hung argued that low turnout among KMT supporters was the main force producing the apparent DPP landslide. However, these missing voters would not be missing forever. In future elections, these voters would turn out and vote for the blue side, so 2016 was merely a blip on the radar (Hung 2016; see also Weng 2016).

At first glance, this argument looks reasonable. Table 2.2 shows that turnout was down 8.1 percent from 2012. In an electorate with nearly 700,000 more eligible voters, over one million fewer votes were cast in 2016. Hung's estimate of

Table 2.2 Comparison of the 2012 and 2016 presidential elections

	2012		2016		Increase	
	Votes	(%)	Votes	(%)	Votes	(%)
KMT (Ma/Chu)	6,891,139	51.6	3,813,365	31.0	−3,077,774	−20.6
DPP (Tsai/Tsai)	6,093,578	45.6	6,894,744	56.1	801,166	10.5
PFP (Soong/Soong)	369,588	2.8	1,576,861	12.8	1,207,273	10.0
Valid votes	13,334,305		12,284,970		−1,049,335	
Eligible voters	18,086,455		18,782,991		696,536	
Turnout		74.4		66.3		−8.1

Source: Central Elections Commission.

1.55 million missing voters seems about right. Hung concludes that the three million vote decline in the KMT's presidential vote was due to 1.5 million voters who did not turn out, 1.2 million voters who turned to Soong, and only 300,000 voters who shifted sides and opted for Tsai. Tsai's aggregate vote only increased a modest 800,000 votes from 2012. Hung argues that 300,000 came from the KMT, and 500,000 were from new voters. The math all works out with only 300,000 voters – less than 5 percent of Ma's 2012 vote base – shifting sides. It is business as usual!

Perhaps not. On the one hand, the tensions within the KMT coalition that would impel nearly half of its voters to stay at home or shift to another blue camp candidate might not simply fade away. On the other hand, these calculations rest on heroic and demonstrably false assumptions. It is assumed that all of the abstainers were KMT supporters, and all of the new voters were DPP supporters. Table 2.3 shows how the 2012 voting coalitions were distributed in 2016.[3] Respondents who reported voting for Ma in 2012 were more likely to stay at home in 2016 than those who reported voting for Tsai. However, the 2016 abstainers were a diverse group. Some of them had voted for Tsai or Soong in 2012, some had not voted at all or had forgotten who they voted for, and some had not been eligible to vote. This survey evidence does not indicate that all

Table 2.3 2012 vote choice and 2016 vote choice (%)

	Chu	Tsai	Soong	Undecided	Abstain	n
Pre-election survey						
Ma (KMT)	35.1	23.1	13.8	17.5	10.6	2,234
Tsai (DPP)	1.0	86.8	3.5	6.9	1.8	1,598
Soong (PFP)	3.4	22.9	52.5	11.9	9.3	118
No response	3.0	22.7	5.0	59.7	9.6	665
Abstained	4.8	29.0	12.0	18.3	36.0	859
Not eligible	10.8	46.5	14.1	12.7	15.9	370
All	15.5	42.8	10.5	19.1	12.1	5,844
Post-election panel survey						
Ma (KMT)	39.6	24.5	15.7	4.4	15.8	1,258
Tsai (DPP)	1.3	90.3	2.0	1.6	4.8	997
Soong (PFP)	10.1	38.0	38.0	2.5	11.4	79
No Response	10.1	50.8	5.2	21.8	12.1	307
Abstained	5.2	36.2	13.3	7.9	37.4	406
Not eligible	11.2	47.5	21.1	2.2	17.9	223
All	18.2	50.4	11.2	5.4	14.8	3,270

Source: TEDS 2016 pre-election and post-election panel telephone survey.

Notes
Rows are 2012 vote choice, while columns are 2016 vote choice. Cells show row percentages. The "Abstain" category includes respondents who cast invalid votes or did not vote. "Undecided" and "No Response" include respondents who forgot who they voted for or refused to answer the question.

1.5 million of the voters who did not turn out in 2016 were part of the 2012 Ma coalition.

Table 2.3 also casts doubt on the idea that most of the DPP's increased support came from new voters. New voters did overwhelmingly support Tsai, but so did the rest of the population. In the pre-election poll, her support rate of 46.5 percent among new voters was not markedly different from her 42.8 percent support in the general population. Likewise, new voters did not differ much from the general population in terms of party identification (Table 2.4). In the aftermath of a period of intense student activism, it is easy to forget that the student demonstrators were only a very small slice of a large, diverse demographic group of new voters. Just as it is not the case that all abstainers were KMT supporters, it is simply wrong to classify all young people as DPP supporters.

If the massive shifts were not caused by monolithic partisan patterns in turnout or generational replacement, there is no escaping the conclusion that large numbers must have changed sides. In fact, the survey data clearly show that this is what happened. According to TEDS surveys, Ma's 2012 coalition fell apart because nearly one quarter of it voted for Tsai and the DPP in 2016. This percentage is significantly larger than the percentage voting for Soong or the percentage abstaining, and it is shockingly close to the two-fifths who ended up voting for Chu, the KMT candidate. Even keeping in mind that these figures are survey estimates and may carry significant error terms,[4] the basic point that large numbers of Ma voters switched sides is beyond dispute.

National identity and party identification

Identity is at the heart of Taiwanese politics, to the point that most analysts consider Taiwan to have only one meaningful line of cleavage defining politics. Whether one identifies as Taiwanese or Chinese largely defines how one will react to most other important questions. Since the party system is based on identity, even issues that are seemingly unrelated to national identity, such as nuclear

Table 2.4 Presidential vote intention and party ID of new voters (%)

	Old voters n = 5,472	New voters n = 369	All respondents n = 5,841
KMT	23.9	22.8	23.9
DPP	34.9	32.5	34.7
Small blue parties	4.5	4.1	4.5
Small green parties	2.7	2.4	2.7
Small unaligned parties	0.5	3.3	0.7

Source: TEDS 2016 pre-election telephone survey.

Notes
Small blue parties include the PFP, New Party, MKT, China Unification, Faith and Hope Alliance, and MCFAP. Small green parties include the TSU and NPP. Unaligned parties include the Green, Social Democratic, and Trees parties. Cells show column percentages.

power or whether to host a flower exhibition, can be consumed by identity. (For more on how identity shapes Taiwanese politics, see Achen and Wang, 2017.)

The standard measure of national identity is a question asking respondents if they think they are Taiwanese, Chinese, or both. Figure 2.1 shows data collected by the Election Study Center on this question since the early 1990s. In this figure, the Chinese and both categories are combined. That is, Figure 2.1 contrasts the population who exclusively identify as Taiwanese with those who have some identification as Chinese. Over the entire period, there was a remarkable decline in Chinese identity. Concentrating on the decade and a half between Lee Teng-hui's re-election as president in 1996 and Ma Ying-jeou's re-election in 2012, the change was moderate though steady. During this period, Taiwanese and Chinese identities were roughly balanced in the population, though the pressure was slowly building on the KMT. After 2012, the gap between the two lines widened considerably. This surge in Taiwanese identity may finally have shifted the tectonic plates too far for the KMT to overcome.

National identity and partisan support are closely related, but they are not the same thing. Not all people with an exclusive Taiwanese identity will support the DPP. Other factors, such as President Chen's corruption scandals, the lure of the Chinese market, President Ma's deployment of government resources, and personal networks enmeshed in KMT local factions have played a role in keeping people with Taiwanese identities inside the KMT coalition. In fact, even with the slow and steady increases in Taiwanese nationalism over the past

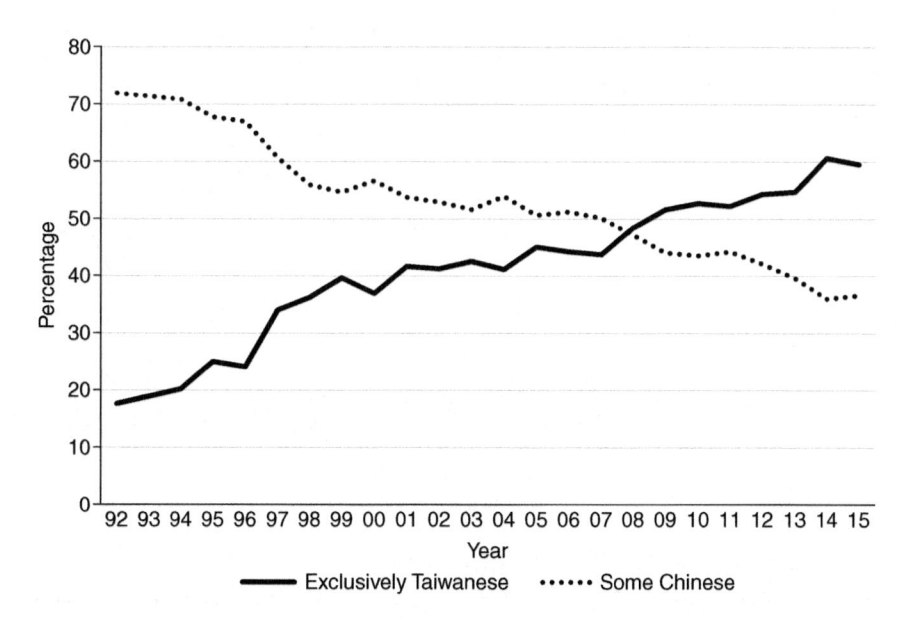

Figure 2.1 Trends in national identity, 1992–2015.

Source: Calculated from Trends in Core Political Attitudes, Election Study Center, NCCU. http://esc.nccu.edu.tw/course/news.php?Sn=166.

two decades, the party system has remained remarkably stable. Figure 2.2 shows changes in party identification over the past decade for the KMT and DPP.[5] From 2005 to 2012, the KMT enjoyed a stable advantage of roughly 10–15 percent over the DPP. The KMT's popularity spiked in December 2011, and its edge over the DPP grew to nearly 20 percent. The December 2011 data was collected during the climax of President Ma's re-election campaign, and it probably reflects his mobilization efforts. Nevertheless, even with this temporary surge in party ID, Ma only won re-election by 6.0 percent of the vote. In retrospect, his re-election looks like a heroic effort requiring all the advantages conveyed by incumbency along with a judicious splash of negative campaigning to hold together the old KMT coalition one last time. (For more on the 2012 campaign, see Batto 2014.)

After the 2012 campaign, the party ID graph changes dramatically.[6] Before the 2011 spike, the KMT had consistently enjoyed party ID from about 35 percent of the population. By September 2012, the spike was gone and the KMT had fallen to nearly 30 percent. It would continue to plunge for the next two years, finally bottoming out at just over 20 percent in December 2014. Meanwhile, the DPP's support grew from the mid-20s to the low-30s. The numbers seem to have stabilized since December 2014, with the DPP holding an

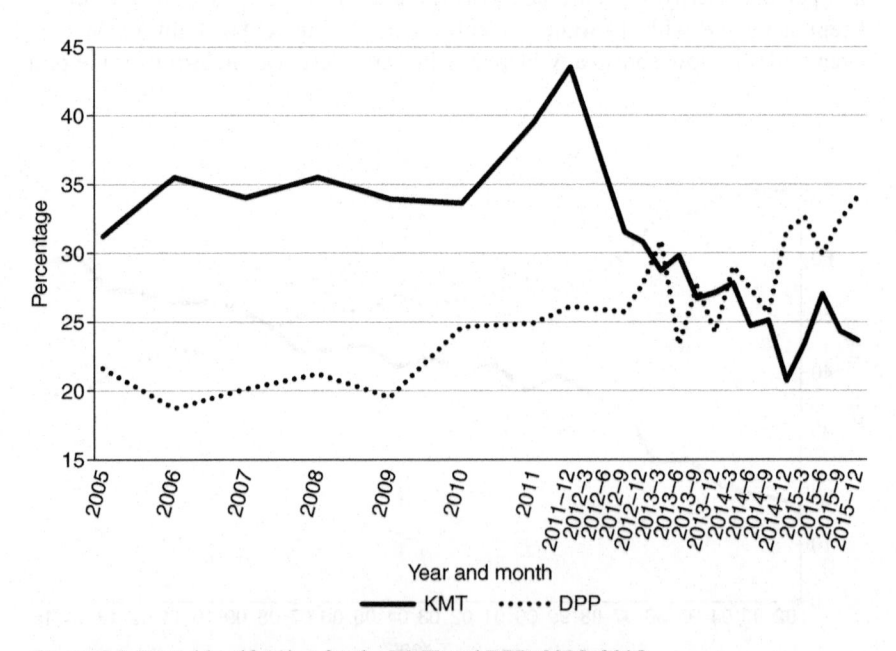

Figure 2.2 Party identification for the KMT and DPP, 2005–2015.

Sources: Data for 2005 to 2011 are taken from Trends in Core Political Attitudes, Election Study Center, NCCU. http://esc.nccu.edu.tw/course/news.php?Sn=165. Data for 2011–12 to 2015–12 are taken from TEDS 2012 and 2016 pre-election telephone surveys and TEDS quarterly telephone surveys. The 2015–12 data point combines the results of the quarterly and pre-election TEDS telephone surveys.

advantage of about 10 percent in four of the five quarterly surveys since then. In short, the party ID numbers indicate that the party system has been turned on its head. Before 2012, the KMT had a consistent 10 percent advantage. Now the DPP enjoys that same edge.

This dramatic shift in party identification is reflected in concrete election results. Presidential races often turn on idiosyncratic factors, and it is instructive to look one level down. After the presidency, mayoral seats (including county magistrate seats) are the most desired elected offices in Taiwan. Most of the KMT and DPP presidential nominees since 2000 have previously served as mayors, and anyone elected to one of these spots in one of the bigger cities can be considered as a contender for the presidency. As a result, these races are mostly contested along party lines. Moreover, since there are multiple races in each cycle, the idiosyncratic factors such as incumbency advantage or candidate charisma tend to even out. This makes the aggregate results of the mayoral races a good snapshot of the partisan balance. In Figure 2.3, the two thick lines show the results of the mayoral races. In the four election cycles from 1997/1998 to 2009/2010, the results are fairly consistent. In each of these cycles, the blue

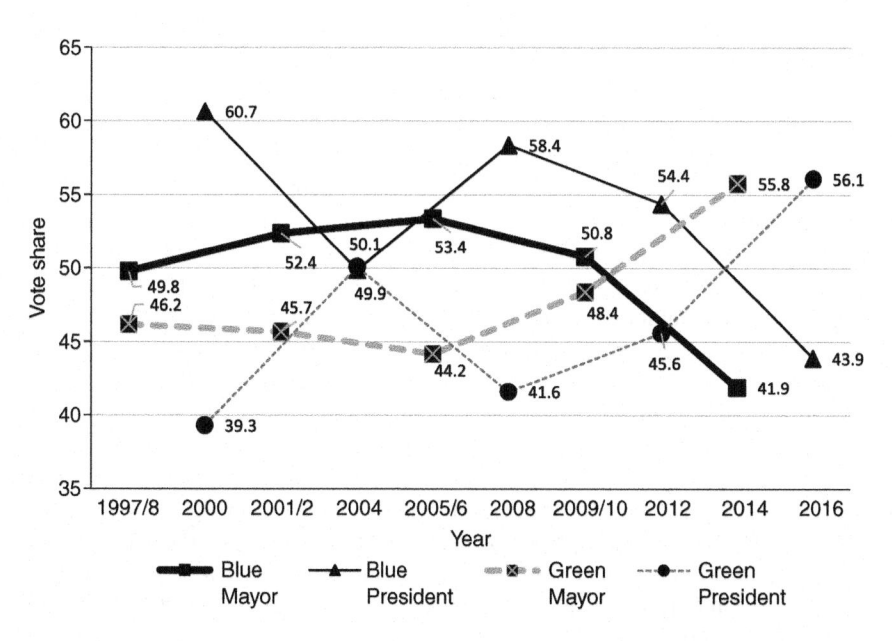

Figure 2.3 Blue and green camp vote shares in presidential and mayoral elections.

Notes
For mayoral and magistrate races, the blue and green camp vote shares include independent and minor party candidates who won at least 10 percent of the votes in their race. Which side the candidate is classified into is the author's subjective judgment based on the candidate's previous partisan affiliation, whether the candidate appealed to traditional KMT or DPP supporters, which major party urged the candidate to drop out, and which major party the media speculated would be hurt by the candidate. For presidential elections, Soong (2000), Lee (2000), Hsu (2000), (Soong 2012) and Soong (2016) are considered to be in the blue camp.

camp enjoys a clear advantage over the green camp of between 2.4 percent and 9.2 percent. However, there is a dramatic shift in the December 2014 elections, when the green camp suddenly leads the blue camp by 13.9 percent. While popular coverage of the 2014 mayoral races focused on the personalities of the individual candidates, the underlying partisan shift was the real force driving those shocking results. The presidential election results, shown by the two thin lines, have historically bounced around a bit more than the mayoral results, reflecting the various strong and weak individual presidential candidates. However, the 2016 results almost perfectly echo the 2014 votes. The DPP's 2016 victory does not appear to be a fluke; it is more likely the new normal.

Which groups of voters shifted sides?

One way to look at where the partisan changes occurred is to examine changes in party ID over Ma's second term. While there is no panel data tracking changes at the individual level from the 2012 election to the 2016 election, it is possible to compare party ID levels in the two TEDS pre-election surveys. These two surveys have relatively large sample sizes that allow a fairly detailed examination of subgroup populations. Table 2.5 shows levels of KMT and DPP party ID across several demographic groups. In the 2012 election, the full sample showed the KMT with 43.5 percent party ID and the DPP with 26.1 percent. In the 2016 pre-election survey, the KMT had plunged to only 23.9 percent while the DPP had risen to 34.7 percent. The KMT's 17.4 percent advantage in party ID had turned into a deficit of 10.8 percent, for a total swing of 28.2 percent away from the KMT.[7]

If one compares the various subgroups, there are a few that have somewhat larger or smaller swings, but the overall trend is that the KMT declined by roughly the same amount among every group. For example, the KMT was much stronger among women than men in both years, but it declined by nearly the same amount among both sexes over the four-year period. In the wake of the Sunflower movement, there was quite a bit of speculation that the youth vote would swing decisively away from the KMT. It is correct that the KMT is less popular (and the DPP more popular) among voters under 40 than among older voters, but this was also true four years ago. In fact, the swing away from the KMT among the youngest group of voters (ages 20–29) was somewhat smaller (–23.3 percent) than the overall average. Similarly, the KMT was stronger among more highly educated voters in both 2012 and 2016, but it lost support fairly evenly among all education levels.

In 2012, the public sector was the KMT's strongest occupational group. It retained this status in 2016. In fact, this was the only occupational group in which the KMT still retained an advantage over the DPP. Nevertheless, the swing away from the KMT was a bit larger in the public sector than in any other occupational group. The smallest swing (–24.2 percent) was among students. Students moved away from the KMT in large numbers, but they tended to turn to smaller parties rather than to the DPP.[8]

Table 2.5 Changes in party ID by demographic subgroups

	n 2012/2016	2012 KMT	2012 DPP	2016 KMT	2016 DPP	Swing
Grand mean	4,806/5,841	43.5	26.1	23.9	34.7	−28.2
Male	2,386/2,882	39.2	29.5	21.4	38.8	−27.1
Female	2,419/2,996	47.8	22.7	26.3	30.7	−29.5
20–29	923/986	39.0	31.9	20.5	36.7	−23.3
30–39	1,018/1,216	42.2	29.4	19.4	37.2	−30.6
40–49	1,004/1,123	49.0	22.8	28.9	32.0	−29.3
50–59	887/1,109	46.0	23.4	27.2	35.0	−30.4
60+	923/1,324	41.9	24.1	24.2	33.8	−27.4
Primary	867/899	33.0	25.4	16.2	35.5	−26.9
Junior high	670/760	40.6	28.1	20.1	41.1	−33.5
High school	1,404/1,639	45.7	26.1	26.3	35.4	−28.7
Technical College	626/723	49.7	22.2	28.6	30.7	−29.6
University	1,226/1,791	46.8	27.7	25.2	33.1	−27.0
Public sector	522/641	57.5	19.7	32.8	29.3	−34.3
Professional, Manager	1,092/1,354	44.5	30.0	25.3	38.8	−28.0
Office worker	761/893	43.1	25.5	24.2	34.4	−27.8
Labor	1,071/1,388	38.0	27.6	18.6	36.7	−28.5
Agriculture	287/290	30.7	29.3	15.5	40.7	−26.6
Student	235/283	46.8	31.5	22.3	31.8	−24.8
Homemaker	787/912	46.0	21.3	26.5	30.2	−28.4
North	1,463/1,796	47.8	25.6	26.7	32.9	−28.4
North-Central	701/869	52.5	19.1	27.4	29.1	−35.1
Central	916/1,114	41.6	21.9	24.5	32.4	−27.6
South-Central	719/859	34.5	32.7	17.7	40.9	−25.0
South	790/948	39.0	32.0	18.8	43.0	−31.2
East	215/256	40.9	26.0	28.9	25.4	−11.4
Hakka	583/706	49.2	23.8	25.4	31.2	−31.2
Min-nan	3,491/4,318	38.8	30.3	20.8	39.1	−26.8
Mainlander	556/551	70.9	5.9	46.8	10.7	−28.9
Indigenous	51/48	54.9	9.8	33.3	14.6	−26.4
Urban	2,742/3,325	47.3	25.7	24.5	35.0	−32.1
Rural	2,021/2,450	39.0	26.3	22.7	34.3	−24.3
Urban Hakka	311/373	52.4	21.5	22.3	35.7	−44.3
Rural Hakka	262/330	46.9	25.2	28.8	26.4	−19.3
Urban Min-nan	1,910/2,376	41.3	31.4	21.0	40.3	−29.2
Rural Min-nan	1,552/1,890	36.0	28.9	20.2	37.6	−24.5
Urban Mainlander	437/429	71.6	5.5	46.4	8.9	−28.6
Rural Mainlander	118/113	67.8	7.6	46.9	17.7	−31.0

Sources: TEDS 2012 and 2016 pre-election telephone surveys.

Notes
Rural townships have a population density of under 2,000 and are not part of a larger metro area.

There are a few regional differences worth noting. The KMT lost the least ground on the sparsely populated and less urbanized east coast. This sheds some light on the fact that the only two counties that Chu won on the main island were on the east coast. For reasons that are not entirely clear, the KMT's old coalition largely held together in this region[9] while it disintegrated everywhere else. The KMT lost the most ground in the north-central area that had previously been its strongest region.[10] Whereas long-time observers have become used to thinking of the blue north, green south, and battleground (though blue-leaning) central regions, the regions are now better described as the overwhelmingly green south, the green central, and the battleground (though green-leaning) north. The east coast is the only remaining blue region on the map.[11]

The last two demographic subgroups must be examined jointly. Among the four major ethnic groups, the swing away from the KMT among Hakkas was a bit larger than among the rest of the population. Likewise, the swing among urban voters was noticeably larger than the swing among rural voters. The rural-urban divide was somewhat evident among Min-nan voters (–29.2 percent among urban Min-nan and –24.5 percent among rural Min-nan), but there was a yawning gap between urban and rural Hakkas (–44.3 percent among urban Hakkas and –19.3 percent among rural Hakkas). While rural Hakkas were more resistant to the changes sweeping the polity, urban Hakkas were at the forefront. In fact, urban Hakkas now look like Min-nan voters in their partisan leanings.

While there have been some variations in party swings across the various demographic subgroups,[12] the most impressive finding is how uniform that change has been. There has been a swing away from the KMT in nearly every group examined, and the great majority of those swings fall into a relatively narrow range. Some 22 of the 31 subcategories in Table 2.5 have a swing within 3 percent of the 28.2 percent overall mean. This is bad news for the KMT. If its losses were due to a sudden drop of popularity in any particular group, it could design a new appeal to woo members of that group. However, its losses are across the board. It cannot regain its former levels of popularity simply by pandering to farmers, Hakkas, students, or Taipei suburbanites. A much more general strategy will be required.

Was President Ma to blame?

In early 2008, the DPP suffered a massive defeat at the ballot box, losing both the presidency and the legislature by overwhelming margins. However, the party recovered fairly quickly from this disaster. By the late 2009 and 2010 local elections, it had recovered its former levels of support, and it was able to mount a credible challenge to the KMT in the 2012 national elections. Moreover, it was able to mount this comeback without making any fundamental changes to its core political positions. Much of the DPP's unpopularity in 2008 stemmed from the widespread perceptions that President Chen was personally corrupt and that he had intentionally and unnecessarily offended China with his aggressive Taiwanese nationalism. Both these problems were largely resolved simply by choosing a new leader. Tsai

Ing-wen had a much cleaner image, and voters no longer had to choose between supporting the DPP and opposing corruption. Her adjustments to the party's China policy were largely matters of style. She did not back away from the DPP's fundamental commitment to Taiwan sovereignty, but neither did she actively go out of her way to incite China's fury. All in all, because the DPP's problems could, to a large extent, be personally attributed to President Chen, its recovery was relatively painless. Changing a leader is much easier than changing or abandoning core ideals.

Is Ma Ying-jeou personally responsible for the KMT's debacle in 2016? Could the KMT make a relatively painless comeback in the next few years just by changing a few faces? On the one hand, Ma was very unpopular. The general public was extremely dissatisfied with Ma's performance in office, and his poll numbers reached nearly unfathomable depths. A media poll published on September 15, 2013 found that his satisfaction ratings had fallen into the single digits (Wang 2013), and critics relentlessly questioned the legitimacy of his every action by reminding him that he was a "9 percent president."

On the other hand, while much of President Chen's unpopularity could be traced to accusations of corruption, character was not President Ma's main problem. TEDS polls show that perceptions of President Ma's character were largely positive (Table 2.6). Early in his second term, about half the population judged his character positively while only about a quarter gave a negative evaluation. Over the next three years, public assessment of Ma's character eroded slightly, but in December 2015 positive judgments still outweighed negative judgments. Personal character was a strength, not a weakness.

Figure 2.4 sheds more light on the roots of dissatisfaction with President Ma. The thick solid black line represents net satisfaction with President Ma's overall performance in office. In the telephone polls taken immediately before Ma's triumphant re-election in January 2012, slightly more people were satisfied than dissatisfied. Very soon after his re-election, this indicator began plunging.[13] By September 2012, his net satisfaction rating was –54.3 percent, and it hovered between –50 percent and –60 percent for most of the rest of his term.

Table 2.6 Evaluations of President Ma's personal character

	Poor (0–4)	*Average (5)*	*Good (6–10)*	*Non-response*	n
2012 December	26.4	17.2	51.7	4.6	1,140
2013 June	24.2	19.7	48.1	7.8	1,072
2013 December	31.7	17.9	42.6	7.7	1,081
2014 June	29.5	20.4	44.5	5.5	1,076
2014 December	33.0	20.1	38.7	8.2	1,081
2015 June	27.8	20.6	46.1	5.4	1,076
2015 December	33.3	20.3	38.4	7.9	1,100

Source: TEDS quarterly telephone surveys.

Note
Respondents were asked to rate President Ma's character 品格 on a scale of 0 (very poor) to 10 (very good).

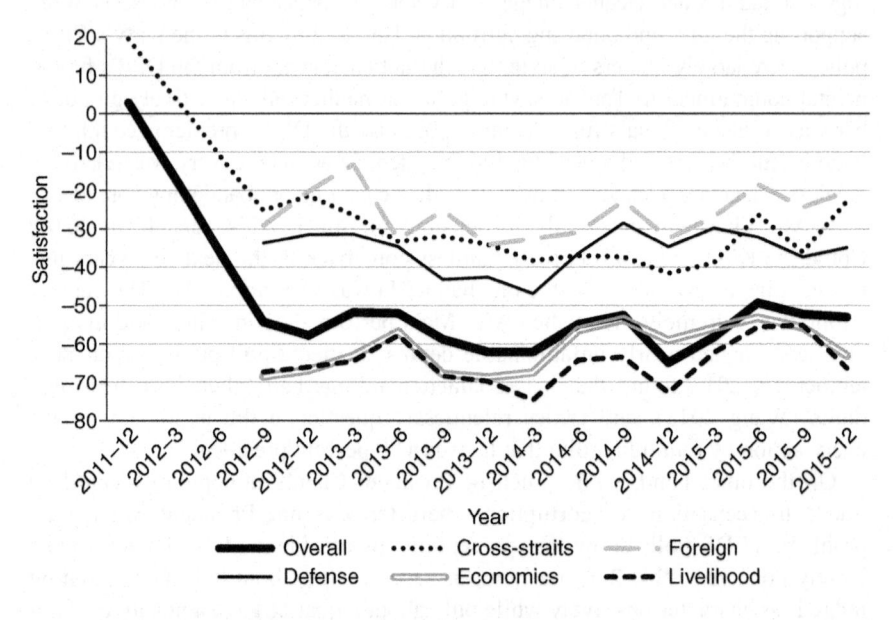

Figure 2.4 Net satisfaction with President Ma's performance in office.

Sources: TEDS 2012 and 2016 pre-election telephone surveys and TEDS quarterly telephone surveys. The 2015–12 data point for overall and cross-Strait satisfaction combines the results of the quarterly and pre-election TEDS telephone surveys.

Note
Net satisfaction is the percentage of respondents expressing strong or moderate satisfaction minus the percentage expressing moderate or strong dissatisfaction.

In addition to general satisfaction, respondents were also asked about Ma's performance in five specific areas. In two areas, promoting economic development and handling people's livelihood issues,[14] Ma's satisfaction ratings were even lower than his already dismal general satisfaction ratings. In another three areas, handling cross-Strait relations, foreign affairs, and national defense, respondents' evaluations were somewhat less negative. Whereas net satisfaction was around –60 percent to –70 percent for economics and people's livelihood, it was usually between –20 percent and –40 percent for cross-Strait, foreign affairs, and national defense.

This appears to be good news for the KMT's future prospects. The KMT's core belief involves Chinese nationalism. The KMT is, after all, literally the "Chinese Nationalist Party." Making fundamental changes to its cross-Strait policy would involve some gut-wrenching choices for the party's true believers about the nature of the ROC and the identity of its citizens. If Ma's poor performance – and by extension the KMT's poor electoral performance – were caused by something else, the KMT might be able to make a comeback without confronting these excruciating choices. Even better, the worst failure seems to have involved people's livelihood issues. Taking care of the people's livelihood is a fundamental pillar of KMT ideology, so this is a problem that, at least in theory, the KMT should want to confront and fix. Such a fix might be as simple as finding a leader better able to express compassion toward ordinary people. If revising its positions on cross-Strait issues is the most painful change for the KMT, adopting new strategies for dealing with people's livelihood issues would be the least painful. It is no coincidence that the KMT tried to focus attention on its failures in dealing with people's livelihood issues. In the middle of the presidential campaign, KMT chair and presidential nominee Eric Chu went on a TV talk show to explain why the public was dissatisfied with the KMT's record in office. He cited three main failings: (1) allowing the prices of electricity and gas to rise; (2) failure to implement universal 12-year education reforms; and (3) the debacle of first passing and then revoking the capital gains tax (Lin 2015). Tellingly, Chu quickly denied that he was trying to break with President Ma (Lee 2015). Since all three problems could be classified as people's livelihood issues and none involved cross-Strait relations or national identity, these were mere policy implementation failures, not indications of flaws in the KMT's core beliefs.

Attitudes and changing sides

A previous section examined changes in party identification among various demographic groups. This section looks at which attitudes were associated with voters who deserted the KMT. In Table 2.3, the top line shows that among people who voted for Ma in 2012, 23.1 percent switched to Tsai and 13.8 percent switched to Soong in 2016. Why did they change? To explore this, I divide Ma voters into four groups: those who stayed loyal to the KMT and voted for Chu, those who switched to Tsai, those who switched to Soong, and those who were either undecided or planned to abstain. This dependent variable is categorical, so a multinomial logit model is appropriate. I set Chu as the default category, so the coefficients for the other categories are in relation to people who voted for Chu.

There are two types of independent variables in the model: demographic and attitudinal. As already seen, most of the demographic variables did not have particularly strong effects on changes in party identification. Once attitudinal variables are added in, the effects of these variables is even weaker. As a result, I have chosen to cull as many as possible, leaving only those that have a significant correlation with the dependent variable. The model includes dummy variables for women, Hakkas, Mainlanders, and people with elementary or less education levels. The reference groups are thus men, Min-nan and Indigenous, and people with junior high or higher education levels, respectively. Age is coded by decade, with people aged 20–29 coded one, 30–39 coded two, 40–49 coded three, 50–59 coded four, and 60 and over coded five.

There are three types of attitudinal variables included in the model: (1) national identity; (2) preference for Taiwan's future status; and (3) satisfaction with Ma's performance in office. I have already mentioned the importance of national identity. Whether a voter considers herself to be Taiwanese, Chinese, or both has been one of the strongest predictors of voting behavior for decades. Ma Ying-jeou consistently expressed pride in his Chinese identity and his policies often reflected that orientation, so a reasonable expectation is that Ma voters with a more pro-Taiwan orientation may have been disillusioned. The model includes a dummy for voters with an exclusively Taiwanese identity, so the reference category is voters with either an exclusive Chinese identity or a dual Chinese and Taiwanese identity. Similarly, attitudes toward Taiwan's future status also have a well-established correlation with vote choices. People who favor immediate or eventual Taiwan independence tend to vote for the green camp, while those who favor immediate or eventual unification with China tend to support the blue camp. Two dummy variables are included for people with pro-unification and pro-independence views. The reference category includes people who favor the status quo indefinitely and those who wish to decide on independence or unification at some later date. Finally, the pre-election survey included two measures of satisfaction, one on Ma's general performance and one on his performance on cross-strait issues. These are measured on five-point scales, with very satisfied coded as two, somewhat satisfied as one, somewhat dissatisfied as negative one, very dissatisfied as negative two, and all non-responses coded as zero.

The results are shown in Table 2.7. There are some similarities across the categories. In all three categories, age is negatively correlated with the vote choice. That is, old people are far less likely to vote for Tsai, Soong, or be ambivalent

Table 2.7 Multinomial logit model of vote intent among 2012 Ma voters

	Vote: Tsai			*Vote: Soong*			*Vote: Undecided*		
	b	*s.e.*	*sig*	*b*	*s.e.*	*sig*	*b*	*s.e.*	*sig*
Constant	0.386	0.263		0.791	0.262	**	0.398	0.221	
Female	−0.268	0.136	*	−0.352	0.142	*	0.257	0.112	*
Hakka	0.215	0.193		0.046	0.214		0.181	0.161	
Mainlander	−0.259	0.072	***	0.040	0.059		0.061	0.046	
Education: Elementary	0.575	0.250	*	−0.119	0.345		0.346	0.201	
Age Group	−0.363	0.064	***	−0.478	0.065	***	−0.170	0.052	**
Taiwanese Identity	0.568	0.142	***	0.062	0.153		0.003	0.119	
Pro Unification	−0.130	0.193		0.091	0.177		−0.412	0.150	**
Pro Independence	−0.581	0.209	**	0.110	0.240		0.120	0.201	
Satisfaction: General	−0.701	0.072	***	−0.598	0.069	***	−0.383	0.052	***
Satisfaction: X Straits	−0.961	0.075	***	−0.425	0.077	***	−0.492	0.063	***

Source: TEDS 2016 pre-election telephone survey.

Notes
$n=2,455$;
LR $Chi^2=1,007.17$;
pseudo $R^2=0.155$;
* $p<0.05$;
** $p<0.01$;
*** $p<0.001$;
The reference category for the dependent variable is intent to vote for Chu (KMT).

than to vote for Chu. To put it another way, younger voters were the most likely to defect from the KMT. Men were more likely than women to defect to Tsai or Soong. Satisfaction with Ma's performance clearly mattered. The coefficients for both satisfaction variables are negative and significant, indicating that dissatisfaction led voters to defect to all three non-KMT options.

However, not all the results are similar across categories. There are also some striking differences. Defectors to Tsai fit the classic profile of DPP supporters. Compared to Ma voters who remained loyal to the KMT, defectors to Tsai were less likely to be Mainlanders, more likely to have an exclusively Taiwanese identity, and more likely to favor independence. Defectors to Soong had none of these characteristics. Defectors to Soong were younger, more likely to be male, and dissatisfied with Ma's performance, but otherwise they looked fairly similar to Ma voters who supported Chu. There is also an important difference in satisfaction. The coefficient for satisfaction on cross-Strait performance for Tsai voters is twice the size of that for Soong voters. Dissatisfaction with Ma's performance on cross-Strait issues mattered much more for erstwhile Ma voters who crossed the blue–green divide.

These results suggest that different types of Ma voters made different choices in 2016. Defectors to Tsai were different in important ways than defectors to Soong. Unfortunately, the TEDS pre-election survey did not ask about satisfaction on the five different policy dimensions, so it is not possible to examine how satisfaction with other policy areas affected the 2016 vote choice.

To delve further into how satisfaction mattered, we now turn to the quarterly TEDS surveys. Unfortunately, those surveys did not ask about 2016 vote intention, so the best we can do is to use party ID among 2012 Ma voters as the dependent variable. Since Figure 2.2 indicates that most of the change in party identification had occurred by December 2014, we can pool the five surveys from December 2014 to December 2015 together as the data set. The dependent variable, party ID, is coded into four categories: KMT or New Party, DPP or TSU, PFP, and all other parties or none. Among 2012 Ma voters, the distribution into these four categories was 58.9 percent, 10.2 percent, 5.2 percent, and 25.6 percent, respectively. We can run another multinomial logit model with the same independent variables as the model in Table 2.7, except for the satisfaction variables. This data set has measures for satisfaction in all five policy areas, so a variable is included for each. Since general satisfaction is highly correlated with each of these measures and would muddy the picture, general satisfaction is excluded from the model. The results are shown in Table 2.8.

The three groups have strikingly different profiles. Compared to Ma voters who still support the KMT, Ma voters who now support the DPP are less likely to be Mainlanders, more likely to have an exclusively Taiwanese identity, more likely to support Taiwan independence, and more dissatisfied with Ma's performance on the cross-Strait issues and the economy. In other words, these voters seem to have discovered that they were on the wrong side of the blue-green divide and changed sides accordingly.

Table 2.8 Multinomial logit model of party ID among 2012 Ma voters

	ID: DPP/TSU			ID: PFP			ID: none/other		
	b	s.e.	sig	b	s.e.	sig	b	s.e.	sig
Constant	−2.513	0.357	***	−2.865	0.452	***	−0.488	0.228	*
Female	−0.327	0.176		−0.443	0.216	*	−0.139	0.118	
Hakka	0.251	0.254		0.294	0.311		0.091	0.174	
Mainlander	−0.278	0.098	**	0.053	0.086		−0.076	0.051	
Education: elementary	1.148	0.311	***	0.797	0.436		1.187	0.217	***
Age group	0.007	0.081		0.067	0.102		−0.100	0.055	
Taiwanese identity	0.627	0.186	***	−0.376	0.245		0.139	0.124	
Pro-unification	−0.445	0.281		−0.318	0.289		−0.357	0.166	*
Pro-independence	0.765	0.240	**	0.146	0.375		−0.034	0.207	
Satisfaction: cross-Strait	−0.648	0.102	***	−0.205	0.117		−0.285	0.065	***
Satisfaction: foreign	−0.158	0.099		−0.079	0.120		−0.171	0.068	*
Satisfaction: defense	−0.157	0.099		−0.119	0.115		−0.266	0.066	***
Satisfaction: economy	−0.248	0.108	*	−0.228	0.125		−0.111	0.064	
Satisfaction: livelihood	−0.167	0.115		−0.407	0.146	**	−0.012	0.067	

Source: Five quarterly TEDS telephone surveys from December 2014 to December 2015.

Notes
$n=1,962$;
LR Chi^2=579.88;
Pseudo R^2=0.141;
* $p<0.05$;
** $p<0.01$;
*** $p<0.001$;
The reference category for the dependent variable is identifying with the KMT or New Party.

PFP identifiers do not look like this at all. In fact, the major difference between PFP and KMT identifiers among Ma voters is that PFP identifiers are more dissatisfied with Ma's performance on people's livelihood issues. This fits with James Soong's image as a competent and compassionate administrator, who had no fundamental disagreement with the Ma administration on the grand strategy of integrating the Taiwanese and Chinese economies. It perhaps also explains Chu's criticism of Ma's three major failures. By focusing on people's livelihood issues, he was trying to reach out to former KMT supporters who had gone over to the PFP, not to those who had defected to the DPP.

The third category is also interesting. Ma voters with no clear party identification were, like DPP identifiers, dissatisfied with Ma's performance on cross-Strait issues. However, they were also dissatisfied with his performance in another area: national defense. Perhaps Ma's decision to cut defense spending or the massive but explicitly non-partisan protests over the death of Corporal. Hung Chung-chiu caused some Ma voters to turn away from the KMT but did not inspire them to move toward either the DPP or PFP.

The findings in this section suggest that the KMT will probably not be able to regain its former majority status simply by changing a few faces and making some minor and relatively painless policy adjustments, though it might be able to consolidate leadership of the blue camp with these sorts of minor changes. Ma voters who defected to Soong or identify with the PFP do not seem to have any fundamental differences with KMT ideals. They could conceivably be wooed back by a new, more compassionate leader who placed a greater emphasis on bread-and-butter issues for everyday people. However, the blue camp is no longer the majority coalition in Taiwan. The Ma voters who defected to Tsai and the DPP seem to have made the decisive jump across the central dividing line because their attitudes were closer to mainstream green camp core beliefs. To win these voters back, the KMT might need to make significant and extremely painful adjustments to its positions on identity and the relationship between China and Taiwan.

The 2016 legislative elections: still a blue and green world

This chapter has focused on the presidential results for two main reasons. First, with fewer contestants, presidential elections are simpler and easier to understand. Second, while the legislative elections are more complex with a variety of local idiosyncrasies, the big picture is the same. There is one fundamental cleavage line that divides the electorate in almost exactly the same way as in the presidential elections.

Table 2.9 shows the results of the 2016 legislative elections. For the first time, the DPP has a majority in the legislature and thus control over both the executive

Table 2.9 Results of the 2016 legislative Yuan election (%)

	District votes	District seats	List votes	List seats	Total seats
Democratic Progressive Party	44.6	50	44.1	18	68
Kuomintang	38.9	24	26.9	11	35
People First Party	1.3		6.5	3	3
New Power Party	2.9	3	6.1	2	5
New Party	0.6		4.1		
Green/Social Democratic Alliance	1.7		2.5		
Taiwan Solidarity Union	0.8		2.5		
Faith and Hope League	0.6		1.7		
Minkuotang (Republican Party)	1.6		1.6		
Other parties	1.3		3.9		
Independent candidates	5.7	2			2
Blue camp	39.7	25	41.1	14	39
Green camp	51.4	54	53.3	20	74
Valid votes/sum	12,148,872	79	12,190,139	34	113

Source: Central Elections Commission and author's calculations.

Notes
The camp district votes represent the main blue camp or green camp candidate in the district. The camp list shares are coded as follows. The blue camp includes the KMT, PFP, New Party, Non-Party Solidarity Union, MKT, MCFAP, and China Unification Party. The green camp includes the DPP, TSU, NPP, Free Taiwan Party, and Taiwan Independence Party.

and legislative branches of government. Moreover, its majority is large enough that, unless discipline totally breaks down, it should have enough votes to win almost all fights in the legislature. This should make President Tsai's hand much stronger than President Chen's ever was, since Chen always had to face a blue camp majority in the legislature.

From the perspective of aggregate votes, it is interesting that the green camp won roughly 12 percent more votes than the blue camp in the presidential, district, and list races. This is the case even though the two camps won very different levels of the total vote in the three different ballots. In the presidential race, there were only three choices on the ballot, all associated with either the blue or green camp. In the district races, there were many strong independent or third party candidates who siphoned votes away from the two main contestants. In the list tier, there were a gaggle of small parties to choose from, but there were no locally entrenched independent candidates. As such, the two camps took 100 percent of the presidential vote, roughly 95 percent of the party list vote, and only about 90 percent of the district vote. The green camp's 12 percent edge in each of these ballots suggests that the green camp advantage does not depend on specific conditions, such as a certain level of turnout or a particular set of candidates or alliances.

At the individual level, there is also quite powerful evidence that most voters are either blue or green. Table 2.10 looks at reported votes in the TEDS post-election panel survey. Not surprisingly, the levels of straight-ticket voting are highest if one only looks at the two ballots that were the same nationwide. Some 31.7 percent of the sample reported voting for the blue camp on both the presidential and party list ballots, while 55.4 percent said they had voted for the green camp on both. Less than one in ten (8.9 percent) reported having split their votes between the blue and green camps. Levels of split-ticket voting rise a bit when district legislators are also considered. Still, nearly three-quarters (74.5 percent) of all voters cast a straight green or straight blue vote on all three

Table 2.10 Straight- and split-ticket voting by camp in the 2016 elections (%)

	Straight blue	Straight green	Split blue/ unaligned	Split green/ unaligned	Split blue/ green	Number
President, LY District	27.7	53.2	2.3	2.1	14.7	2,327
President, LY List	31.7	55.4	1.3	2.7	8.9	2,501
LY District, LY List[†]	28.4	50.2	2.9	3.7	14.0	2,299
All three ballots	25.5	49.0	2.6	3.5	19.4	2,265
Ma voters: all three	53.7	16.9	4.1	1.1	24.1	874

Source: TEDS 2016 post-election panel telephone survey.

Notes

This table does not include respondents who did not vote or did not reveal their vote in any of the relevant races. The blue camp includes the KMT, PFP, New Party, Non-Party Solidarity Union, MKT, MCFAP, and China Unification Party. The green camp includes the DPP, TSU, NPP, Free Taiwan Party, and Taiwan Independence Party. [†]There were also 0.9 percent who voted for an unaligned party on both the district and list ballots.

ballots, and only 19.4 percent of the sample reported having split their support between the two main camps.

People who reported having voted for Ma in 2012 might be expected to have lower levels of straight ticket voting. As we have seen, these voters splintered in many different directions and might have been expected to be more conflicted than other voters. However, even in this group, levels of split-ticket voting were not particularly high. Of the respondents who reported a vote on all three ballots, over 70 percent reported a straight blue or straight green ticket. Notably, 16.9 percent reported having voted straight green. To put it another way, more than half of the Ma voters who defected to Tsai went even further and cast a straight green ticket. The previous section looked at attitudes, finding that a large group of Ma voters sympathized with green ideas and switched sides. These data points show a parallel change in behavior, with a large group of 2012 Ma voters casting all three of their 2016 votes against Ma's KMT.

Conclusion

The 2016 election marked a major shift in Taiwan's political landscape. Large numbers of voters who had previously supported the KMT switched sides and threw their weight behind the DPP. Survey evidence shows that the voters who made this shift did so because they found themselves at odds with the KMT on very basic points, such as national identity, Taiwan's future status, and cross-strait policy. These issues are at the heart of the dominant political cleavage that defines Taiwan's political spectrum, so there is little reason to think that the KMT could woo these voters back to its side with new faces or new policies on less important issues. It is more likely that these votes have made a permanent shift and will continue to be part of the DPP's coalition. If this is the case, the DPP will have a solid majority for the foreseeable future.

One can point to the events of President Ma's tumultuous second term, including waves of intense protests, a series of food scandals, and a paucity of good economic news, as the triggers driving large numbers of 2012 Ma supporters to change sides. However, these immediate factors were embedded in a much deeper shift in national identity that has been building for several decades. Until 2008, the share of the electorate with some Chinese identity had always been greater than the share with an exclusively Taiwanese identity. Since 2008, the reverse has been true, and by 2016 the gap had grown to over 20 percent. Given the fundamental importance of national identity in Taiwanese politics, this augurs poorly for any revival of KMT fortunes unless the KMT revises its stance on the relationship between Taiwan and China in order to appeal to voters with an exclusive Taiwanese identity, something that would be extremely painful for many of its members.

In the aftermath of the 2016 election, the KMT has made no moves to moderate its stance toward China in order to appeal to the new median voter. After Eric Chu resigned as party chair, members chose hardliner Chinese nationalist Hung Hsiu-chu to fill out the remainder of his term. As the KMT's presidential candidate, Hung's extreme positions had been so unpopular with the general public that the KMT had to revoke her nomination just three months before the election. In the May 2017 election for party chair, the KMT turned to former Vice President Wu Den-yi. While Wu is more moderate than Hung, he does not advocate any overhaul of established KMT doctrine. Rather, Wu's leadership is predicated on the idea that the KMT's old coalition still exists,[15] so he favors a return to the KMT's positions in the 2008 and 2012 elections, including a strong commitment to the 1992 Consensus. Wu is acceptable to almost all members of the blue camp, and his election makes new splinter parties far less likely. However, even if he is able to bring all blue camp supporters back into the KMT fold, the arguments presented in this chapter suggest that the blue camp is no longer large enough to win a majority.

This does not mean that the KMT is necessarily doomed. There seems to be no danger of it losing its position as the undisputed leader of the blue camp, and there are two important reasons that the blue camp will continue to have an important political presence. On the one hand, one-third of the electorate continues to express an identity as at least partly Chinese. One-third is a sizeable fraction of the population, and it is certainly large enough to support the main opposition party. On the other hand, many large Taiwanese businesses want policies that create more predictable terms of trade with China and increase their access to the Chinese market. This combination of a sizeable set of voters and a solid financial foundation should ensure that the blue side of the political spectrum will not simply shrink into irrelevance.

Nonetheless, for the first time in Taiwan's post-war history, the KMT is starting an election cycle as a clear underdog. In the past, the DPP needed to consolidate all of its strength and then have several other things go right to win a national election. Now, the KMT finds itself in that position. We have entered a new era in Taiwanese politics.

Notes

1 From the standpoint of legislative and mayoral seats, there is a plausible argument that the KMT is now weaker than the DPP has ever been since complete legislative elections began in 1992. The KMT currently holds 31.0 percent of the legislature and its local governments govern 24.6 percent of the population. At the beginning of the democratic era in 1992, the DPP won 31.7 percent of legislative seats and its local governments covered 35.2 percent of the population. After the DPP's 2008 debacle, it held only 23.9 percent of legislative seats, but DPP local governments encompassed 30.8 percent of the population.

2 Since around 2000, it has been common to divide the political spectrum into the blue camp, which is led by the KMT and is oriented toward Chinese nationalism, and the green camp, which is led by the DPP and is oriented toward Taiwanese nationalism.

3 This chapter draws on a variety of survey data from the Taiwan Election and Democratization Studies (TEDS) project. TEDS is a multiyear project funded by the Taiwan's Ministry of Science and Technology and led by Chi Huang. Surveys analyzed include the 2012 and 2016 pre-election and post-election panel surveys (TEDS2012-T, NSC 100–2420-H-002–030; TEDS2016-T, MOST 101–2420-H004–034-MY4) and quarterly surveys from September 2012 to December 2015 (TEDS2012_PA09

through TEDS2015_PA12, MOST 101–2420–H004–034–MY4). For more information, see the TEDS website at www.tedsnet.org. All descriptive statistics, such as percentages, use weighted data. The models in Tables 2.7 and 2.8 use unweighted data.

4 Two types of error may be especially pertinent. One, it is well known that respondents tend to over-report voting for a winner. Perhaps the number of people who claimed to vote for Ma in 2012 or Tsai in 2016 is inflated. Two, the sample may not adequately cover the entire population. A large number of Taiwanese voters live outside Taiwan, so surveys would not normally be able to reach them. In fact, given the final results, it seems plausible that the actual fraction of 2012 Ma voters who voted for Tsai in 2016 was somewhat less than one-quarter and the actual fraction who voted for Chu was quite a bit more than two-fifths.

5 This figure begins in 2005 because that is when the PFP's support fell below 5 percent and the KMT assumed a near monopoly over support in the blue camp. However, if one considers the entire blue and green camps, the graph would show that the blue camp has enjoyed a similarly sized advantage over the green camp since the late 1990s.

6 Unfortunately, TEDS did not begin doing quarterly surveys until September 2012, so we cannot see exactly when the KMT's support began falling. Evidence from other sources suggests that the drop began soon after Ma's January re-election. TISR surveys show that the spike in party ID was gone by his second inauguration in May. See www.tisr.com.tw/.

7 Note that about two-thirds of the swing was caused by a drop in KMT popularity while only about a third came from a rise in DPP popularity. To some extent, this is an artifact of the pre-election temporary spike in KMT party ID in 2012. If one assumes that the 2012 spike was a statistical blip rather than evidence of a solid and enduring state of public opinion, the KMT's baseline should have been closer to 35 percent. In that case, the swings would be somewhat smaller and about half would be due to a decline in KMT popularity and half due to a rise in DPP popularity. However, the relative changes among each demographic subgroup would probably be about the same.

8 Among the entire 2016 sample, 7.9 percent of respondents identified with a third party. Among students, 14.4 percent did. By contrast, in 2012 students were slightly less likely to identify with a third party (4.7 percent) than the population at large (6.4 percent).

9 However, the DPP won the legislative seats in both Taitung and Hualien counties. Since the KMT won the presidential races and the blue camp had a clear advantage in the party list vote in these two counties, I suspect the DPP's victories in the district seats were mostly due to the personal qualities of the candidates.

10 The two most stunning election results in 2014 came in this region when the DPP won the mayoral seats in both Taoyuan and Hsinchu Cities. These party ID figures suggest that while most pundits were caught unaware, these two victories were not flukes. The DPP is now on an even footing with the KMT in party ID in these two cities.

11 There are, of course, enclaves within each of these regions that vote differently from the wider region.

12 The missing demographic category is income. Given the complaints about the state of the economy, the economic component to the Sunflower protests, and rising housing prices, it is reasonable to wonder if the shift in partisan loyalties is rooted in income disparities or class cleavages. Unfortunately, TEDS does not ask about respondents' income levels in telephone surveys since that is a relatively sensitive topic.

13 As with party ID, it is hard to pinpoint exactly when Ma's satisfaction ratings began plummeting. Media polls show that most of the plunge had already occurred before his second inauguration on May 20, 2012. See www.tisr.com.tw/wp-content/uploads/2016/05/20160513_P1.png.

14 People's livelihood refers to the everyday welfare of ordinary people. For example, rising prices of basic commodities such as vegetables, electricity, or public transportation are classic people's livelihood issues. The term comes from Sun Yat-sen's doctrine of the Three Principles of the People, which is the official ideology of the Republic of China. The other two principles are nationalism and democracy.

15 Wu even reiterated the idea that the reduction in turnout was entirely due to KMT supporters staying home, and that the KMT could win a majority if it could back these abstainers and the voters who had turned to Soong (Hsieh 2017).

References

Achen, C. and Wang, T. Y. (eds.) (forthcoming). *The Taiwan Voter*. Ann Arbor, MI: University of Michigan Press.

Batto, N. F. (2014). "Continuity in the 2012 Presidential and Legislative Elections." In Cabesan, J. P. and De Lisle, J. (eds.) *Political Changes in Taiwan under Ma Ying-jeou: Partisan Conflict, Policy Choices, External Constraints, and Security Challenges*. London: Routledge, pp. 15–37.

Hsieh, C. L. (2017). "Wu Dun-yi: Cong jintian kaishi buneng zai cuotuo" [Wu Den-yi: Starting Today We Cannot Slip Up Again]. *Central News Agency*, June 14.

Hung, Y. T. (2016). "Lan haishi lan, lu haishi lu, zhengzhi bantu mei yiwei" [Blue Is Still Blue, Green Is Still Green, the Political Map Has Not Shifted]. *United Daily News*, January 18.

Lee, K. Y. (2015). "Pi zhizheng san cuo yu Ma qiege? Zhu: "yiding yao Ma zhantai" [Is Chu Separating Himself from Ma by Criticizing Three Governing Flaws? Chu: "I Will Definitely Ask Ma to Campaign for Me"]. *United Daily News*, October 29.

Lin, T. Y. (2015). "Zhu Lilun: Guomindang zuida kunjing renmin buman zhizheng" [Eric Chu: The KMT's Biggest Obstacle Is the People Are Dissatisfied with Its Governing]. *United Daily News*, October 29.

Wang, C. (2013). "Ma's Approval Rating Plunges to 9.2 Percent." *Taipei Times*, September 16.

Weng, D. L. C. (2016). "Daying 300 wan? Bie wuhuile" [A Huge Three Million Vote Win? Don't Be Misled]. *United Daily News*, January 24.

3 The role of democracy in the rise of the Taiwanese national identity

Frank Muyard

Taiwan's contemporary political history has been characterized by two phenomena: democratization and the rise of a new national identity. Since the last quarter of the twentieth century, a series of political events and profound social evolutions in Taiwan have changed the national picture of the country with a new perspective on who were the Taiwanese, nationally, politically, and culturally starting to take hold in the 1980s. The shift in "national imagination" from a Chinese nation to a Taiwan-centered national polity was prepared by the growing political opposition to the Kuomintang (KMT) dictatorship and request for the self-determination of the Taiwanese since the mid-1970s, as well as facilitated by the gradual international, then domestic, delegitimization of the Republic of China (ROC)'s claims to represent the Chinese nation (Cheng and Haggard 1992; Hsiau 2000; Wang 2013a, 2013b). But it is only in the 1990s that the country's democratization, alongside China's own socio-political evolution, have fully reshaped the way Taiwanese look at themselves, their Chinese neighbor, and the world. The democratization of Taiwan's political institutions that spanned the years 1991–1996, with the establishment of freedoms of opinion, expression, and political participation, led to the renewal of the formerly China-centered institutions of the 1947 ROC Constitution through the election of the National Congress and Assembly by, and only by, the Taiwanese population, as well as the direct and free election of all national and local executive and legislative political positions by the Taiwanese electorate (Lee and Wang 2003; Jacobs 2012). Soon, the formerly taboo topic of Taiwanese nationalism emerged publicly and the question of how to evaluate the reality, nature, and authenticity of the emerging new national identity became an intense focus of political and academic debate.

These two concomitant developments raised many questions about their compatibility, especially since nationalism and democracy are often seen in liberal academia as being in conflict. Some scholars of nationalism have underlined the positive contribution and inherent role of nationalism in the historical development of modern democracy (Nodia 1992; Yack 1999; Calhoun 2007), while liberal nationalists, like Yael Tamir and David Miller, argue that nationality is necessary for the functioning of liberal democratic states (Dzur 2002; Abizadeh 2004). However, suspicion of nationalist movements and expressions of national

36   *Frank Muyard*

identity remains widespread among liberal academics, including major students of nationalism like Hobsbawm, who stand opposed to the ideology of nationalism and are critical of anything that raises the specter of potential ethnic conflict. Together with the usual dislike by state authorities of any popular movement that challenges the establishment and the status quo, such attitudes often result in painting a picture of illegitimacy or danger over the development of "new" national identities and nationalist movements. This was the case at the time of the collapse of the Soviet Empire at the turn of the 1990s (Nodia 1992), but it is still true today in Asian Studies, notably in the perception and study of Taiwan's rising national identity.

Yet the national issue did not unsettle Taiwan's democratization. As Schubert stated, "Taiwan's democracy has remained stable, and it is reasonable to argue that the 'identity divide' on the island has not severely undermined the political system so far" (2006: 28–29). Rather, democratic transformation has certainly allowed the peaceful expression of the ethnic and national issue. Meanwhile, democratization was also fueled and supported by the very sense of ethnic and national entitlement that the native Taiwanese brought with them when they decided to fight for the establishment of democratic rule and politics (Wang 2008, 2013b).

The issue is not only that democracy needs some kind of national framework to flourish since it needs a people (*demos*) (Calhoun 2007; Helbling 2009). It is also, first, that all modern democracies are bathed in the national ideology since birth; and, second, and more importantly, that democracy, by its inner dynamics and procedures, feeds national identity and a national habitus in the community or society where it operates. As a result, the national identity may also change in scope and content to reflect more accurately the democratic society it is associated with. This is precisely what has been happening in the past 25 years in Taiwan with the rise of a new Taiwanese national identity that has reinvented the identity of the state and the meaning of being Taiwanese for its inhabitants.

This chapter attempts thus to look back at the emergence of this new Taiwanese identity under democracy in a different way: as a logical, and even necessary, consequence of democratic practice and socialization. I review first the reality of the rise of Taiwanese national identity through analysis of opinion polls numbers on two relevant series of questions on self-identification and preference for political status of Taiwan. I discuss then the issue of genetic links, and the complementarity or dependence, between democracy and nationalism. Finally, I assess whether the natio-genesis nature of democratic dynamics may be illustrated through the political expression of people educated under democracy, the young generations. I hope this may help to replace Taiwan and Taiwan nationalism in the wider discussion about nation, democracy, and modernity, as well as understand future political developments in Taiwan, Hong Kong, and other polities in the region.

The rise of the new Taiwanese national identity

In all kinds of society, but above all in a democratic society, an individual's representations of their identity and their nation are not passive reflections of the state or political elites' discourses and policies. The power of their agency directly affects the country's political life through voting and participation in social movements, and their political preferences and choices may anticipate, support, or resist the dominant and changing social discourses on their state and nation's definition. Among the various ways to assess a society's national identity, the longitudinal analysis of opinion polls may provide a direct picture of these representations about national and political identity, helping us to track their evolution through time. It completes studies about the nationalist agenda of political parties and leaders, and long-term phenomena of cultural nationalism that have already well documented the struggle between Chinese and Taiwanese nationalisms in Taiwan since the 1980s.

Surveys and polls concerning the major political issues of national identity and preferences about the recognized status of the Taiwanese state have been conducted regularly and with increasing detail since the early 1990s. The aggregated results offer a clear picture of the evolution of public self-identification with Taiwan and China as well as the Taiwanese's preferred choice for political relationships between the polities facing each other across the Taiwan Strait.

The rise of the Taiwanese identity

We look first at two series of polls run by an academic survey center (ESC, NCCU) since 1992, and the pro-KMT TVBS media group since 1999 about the self-identification of the Taiwanese. The classic question in these polls has been to ask respondents to identify as Taiwanese (台灣人), Chinese (中國人), or both (都是). ESC polls bi-yearly figures have been regrouped in multi-year averages to reflect the level of each of these groups under the six successive presidential terms of Lee Teng-hui (1988–2000), Chen Shui-bian (2000–2008), and Ma Ying-jeou (2008–2016).[1] As Table 3.1 shows, three different trajectories characterize the evolution of people's identity preferences.

First, the Chinese identity, which was chosen by a quarter of respondents up to the mid-1990s, has followed a continuous and steep slide up to now, with the 2016 latest figures at 3.4 percent. Second, the Taiwanese identity category, which in 1992 attracted fewer supporters than the Chinese identity, has seen a constant rise in the past 20 years. It grew to one-third of the respondents in the second half of the 1990s, passed the 40 percent threshold under Chen's first term, but it only reached its maximum under Ma Ying-jeou, gaining an absolute majority under his first term, then exceeding 60 percent in 2014. In 2016, it is slightly lower at 58.2 percent. Finally, the dual category of both Taiwanese and Chinese identity has been extremely stable from the early 1990s up to 2008, with multi-year average ranging from 43–46 percent. It is only after Ma's first

Table 3.1 Taiwanese/dual/Chinese identity, 1992–2015, results from the National Chengchi University (NCCU) Election Study Center (ESC)

Date/leader	Taiwanese (%)	Both (%)	Chinese (%)	N.A. (%)
June 1992*	17.3	45.4	26.2	11.0
1992–1995 average **	20.9	46.0	24.1	8.9
1996–1999 average	33.5	43.2	16.3	7.0
2000–2003 average	40.6	43.6	10.2	5.7
2004–2007 average	43.5	45.2	6.3	5.1
2008–2011 average	51.2	40.8	4.0	4.1
2012–2015 average	*57.9*	*35.0*	*3.6*	*3.6*
Under Lee Teng-hui				
December 1992	18.8	49.1	23.2	8.9
December 1995	25.0	47.3	20.5	7.3
June 1996	23.1	50.9	15.8	10.2
December 1999	39.3	44.1	10.7	5.9
Under Chen Shui-bian				
June 2000	36.9	43.8	13.1	6.2
December 2003	43.2	42.9	7.7	6.3
June 2004	40.6	48.3	6.3	4.9
December 2007	43.7	44.5	5.4	6.5
Under Ma Ying-jeou				
June 2008	46.1	45.4	3.4	5.1
December 2008	50.8	40.8	4.2	3.7
2009[†]	51.6	39.8	4.2	4.4
2010[†]	52.7	39.8	3.8	3.7
2011[†]	52.2	40.3	3.9	3.7
June 2012	*53.7*	*39.6*	*3.1*	*3.6*
2012[†]	54.3	38.5	3.6	3.6
2013[†]	57.1	35.8	3.8	3.3
2014[†]	60.6	32.5	3.5	3.5
2015[†]	59.5	33.3	3.3	4.0
Under Tsai Ing-wen				
2016[†]	*58.2*	*34.3*	*3.4*	*4.1*

Notes
* June or December polling results are half-year polling average as compiled by ESC. ** Multi-year averages calculated by the author based on each year polling average provided by ESC. † Whole year polling average as compiled by ESC. Source: Election Study Center, N.C.C.U., "Taiwanese/ Chinese Identification Trend Distribution in Taiwan (1992/06~2016/12)," in "*Important political attitude trend distribution*," January 12, 2017, http://esc.nccu.edu.tw/course/news.php?Sn=166. For June and December results before 2015, cf. Election Study Center, N.C.C.U., "Important political attitude trend distribution," July 2009, and July 2012.

election as president that this group started to fall markedly, with the 2016 figure at 34.3 percent.

The polls thus show a double, and parallel, transfer of identity from the Chinese to the dual identity and from the dual identity to the exclusive Taiwanese identity. While the first shift allowed the dual identity to maintain dominance throughout the Chen administration, the election of Ma Ying-jeou as president seems to have triggered a new wave of transfer of identification to the Taiwanese identity at the expense of the dual identity category, the Chinese identity staying under 5 percent after 2007.

The TVBS Poll Center's series of surveys since 1999 confirms this analysis. As Table 3.2 shows, the polls indicate that the dual identity group remained dominant until 2004, then roughly on par with, or above, the Taiwanese identity group between 2005 and 2008. Only in 2008 the Taiwanese identification took the lead and passed the 50 percent majority threshold to rise further up to 55 percent in 2013.[2] But their polls add an important layer of information about the preferred identity of the dual group respondents. Table 3.3 presents a complementary series of polls that asked a second question about respondents' identity, limiting the choice between the only two answers of Chinese or Taiwanese identity. In 2000 already 58 percent of respondents favored a Taiwanese identity

Table 3.2 Taiwanese/dual/Chinese identity, 2000–2013 (selection)

Date/leader	Taiwanese (%)	Both (%)	Chinese (%)
1999 July	*35*	*50*	*9*
Under Chen Shui-bian			
2000 April	37	51	9
2002 August	35	52	9
2003 April	33	54	6
2004 March	43	44	7
2005 March	45	44	6
2006 October	39	50	6
2007 June	44	43	6
Under Ma Ying-jeou			
2008 April	46	43	3
2009 March	49	44	3
2011 January	50	43	3
2011 August	52	38	3
2012 March	54	40	3
2012 October	55	37	3
2013 October	*55*	*38*	*3*

Source: TVBS Poll Center, *Opinion Poll on Ma-Xi meeting and national identity*, October 2013.

Table 3.3 Taiwanese vs. Chinese identity, 2000–2013 (selection)

Date	Taiwanese (%)	Chinese (%)	N. A. (%)
2000 June	58	18	24
2008 April	68	18	14
2009 March	72	16	13
2011 August	74	13	13
2012 October	75	15	10
2013 October	*78*	*13*	*9*

Source: TVBS Poll Center, *Opinion Poll on Ma-Xi meeting and national identity*, October 2013.

versus only 18 percent a Chinese one, with a quarter of respondents refusing to answer that question. In 2008, 68 percent chose the Taiwanese identity versus the same number of 18 percent with a Chinese identity. It jumped then to 72 percent in 2009 with the Chinese identity starting to fall to 16 percent, and finally in 2013 the Taiwanese identity reached a high of 78 percent versus a new low of 13 percent for the Chinese identity category. This indicates that, among the people choosing the dual identity category, a much larger number, and increasing since 2008, actually favors their Taiwanese identity part rather than their Chinese one. These results also show that contrary to analyses that ascribed the rise of Taiwanese identity to "political manipulations of the masses" by unscrupulous politicians under the Lee Teng-hui and Chen Shui-bian administrations, the most significant increase came again after the election of Ma Ying-jeou and in spite of his administration's propaganda in favor of Chinese nationalism and identity.

Criticisms of the polling methodology, the questions asked, and the terms used have been regularly expressed, leading to some refinement and additional questions or categories in the polling. *In fine*, these surveys all confirm the main trends: the Taiwan people express a distinct political Taiwanese identity, while they may also recognize themselves as culturally and ancestrally part of a larger Chinese or Sinitic community and civilization, but under the name *huaren* (華人, people of Chinese ancestry), and not *zhongguoren* (中國人, Chinese people) (Le Pesant 2011, 2012; Muyard 2012). The Ma administration's emphasis on the "blood" relation of the Taiwanese with the "Chinese ethnic nation" (中華民族), or their common belonging with the Chinese to the descendant group of the Yan and Yellow Emperors (炎黃子孫) may have given some solace to the Chinese nationalists in the Kuomintang or in China, but they have not changed the political identity and national choice of the Taiwanese one bit. Actually, the classic polling question which does not distinguish between 華人 and 中國人 may misidentify the nature of the Chinese aspect of the "dual Taiwanese and Chinese" group, taking an identification with the "Chinese/Sinitic world/civilization" (as 華人) as a potential sense of belonging to a Chinese political community (as 中國人), which actually remains the choice of only a minority of the dual identity group.

Finally, the 13 percent of people claiming Chinese identity in TVBS polls seems to represent the maximum level of Taiwanese holding onto a Chinese national, or racial/ethnic, primary identity and imagination. It is slightly superior to the number of Mainlanders (*waishengren* 外省人) in Taiwan (around 10 percent since the mid-2000s, cf. Council for Hakka Affairs 2008) and should not therefore be equated with them, especially since the younger generations of both Mainlanders and native Taiwanese ancestry are increasingly expressing a sole Taiwanese identity (see below). Analysis of academic surveys on the nature of national identification in both groups indicates nonetheless that Mainlanders represent the largest part of the group of Chinese nationalists and Chinese identifiers (Shen and Wu 2008; Muyard 2012). Alongside northern Taiwan Hakkas, they are also consistently offering the highest electoral support for the KMT and the Blue camp (in the range of 80–90 percent for Mainlanders and 56–68 percent for Hakkas in the presidential elections from 1996–2012, see Wang (2014: 110)).

Support for eventual independence since 2000

The second kind of poll that is most relevant to the study of national and political identity of the Taiwanese is another set of choice answers about their preference for the present and future type of relationships of their state (the ROC in Taiwan) with the Chinese state (the PRC), namely: formal unification, formal independence, or continuation of the so-called status quo. Notwithstanding its constant evolution, preserving the status quo fundamentally represents for all Taiwanese that no move should be made to change the present state of separation of Taiwan and China, de facto independence of Taiwan as the ROC and full sovereignty of the ROC in Taiwan.

The ESC series of polls offer the classic range of six possible answers from immediate to eventual independence or unification, and temporary or ad infinitum status quo. When all answers supporting status quo are tabulated, the result is an overwhelming support for the present cross-Strait state of affairs of between 80 percent and 86 percent since the mid-2000s. This large consensus behind the status quo is not, however, conducive to understanding the Taiwanese's real desire for the political status of their country beyond the present state of affairs, or how such wishes are feeding, or are coherent with, their expression of national and political identity. In order to better understand the Taiwanese positions toward the independence-unification issue, a more detailed analysis of these polls is required, highlighting the change occurring since the 1990s and the meaning of each category of answer. First, the polls show a jump for the "status quo indefinitely" answer from 9.8 percent in 1994 to 27.7 percent in 2012, and 26.1 percent in 2016, together with very stable levels in support of preserving the status quo now and postponing any decision to a future time, this category scoring between 29 percent and 38 percent since 1994, and staying within a 33~36 percent range since 2008. At the same time, there is an important decrease in support for unification, be it now or later, with this group's numbers halved between 2000 and 2015 and falling to 9~10 percent since 2008. On the other side of the political spectrum, support for independence has doubled from 11.1 percent in 1994 to 22.9 percent in 2016, with levels hovering between 19 percent and 24 percent since 2008 (see Table 3.4).

The current status quo meaning concretely Taiwan's de facto independence and its political separation from China, the category "status quo indefinitely" may be considered to be composed of closet independence supporters, be they wary of a military conflict with China and ready to settle for a practical independence under the ROC name as long as nothing changes, or at least political supporters of the separate identity of the ROC in Taiwan with no interest in any kind of unification with a present or future China. In 2016, counted together with the avowed independence supporters, they constitute 49 percent of the population supporting forever separation of Taiwan and China, not including those who prefer to decide later, versus only 10.2 percent expressing support for changing the status quo and achieving unification today or in the future.

Behind the explicit support for the maintenance of the status quo, appears thus a strong trend in favor of Taiwan independence, belying most analyses

Table 3.4 Independence, status quo, or unification, 1994–2016, from NCCU ESC surveys (%)

Date	1 Independence asap	2 Status quo – toward Independence	Total independence (1 + 2)	3 Status quo indefinitely	4 Status quo decide later	Total unification (5 + 6)	5 Status quo – toward unification	6 Unification asap	N.R.
1994	3.1	8.0	11.1	9.8	38.5	20.0	15.6	4.4	20.5
1996	4.1	9.5	13.6	15.3	30.5	22.0	19.5	2.5	18.6
1998	5.7	11.5	17.2	15.9	30.3	18.0	15.9	2.1	18.7
2000	3.1	11.6	14.7	19.2	29.5	19.3	17.3	2.0	17.4
2002	4.3	13.8	18.1	15.0	36.2	18.2	15.7	2.5	12.4
2004	4.4	15.2	19.6	20.9	36.5	12.1	10.6	1.5	11.0
2006	5.6	13.8	19.4	19.9	38.7	14.1	12.1	2.0	7.9
2008	7.1	16.0	23.1	21.5	35.8	10.2	8.7	1.5	9.4
2010	6.2	16.2	22.4	25.4	35.9	10.2	9.0	1.2	6.1
2012	4.8	15.1	19.9	27.7	33.9	10.4	8.7	1.7	8.1
2014	5.9	18.0	23.9	25.2	34.3	9.2	7.9	1.3	7.3
2015	4.3	17.9	22.2	25.4	34.0	9.6	8.1	1.5	8.8
2016	4.6	18.3	22.9	26.1	33.3	10.2	8.5	1.7	7.4

Source: Election Study Center, N.C.C.U., "Taiwan Independence vs. Unification with the Mainland Trend Distribution in Taiwan (1992/06~2016/12)," in "Important political attitude trend distribution," January 12, 2017, http://esc.nccu.edu.tw/course/news.php?Sn=167.

about the indecisiveness or hedging of the Taiwanese, and rather uncovering the constrained nature of their support for the status quo. This is also confirmed by the underestimation of the real number of supporters of independence in Taiwan in the ESC polls as other surveys, with answers restricted to the two choices of independence or unification, or offering specific conditions for independence or unification, demonstrate.

This is illustrated by the TVBS polls on the issue of independence and unification. According to the polls in columns two to four of Table 3.5, in late 2013, a large majority indeed desired the maintenance of the status quo, although a bit inferior to the ESC figures: 64 percent of Taiwanese supported the status quo, 24 percent the independence of Taiwan, and 7 percent unification with China. These results have been rather stable since 2007 beyond occasional ups and downs. However, when the TVBS pollsters reduce the possible answers to only two choices, respondents increasingly and overwhelmingly opt for Taiwan's independence (cf. Table 3.5, columns five and six): in 2007, already 55 percent supported independence versus 25 percent for unification; in late 2013, 71 percent favored independence versus 18 percent in favor of unification. It means that among those who favor the status quo (64 percent of all respondents), only 17 percent wish unification, while 73 percent in fact support the country's independence.

Yet the support for independence or unification, and the desire to stay separate from China in the future, may also be determined by the present political and economic circumstances across the Strait with, on the one hand, the PRC's dictatorship, lack of freedom, and lower socio-economic levels in China, and on the other hand, the open threat of war by Beijing if Taiwan declares formal

Table 3.5 Independence, status quo, or unification polls, 2000–2013

Date	Independence (%)	Status quo (%)	Unification (%)	Independence (%)	Unification (%)	N.R. (%)
2000	16	55	14			
2004	19	64	10			
2007 March	15	62	9	55	25	20
2007 August	23	58	8	65	21	13
2008 June	19	58	8	65	19	16
2008 October	24	58	5	68	14	18
2009 March	19	64	5	66	17	18
2009 December	20	64	4	68	13	19
2011 January	21	61	9	68	18	14
2011 August	16	67	5	65	17	18
2011 October	20	62	6	67	17	17
2012 March	19	68	5	69	16	15
2012 October	18	65	7	65	17	18
2013 June	22	62	8	68	18	14
2013 October	24	64	7	71	18	11

Source: TVBS Poll Center, *Opinion Poll on Ma-Xi meeting and national identity*, October 2013.

independence. To understand the weight of these circumstances, we must turn to other surveys that offer some rather clear answers.

First, surveys providing additional questions to the respondents on what would be their wish for present and future political relationships with China demonstrate that most supporters of the status quo would shift their choice to independence for Taiwan if such independence would not trigger war with China. This is illustrated by the research done by Wu Nai-teh, who developed a poll questionnaire in the 1990s asking specifically whether one would support unification if the socio-economic and political conditions were the same in Taiwan and China, and whether one would support independence if it did not trigger war with China (Wu 2012, 2013, 2014). The results indicate that those in favor of ultimate unification under the same conditions of development decreased from 66.6 percent in 1992 to 29.2 percent in 2013. Meanwhile, the supporters of independence under peaceful conditions rose from 36.7 percent in 1992 to 55 percent in 2013 (Wu 2014). As significant as these results are those indicating *opposition* to unification or independence. In 2013, Wu's survey showed that 63.8 percent of Taiwanese opposed unification with China even if there were no differences in political and economic conditions across the Strait, while only 38.5 percent of people opposed the declaration of independence even if it did not trigger war.

Wu's survey results are confirmed by public polling run by the (Kuomintang-leaning) *Global Views* magazine. Between 2008 and 2011, these polls indicate that only 12–16 percent of Taiwanese respondents would favor eventual unification with China in the future if both sides have similar levels of economic and political development, versus around 67 percent who don't see the need for it (GVRSC 2011). Similarly, between 2008 and 2014, 60–69 percent opposed the idea that Taiwan and China should ultimately be unified (versus 15–24 percent in favor), while 45–51 percent agreed that Taiwan should ultimately become an independent country (versus 30–38 percent who oppose it) (GVRSC 2014). The latest iteration of this type of poll in May 2016, by independent pollster TISR, confirms the stability of these numbers and of the Taiwanese's position towards unification: 66.4 percent oppose ultimate unification, and 18.5 percent support it, while 52.6 percent support ultimate independence with 30.9 percent opposing it (TISR 2016).

These results show the preference for the status quo expressed by the Taiwanese is clearly a secondary choice or a forced choice under the present cross-Strait situation with Beijing threatening war to prevent the formal declaration, or recognition, of the independence of the current polity in Taiwan as a Taiwanese nation-state. It hides a preferred choice for independence, which is not only overwhelmingly shared among the population but also has been constantly growing since 2000. Conversely the option of eventual unification, even under the best conditions of socio-political and economic similarity and peaceful means, has gradually lost its appeal for the Taiwanese to the point that in the 2010s around two-thirds are opposed to it, while less than 25 percent would consider it.

Finally, a different set of polling questions makes clear how the Taiwanese define their country relative to China. When asked by the TISR polling center about the nature of their state and its relationship with the Chinese state, 78 percent of respondents indicated in September 2014 that they considered Taiwan and China to be two distinctly developed countries (*guojia* 國家), while 5.1 percent believed both sides belonged to a divided Republic of China (ROC) and 2 percent to a divided People's Republic of China (PRC) (TISR 2014). This means that only 7.1 percent of Taiwanese support the KMT and CCP's interpretation that both Taiwan and Mainland China belong to one country called China. Conversely, an overwhelming majority quietly states that Taiwan is an independent country separate and distinct from the "real China." In that sense, the fact that the majority of Taiwanese may accept that Taiwan is the Republic of China means that they also consider that the Republic of China is Taiwan and only Taiwan at the exclusion of Mainland China.

The persistence of a stable residual minority of 13–18 percent of politically Chinese identifiers and supporters of ultimate unification since the mid-2000s needs, however, to be emphasized too, indicating that there indeed exists a Chinese nationalist group in Taiwan. The fact that they are mainly concentrated in the North and Taipei, and over-represented at the highest levels of the state and administrations and in the economic, social, and cultural elites – as the Ma Ying-jeou government exhibited weekly between 2008 and 2016 – have some significant political effects, in Taiwan and abroad. By virtue of being in powerful positions (largely inherited from the period of Mainlanders and KMT's domination of the state), this China-oriented group has given a distorted image of the Taiwanese people's perspectives on the issues of national identity and relations with China, and has been in position to develop policies that were increasingly disconnected with the needs and interests of the rest of the population while favoring the benefits of the few, especially the industrialists and the upper-middle class linked to China-based interests. The phenomenon of plutocratic behavior, increasingly denounced since the 2000s in Western democracies, therefore, takes in Taiwan a tint of minority nationalism and outsider interests which have added to the growing frustrations and anger of the civil society toward an unresponsive government elite, and which exploded in the Sunflower Movement and then the KMT's series of electoral debacles in the 2014 local elections (Muyard 2015) and the 2016 general elections.

Today, the Taiwanese national identity and its mainstream civic nationalism are dominant and established facts. Taiwanese identity and the support for independence will not go away in the forthcoming decades since, as we will show below, younger generations are even more Taiwan-centered than the older generations, belying the discourse that Taiwan identity and rejection of subordination of Taiwan to China would be stronger among the generations born before 1945. Resistance, coming mostly from an entrenched political and cultural Chinese nationalist elite, has repeatedly questioned and challenged the validity of these evolutions, on statistical, political, or moral grounds. In a rather surprising turn to many, these trends have persisted and intensified under

Ma Ying-jeou's administration, and against his wishes, toning down most of the critics about these data. Now, what is appearing more clearly is that the genetic links between nationalism and democracy may be central to the emergence of the contemporary Taiwanese national identity.

Democracy and the building of a national habitus

The impact of democratization on the self-recognition of the Taiwanese people has been devastating for the former authoritarian state ideology of Chinese nationalism and Chinese identity. That the China the Kuomintang has claimed to represent since 1949 has all but disappeared, except in Kuomintang Chinese nationalists' minds, while the real China concretely appeared so radically different from the Taiwanese society and increasingly threatening to Taiwan's new democratic way of life are two major factors behind the rejection of Chinese identity among most Taiwanese. But this *out-group* factor must be perceived together with several *in-group* dynamics. The main reasons usually suggested to explain the change in Taiwan's national identity include the KMT party-state's repression of the native Taiwanese (Holo and Hakka, or *benshengren* 本省人), the "localization/Taiwanization" politics of Lee Teng-hui, the DPP's nationalist policies, and international influence (for a review, cf. Muyard 2012; Wang 2008, 2013b).

In many ways, Taiwan follows a classic model of national self-determination under economic modernization and moving out of colonization/ruling minority power after decades of political repression (cf. Gellner 1983). The emergence of a distinct national consciousness among the people of Taiwan, at least in part of the elite groups, is indeed not new, and can be traced to the 1930s in the context of Japanese colonization. It spread more widely after 1945 and the conflicts between the ROC authoritarian regime and the local Taiwanese population over the questions of access to political power and representation of the native Taiwanese political, economic, social, and cultural interests (Chang 2000). But it is not sufficient to explain the nature of the new Taiwanese nation in the making. Similarly, Beijing's direct or indirect actions, including the impressive rise of the Chinese economy, may have accelerated societal changes in terms of divergent national identities. They are not, however, their direct cause, which is rather to be found, I would suggest, in the dynamics of democratic discourse and practice, which generate *quasi-automatically* a process of local or grassroots-based community-building that, if not in resonance with the nationalist ideology and politics at the state level, may emerge as a distinct national identity and self-determination movement. It is, therefore, necessary to look into the dynamics of democratic change, how it transforms the relations between the state and civil society toward more power for individuals and local interests, and is conducive to introducing the formation of a distinct society and identity through belonging to a democratic community of life.

Modern nations and democracy

Two intertwined political characteristics have defined the modern state – and modern times – since their inception in mid-seventeenth-century England, and furthermore after the French Revolution: (1) democracy, or the representation of the people's interests and needs at the highest levels of state power; and (2) the nation and its corollary, nationalism.

Ideologically, the modern nation represents the symbol, the voice, and the will of an undivided people sharing some common history, culture, political and economic interests, and united by political rights under the principles of liberty and equality. It locates its symbolic person and power in the modern state institutions. The nation-state then claims to represent the public good and interests, integrating and superseding all individual and local/community-based interests. This ideological construct only works fully if these individual and local, community-based, interests are really taken care of, and are represented at the main levels of power that are the state/national and local governments. In other words, the legitimacy of the nation and its state depends on the proper representation – in practice, the democratic representation – of the changing and specific interests and needs of all the members of the society under the state's control. Failure by the state to fulfill these requirements will turn its national discourse into an empty ideology and open the door to the formation of a new locally based political consciousness.

For centuries, these two processes have taken the form of movements for national self-determination and growing legal recognition of individual political rights, with a gradual widening of "the people" involved, until all these principles were officially recognized as universal in the Charter of the new United Nations Organization in 1945. As Armitage observes in his global history of independence movements, since the American Declaration of Independence, the world has witnessed "a contagion of independence and sovereignty" (Armitage 2007: 138) and a proliferation of new nation-states in four major waves: 1790–1848, 1918–1920s, post-1945, and post-1990. Most of these new states were created in the twentieth century and under the call for the self-determination of their core constitutive nation. Yet, due to the devastating wars partly waged under the flags of nationalism and racial segregation during the twentieth century, a growing abhorrence toward nationalism and the nation developed among liberal academia and left-wing intelligentsia and political parties. As Laitin (2007) noticed, it is received wisdom among the educated public and social scientists that nationalism is dangerous and prone to lead to violent conflict. Today's vulgate is that nationalism is "bad" and opposed to the spirit of democracy, especially liberal democracy. Nielsen (1999) observes that self-described, liberal, anti-nationalists believe that nationalism cannot but be xenophobic, authoritarian, exclusivist and, where it has the opportunity, often expansionist as well. Ironically, anti-nationalist liberals and leftists have adopted as their general definition of nationalism the ultra-nationalist and racist perversion of the national idea. Non-democratic, criminal, and racialist behavior that predates the modern nation are thus attributed to the nature of nationalism rather than to well-entrenched power politics in traditional and authoritarian states. While nationalism has indeed often been used as a pretext for violence or war in order to hide concrete economic, political or class interests, it does not appear by itself conducive to violence. Quantitative studies analysed by Laitin (2007) show that there is no affinity between national differences and violence, and also, contrary to the standard view that ethnic conflict is a worldwide phenomenon, that the world reality is a near ubiquity of ethnic cooperation.

The salient issue here is whether nationalism is by nature as "bad" as the liberal orthodoxy frames it, and how it relates to the cohesiveness of a state and a society, especially the democratic ones (Nodia 1992; Calhoun 2007). Classic views on nationalism and the nation have largely focused on the levels of state power and domestic politics, their use of nationalism as a political tool, on their analysis as political ideology, or the wreckage that authorities using extreme and racist nationalist ideologies have done in wars and domestic political persecutions (e.g. Hobsbawm 1990). Too often, however, societies and their historical and societal developments are overlooked, as if people – and masses – were by definition lacking agency and ready to be manipulated by governments and political groups – a vision which is itself rather contemptuous of the spirit and practice of liberal democracy. Nodia even suggests it reflects the "old liberal fear of the people," of the "populace" by the liberal elites, which "takes now the more respectable form of aversion to nationalism" (1992: 14). Concurrently, the genetic links between the dynamics of democracy and nationalism are mostly excluded from the discussion, as a blind spot of the political analysis, and little research has been published on them (Noiriel 1991; Nodia 1992; Helbling 2009).

What is often ignored, is that nationalism and national identity are at the very core of the liberal democratic Western modern states. Currently, all contemporary democratic states (genuine nation-states or not[3]) are built on the firm bases of a "sovereign people," a state-engineered nationalism (even if called patriotism), and a "new" national identity mostly constructed since the nineteenth century (and often later) by intellectual elites and the state (Anderson 1983; Gellner 1983; Thiesse 1999). As stated by Yack (1999: 115): "The age of liberal individualism has also been the age of nationalism; liberal practices have been realized, for the most part, within the framework of national communities."

Yet it is not only at the symbolic level that democracy calls for and generates a national habitus. In practice, in opening the public space to the multiplication of horizontal contacts and relationships, directly or through media of information and communication (Anderson's print capitalism for the eighteenth and nineteenth centuries, social media today), beyond the limits of the family or ascriptive groups, the dynamics of democratic practice (together with economic modernization) are a powerful driver of the formation of new political and national consciousness. Concurrently, the very procedures and spirit of democratic behavior may also dampen potential communitarian or "ethnic" conflicts (especially when non-territorialized), through the recognition of and respect for the rights of all to be part of the debate and the common determination of the state policies and national issues.

Democratic discourse and practices thus provide much more than elections and political legitimacy for the ruling group. They also bring an institutional and practical recognition of the horizontal links criss-crossing society, and of local-ized (as opposed to state or centralized), community-based, common interests and needs that demand to be fully represented at the highest levels of power and in national policies. Democracy is also always about defining who is part of the political community, who are the citizens allowed to cast a vote on the state identity and policies. It calls for a distinct body of citizens and would-be nation-als on a delimited territory. Finally, it generates demands for, and generally translates into, increase in the power of local administrative authorities seen as representing and better promoting the local, or specific, communities, interests, and needs. In that context, factors of economic growth and development, com-petition among groups for state resources, and social redistribution of the overall wealth play major roles.

Recent cases of independence movements and political secession among Western democratic countries also illustrate the persistence of these nation-genesis processes and highlight how democratic practice and administrative devolution and autonomy may lead to demands for even higher autonomy and outright independence. They are usually based on lasting feelings of historical, social, and cultural distinctiveness and lack of adequate representation of their distinct interests and needs at the level of the union/federal/central government, including inadequate economic benefits, returns, or redistribution from this gov-ernment's coffers.[4]

Democratic practices as such do not necessarily lead to nationhood. But since they require and frame a community of citizens united by common interests, needs, and values, and constantly reactivate horizontal and vertical links between the participants and the elected officials in democratic procedures, these prac-tices anchor the necessity of direct political representation of the local com-munity/body at the highest level of government. Democracy appears indeed like a Pandora's box for all established powers and takes on a life on its own once the people participate in its institutions and identify with its processes, proced-ures, and spirit. For that reason, lack of appropriate representation of the local, majority, or national community at the political decision-making level, together with acts or expressions of cultural oppression or contempt by the ruling group toward the majority, and growing economic and wealth imbalances between social groups and classes, especially among the middle class, are strong fuel for the formation of a territorially-centered identity.

That is why Nodia insists that "democratic transitions (and not just industrial-ism or capitalism) engender nation," and that "in emergent democracies, move-ments for democracy and movements for independence are often one and the same", since both "are acting in the name of 'self-determination'" (1992: 9). In Helbling's terms:

> Democracy and nationalism constitute not complementary but rather mutually dependent logics in the sense that nationalism tells us who is allowed to participate in a democratic system, and democracy constitutes a process during which the cultural boundaries of a nation are defined.
>
> (2009: 11)

The state also plays a major role in the process. Noiriel remarks thus that:

> The essential factor in the construction of a national group lies in its progressive institutionalization through the welfare state [*état social*], which conveys the national norms throughout the whole society, but also succeeds in inducing individuals to interiorize them (and thus inherit them unconsciously).
>
> (1991: 93)[5]

Furthermore, with the emergence of the welfare state, new social rights based on citizenship criteria and financed by the national body of citizens, are added to the political rights, reinforcing the integration of all individuals, regardless of class or origins, into the national community. The Taiwanese case seems to well illustrate this construction of a new national habitus after democratization, together with state-sponsored processes of national assimilation of all groups, under a territorially delimited political and new welfare state.

Democracy in Taiwan and the new national identity

In 1991–1992, the ROC electorate was redefined as being only the people of the free area of the ROC, meaning Taiwan, Kinmen, and Matsu. The stage was thus set to generate a national identity focused only on this territory and the people who inhabit it, together with the redefinition of the meaning of these inhabitants as *Taiwanese* in two ways: politically and nationally, as first, or only, Taiwanese, and no longer Chinese; and as democratic citizens, including all of the territory's inhabitants regardless of their origins, ethnic groups, country of birth, previous citizenship (as long as they fulfill the administrative requirements to be citizens of the ROC as defined by the democratic state). This was, however, just the start of a process, as it requires time and practical participation in common democratic procedures for a national community to crystallize.

What happened after the beginning of democratization was first the freedom to publicly advocate the majority's interests and the old Taiwan-centered consciousness of the *benshengren* 本省人 (Holo and Hakka). It also spurred the growing public recognition of the specific culture, history, and society of the native Taiwanese (and later of Indigenous peoples, and even of less-privileged Mainlander communities), which had been repressed for 40 years. Through active interaction between state and party leaders and civil society, democratic dynamics led the transformation of this consciousness and this self-identity from exclusive and ethnic-based, to an inclusive civic national identity. The policies of state localization and Taiwanization promoted by Lee Teng-hui and followed by the DPP also contributed to developing a new framework of citizenship under the concept of "new Taiwanese" (*xin Taiwanren* 新台灣人) embracing all ROC citizens, including Mainlanders (*waishengren* 外省人) and new immigrants. This new framework, first publicly proposed by Annette Lu Hsiu-lien in 1979 (Wang 2013b: 94), has defined the emerging new Taiwanese nation as based on territorial and political criteria, democratic values, community of fate and of life, and recognition of the four, then five, main ethnic groups and their respective cultures and memories as all parts of Taiwan's national heritage.

Out of the former native Taiwanese identity built in differentiation from the Japanese identity between 1895 and 1945, then reinforced by the struggle against the KMT-imposed Chinese national identity under the structural social discrimination of the native Taiwanese, Taiwanese national identity transformed into an all-encompassing, multi-ethnic, multicultural identity, including Holo, Hakka, Mainlander and Austronesian Indigenous peoples groups, together with their histories and cultures. Being Taiwanese today does not thus imply rejecting one's putative Chinese history, culture, or ancestry, but on the contrary, means to recognize it as part of the wider Taiwanese culture based on the unique fusion of traditional Chinese culture, Taiwanese specific local culture, Austronesian culture, as well as foreign cultural input, from Japan or the USA, or even the culture of the new and fifth "ethnic group" formed by the South-east Asian immigrants and spouses, inasmuch as it has marked the specific history of Taiwan.

At the same time the Taiwanese cultural identity was changing from being perceived as restricted to Holo-speaking people (and their popular culture and language long decried as uncouth by educational and cultural authorities during the one-party era) to being redefined as all-inclusive, territorially-based, non-language-specific, and expressing the Taiwanese democratic society and experience, the perception of the *Chinese* culture in Taiwan has become more and more associated, on the one hand, with the ancient imperial Chinese culture and the high, often conservative, culture imposed under the KMT dictatorship, and, on the other hand, with contemporary Chinese culture as developed in the People's Republic of China (PRC) since 1949. The growing sense of distinctiveness of the Taiwanese from the PRC society that went along with the discovery of the "real China" since the legal opening of cross-Strait contacts in 1987 has thus contributed to push the Taiwanese to differentiate themselves even more from being seen as Chinese or associated with Chinese people's behavior and culture, be it in Taiwan, in China, or internationally (Chang 1991; Wang 2000; Lynch 2002).

Taiwan's contemporary political change can also be seen as a case of the slow building of a national and democratic habitus. Taiwan's electoral dynamics since democratization have indeed been far from following a simple pattern of opposition between Chinese and Taiwanese nationalism or between ethnic groups (Fell 2011, 2012). By contrast to many countries of the Third democratic wave, Taiwan's democratization did not immediately result in the rejection of the political party in power under the previous dictatorship, but on the contrary, saw this party maintaining and even increasing its electoral success during and after the 1990s. Nor did the liberation of speech and full democracy result at once in a large embrace of Taiwanese nationalism. In many ways, the middle-of-the road and unassertive expression of political identity of most Taiwanese has been reflecting the still recent experimentation with political and opinion freedoms, and the weight of the legacy of 40 years of imposed Chinese nationalism and Sinicization policies, especially in educational, cultural, and state institutions. It also corresponded to the specificity of the 1990s political era where a native Taiwanese president and KMT chairman symbolized the democratization of the country and gradually acknowledged in public discourses and state and educational policies the distinct identity and history of the country's people against all the political history of his very own party.

The first transition of power, with Chen Shui-bian's victory at the presidential poll in 2000, only came under very specific political and electoral circumstances and is better understood as one event in a continuum of socio-political changes that informed the gradual shift in national imagination or national identity of the Taiwanese electorate, rather than a radical electoral turn or a one-time change. In 2000, the national identity of the Taiwanese was still largely seen as in flux and in play, undetermined or confused, both in responses to their self-ascription as Taiwanese or Chinese, or regarding their wishes for Taiwan's formal and eventual political status, and was assumed by most domestic and foreign analysts to be for the large majority still somehow "fundamentally" Chinese. Whereas academic surveys were already showing a rise of Taiwanese identity and decline of Chinese identity, it was often explained away by "period effects" or specific political events in the 1990s involving negative actions by China against Taiwan and Taiwanese, and seen as reversible by future positive events (Liu and Ho 1999; Ho and Liu 2003).

After 2008, the Lee Teng-hui "new Taiwanese" policy was formally continued under Ma Ying-jeou's KMT administration, with he himself as one of the first, as a "new Taiwanese," to politically benefit from this inclusive definition of Taiwaneseness. At the same time, a major official shift happened, where this Taiwanese identity came to be redefined by the government as only a part of, and subordinate to, a larger Chinese identity, which would represent the country's genuine national identity, according to Ma and his fellow KMT Chinese nationalists. For Ma, both sides of the Taiwan Strait belong to one Chinese ethnic-race nation (*zhonghua minzu* 中華民族) beyond their distinct citizenships, histories, and political trajectories (Ma 2008). However, neither this concept, nor Ma's reading of the merely local or provincial nature of the Taiwanese identity, have taken hold in society, and rather marked him as detached, and his policies as undermining the majority's wishes for an independent future for the whole Taiwanese community.

The growing discrepancy between the Taiwanese's perception of their national identity and Ma and Beijing's insistence on a blood-based Chinese nation as one big family actually illustrates the difference between a modern nation and an ethnic community. As Nodia observes, the concept of nationhood has an intrinsic link to the idea of an autonomous personality, which is also central to liberal democracy.

> [It is] what distinguishes modern self-conscious nationalism from primordial ethnicity. The essence of ethnicity lies in its extension of the idea of *family* to the macrosocial level. Community is "imagined" as a big family stemming from the same ancestor. When a nation "imagines" itself, however, it sees not a family, but a unique personality with a distinct character.
>
> (Nodia 1992: 11)

National identity in a democratic society: generations educated after the end of authoritarianism

Academic surveys targeting the political attitudes of young Taiwanese only started to appear regularly in the mid-2000s. Similarly, the publication of specific age demographics for public poll results occurred quite late, around 2006. Both expressed a new interest in knowing what the generations raised under a democratic regime thought and felt about the country's future and identity. Since then, more in-depth studies of the younger generations' (usually aged 20–29, the voting age in Taiwan being 20) political opinions and values have been conducted, including large-scale questionnaires and focus groups among university students (e.g. Rigger 2006, 2007; Cabestan and Le Pesant 2009; Le Pesant 2011, 2012, 2014; Lin 2013, 2014), while reasonably regular polling results on the political views of the younger generations are available only since 2012.[6] These studies have often emphasized some significant differences in the youth's perception of politics, nationalism, ethnicity, and relationship with China compared to older generations. Rationalism and pragmatism, individual economic achievement, and rejection of party politics, ethnic identity, and nationalist disputes have, for instance, often been seen as major characteristics of these generations (Rigger 2006, 2007; Le Pesant 2011). The growth of youth-based social and political movements since the early 2010s culminating in the Sunflower Movement in March 2014 came therefore as a surprise to many politicians and political analysts. However, attentive analysis and blogs and polls readings since 2008 had already indicated that these new generations were actually not only identifying more with Taiwan as their country and political community than their elders, but also were deeply concerned by issues of social justice and economic inequality (Cole 2012, 2013, 2014; Le Pesant 2012; Lin 2013, 2014).

The division of the population into different age groups by polling centers does not necessarily match demographic or sociological generations, whose determination is still very much in debate among social scientists. Polls taken today classify the population into five or six age groups, from 20–29 years old to 30–39, 40–49, 50–59, and over 60 years old (also divided into 60–69 and over 70 years old age groups). It does not include the young below 20 years old, although students start undergraduate school around 18. In 2015, the

20–29-year-old group members were born between 1986 and 1995, while the 30–39-year-old group were born between 1976 and 1985. People born under full democracy (since 1992) are only starting to appear in the polling data (aged under 23 years in 2015) but constitute the entire body of today's college students. Future survey data should then gradually be able to give a more comprehensive picture of this sociological generation.

Studies by Le Pesant conducted between 2005 and 2012 among university students have repeatedly shown the deep attachment of young Taiwanese to Taiwan as their nation and their support for independence. He stresses that they are often reluctant to be drawn into issues of identity,

> not because they do not consider them important, but because they feel that identification with Taiwan is a given, that it is shared by the overwhelming majority of the population and that they therefore refuse to join in with the 'game of manipulation and division of identity' played by both sides of the political divide.
>
> (Le Pesant 2012: 76)

Lin Thung-hong's (2013, 2014) analyses of Taiwanese political attitudes by age groups also show a growing identification as Taiwanese, growing support for Taiwan independence under the right conditions, and lower support for unification among younger generations throughout the 1995–2010 period.

When we look at the demographics of opinion polls results on national identity issues, all the trends analyzed above for the whole population are markedly more pronounced for the younger generations, with up to 75.8 percent choosing Taiwanese identity in the classic three-choice poll in March 2015 (Table 3.6). When compared with data from academic-run surveys, these high numbers appear reliable for the post-2010 period. It is also confirmed by the results of the Taiwanese vs. Chinese identity choice, which eliminates the "cultural Chineseness/Taiwaneseness" dimension often included in the choice for a dual identity (Table 3.7). Here the polls run by TVBS in 2012 and 2013 show a marked

Table 3.6 Taiwan youth (20–29 years) Taiwanese/dual/Chinese identity, 2006–2015 (%)

Date	Taiwanese	Both	Chinese
Liberty Times 2006	62.1	17.9	8.9
CommonWealth 2009*	75.0	14.0	7.0
TVBS 2012 March	56.0	42.0	2.0
TBT 2014 March	64.6	33.2	2.2
TBT 2014 June	72.9	21.2	0.7
TBT 2015 March	75.8	24.2	0.0

Sources: Polls by *Liberty Times* (2006), *CommonWealth Magazine* (2009), TVBS (2012), TBT (2014, 2015a).

Note
* 18–29-year-olds.

Table 3.7 Taiwan youth (20–29 years) Taiwanese vs. Chinese identity, 2012–2015 (%)

Date/detailed by age-groups	Taiwanese	Chinese	N.A.
TVBS 2012 October/All	75	15	10
20–29 years	87	9	5
30–39 years	84	12	4
40–49 years	74	17	9
50–59 years	63	20	17
+60 years	69	16	14
TVBS 2013 June/All	73	17	11
20–29 years	88	7	5
30–39 years	74	19	5
40–49 years	71	15	9
50–59 years	67	22	4
+60 years	63	20	10
TVBS 2013 October/All	78	13	9
20–29 years	89	11	0
30–39 years	83	11	6
40–49 years	75	16	10
50–59 years	76	14	10
+60 years	69	14	18
TBT 2014 June/All	89.2	6.7	4.1
20–29 years	92.0	4.8	3.2
30–39 years	91.3	4.7	3.9
40–49 years	90.1	7.8	2.1
50–59 years	88.2	8.2	3.6
60–69 years	89.3	6.5	4.3
+70 years	84.5	9.7	5.7
TBT 2015 June/All	87.8	7.0	5.2
20–29 years	94.9	0.7	4.4
30–39 years	96.2	2.1	1.7
40–49 years	82.8	10.2	7.0
50–59 years	84.5	10.3	5.2
60–69 years	82.7	10.0	7.4
+70 years	82.0	10.7	7.3

Sources: Polls by TVBS (2012, 2013), TBT (2014, 2015b).

difference between the whole-population levels of Taiwanese identity and Chinese identity and the preferences indicated by younger age groups, highlighting a generational effect in the data. In October 2012, 87 percent of 20–29-year-olds opted for the Taiwanese identity, the highest among all groups, and 12 percent more than the whole population average, and only 9 percent identified as Chinese versus 15 percent for the whole population. One year later, the 2013 TVBS poll indicates that the Taiwanese identity choice has increased slightly to almost 90 percent of the 20–29-year-olds, a growth mirrored in the rising level of this choice for the whole population and most other age groups. The June 2014 TBT poll, conducted after the Sunflower movement, showed an even higher identification as Taiwanese, both for the 20–29-year-old age group (92 percent) and for the all-groups average (89.2 percent). Of significance, in all polls, the two age groups of 20–29-year-olds and the 30–39-year-olds score higher for Taiwanese identity and (with one exception) lower for Chinese identity than the whole population average, indicating that the overall rise in Taiwanese identity is in recent years led by the younger age groups, especially the 20–29-year-olds, and then reflected in the older generations.

Age demographic data from polls about Taiwan's status in relation to Mainland China and the independence vs. unification outcome are much less publicly available. Academic surveys and Green camp think tanks polling offer some indications that the results about both issues are similar or higher in support for independence among the young generations compared to the whole population. Confirming Lin's studies based on 2010 data (Lin 2013, 2014), figures from a distinct 2010 academic survey (Le Pesant 2014) indicate that 80 percent of the 20–25-year-old age group favor independence if it does not trigger war (+5.4 percent compared to a similar 2005 survey), only 33.7 percent support unification with China under similar level of political and economic development (–12.4 percent), and 45.7 percent manifest a complete opposition to any future unification (+12.3 percent).

The 2014 and 2015 TBT polls also give recent data about the younger generations' views on independence and unification (Table 3.8). The results show that, in June 2014, support for independence rose to 40.8 percent, compared to 48.6 percent for the status quo and 7.8 percent for unification among the 20–29-year-olds, whereas the 30–39-year-old group is closer to the whole population average. When reduced to only two choices, the overall figure for independence

Table 3.8 Independence, status quo, or unification by age groups, 2014–2015 (%)

Age groups	Independence	Status quo	Unification	Independence	Unification	N.R.
TBT 2014 June						
All	28.3	55.8	7.8	65.1	18.6	16.3
20–29	40.8	48.6	7.8	71.1	18.9	10.0
30–39	31.9	55.3	8.5	69.2	20.7	10.1
40–49	27.7	61.2	8.8	64.9	21.5	13.5
50–59	23.9	59.4	7.9	63.9	16.4	19.7
60–69	19.4	61.4	5.8	57.5	19.9	22.6
+70	23.6	46.9	7.6	63.0	11.6	25.4
TBT 2015 July						
All				69.5	13.7	16.8
20–29				84.1	7.5	8.4
30–39				76.0	13.4	10.6
40–49				62.0	22.1	15.9
50–59				67.0	11.6	21.4
60–69				62.2	13.5	24.4
+70				61.7	13.1	25.2

Source: Polls by TBT (2014, 2015b).

was 66.1 percent (inferior to similar TVBS polls' results discussed above but with a higher non-response rate), with both 20–29-year-old and 30–39-year-old age groups scoring above the average at 71.1 percent and 69.2 percent. Support for unification is rather similar among younger groups and the whole sample at 18–20 percent. In July 2015, 84.1 percent of the 20–29-year-olds expressed support for independence with only 7.5 percent in favor of eventual unification; in the 30–39-year-old age group, 76 percent chose Taiwan's future independence versus 13.4 percent for unification.

All these polls show a cline in opinions along the generations, indicating higher support for Taiwanese identity and independence among the younger age groups educated under democracy than in the Taiwanese population as a whole, while older generations express more support for dual and Chinese identity, status quo, and unification. The younger generations, born since 1980, thus appear more cohesive and less diverse in political views about the Taiwanese nation than older generations. Public discourse analysis and observant participation by this author indicates that they also show deep attachments to the principles of democracy, equal human and social rights, and social justice for all, which are mainstay values of liberal democratic societies, as well as a strong loyalty to both the national and local territories. They reject ethnic ascription, racial distinction, and any kind of social and political discrimination. They are also more internationalized, in touch with the rest of the world, and more traveled than older generations. At the same time, they are, for most, intensely rooted in the Taiwanese territory (*Taiwan tudi* 台灣土地), their multicultural society, and the values both represent. As such, they exhibit a rather successful integration of progressive and democratic education's values, with additional strong localization and globalization dimensions.

Conclusion

Political analyses of the national identity debate during the 2000s have often misread the depth, causes, and dynamics of the identity change by overly focusing on political parties and government actions, the alleged indecisiveness of opinion expressed in public opinion polls, or the inadequacy of these polls to assess national identity change. Ma Ying-jeou's victories at the presidential polls in 2008 and 2012 have also been described as a rebuke to both the DPP-supported Taiwanese nationalism and to academic analyses highlighting the political significance of Taiwanese citizens' identity shift. Since then, eight years of Ma's administration with its Chinese nationalist ideology, economic and political rapprochement with China, and its official anti-Taiwanese nationalism policies, have offered a real-life test of the strength, lasting validity, and multiple motives of the contemporary shift toward a new Taiwanese national identity and imagination.

As a result, and contrary to the views of many in the 2000s, the issue of Taiwan's national identity is now clearly settled: a new Taiwanese national identity defined by civic nationalism and multiculturalism has emerged in the past two decades and become prevalent in the majority of the population, especially among the younger generation. Such an outcome has its roots in a long process of growing political assertion of a distinct Taiwanese identity and sense of specific community, then nationhood, among the Taiwanese people that started as early as in the 1930s. But it is also the result of the implementation of an inclusive view of the nation and what, and who, constitutes the Taiwanese citizens and people that was offered and developed under democracy since the 1990s.

Notwithstanding other inputs, since this past quarter of a century has been characterized by the full democratization of Taiwan, a correlation between democratic practice, including the freedom of opinion, expression, and participation in free elections for national and local political offices, and the growing assertion of Taiwanese national identity may be inferred. It is corroborated by the highest support for Taiwanese identity and eventual independence among the younger generations raised under democracy compared to the older age groups. This also highlights that, even though as a whole the Sinicization of Taiwan under the KMT dictatorship failed to remake the Taiwanese people into Chinese nationalists, it worked best among the generations which were schooled and socialized between the 1960s and the mid-1980s, at the height of the repressive and nationalistic policies of the authoritarian regime, and who are now aged between 40 and 65 years old. In the past 25 years, through its democratic system and practices, Taiwan has built a new Taiwanese national imagination, which is supported by the overwhelming majority of the Taiwanese, and has effectively left behind the intellectual and symbolic framework of Chinese nationalism. With the new generations deeply attached to their Taiwanese and democratic identity, it is difficult to see how this situation could change or reverse in the coming decades, whatever the future political evolution of the PRC.

Notes

1 After succeeding Chiang Ching-kuo after his death in 1988 due to his position as vice-president, Lee's first own presidential term started in 1990, when he was elected by the then National Assembly. The first direct election for presidential office in Taiwan took place in 1996. No ESC data is available before 1992.
2 Contrary to the ESC surveys which have been regularly conducted and aggregated at the same time of the year since at least 1994, the TVBS Poll Center does not run polls on identity at regular intervals, but follows important political events or its own peculiar schedule. Between 2000 and 2013, it conducted more than 15 surveys on this issue at a maximum interval of 22 months. However, since October 2013, TVBS has not run any survey on Taiwan's people's identity, or about people's desire for independence, unification or status quo, with no apparent explanation why the surveys have stopped.
3 On the rarity of genuine, congruent, nation-states in the modern world, see Connor (1978).
4 These movements are not necessarily successful in creating new nation-states. Actually, independence of new nations by democratic means is probably harder to achieve when set within an already democratic state: Quebec, twice, and Scotland have experienced failed referendums to secede from Canada and the United Kingdom. Catalonia is the next test for a independence referendum in a state that is already democratic.
5 Translation by the author.

6 All the public polls' numbers for specific age groups must be read with caution, since the margin of errors rises significantly with small sampling, and most of the time the 20–29 age group constitutes only a minor part of the whole poll sample (in general ±1,000 persons). They are therefore better taken as general trend indicators to be confirmed by more in-depth surveys and other scientific assessments of young generations' political ideas and values.

References

Abizadeh, A. (2004). "Historical truth, national myths and liberal democracy: On the coherence of liberal nationalism," *Journal of Political Philosophy*, 12(3): 291–313.

Anderson, B. (1983). *Imagined Communities: Reflections on the Origin and Spread of Nationalism*, London: Verso.

Armitage, D. (2007). *The Declaration of Independence: A Global History*, Cambridge, MA: Harvard University Press.

Cabestan, J. P. and Le Pesant, T. (2009). *L'esprit de défense de Taiwan face à la Chine. La jeunesse taiwanaise face à la tentation de la Chine*, Paris: L'Harmattan.

Calhoun, C. (2007). "Nationalism and cultures of democracy," *Public Culture*, 19(1): 151–173.

Chang, H. (1991). "Impressions of Mainland China carried back by Taiwan visitors," in Myers, R. (ed.) *Two Societies in Opposition: The ROC and the PRC after 40 years*, Stanford, CA: Stanford University Press, pp. 141–155.

Chang, M. K. (2000). "On the origins and transformation of Taiwanese national identity," *China Perspectives*, 28: 51–70.

Cheng, T. J. and Haggard, S. (eds.) (1992). *Political Change in Taiwan*, Boulder, CO: Lynne Rienner.

Cole, J. M. (2012). "Taiwan's youth fights for democracy, again: Students concerned about the erosion of free speech take to the streets to halt a mogul's media buying spree," *The Wall Street Journal*, December 13.

Cole, J. M. (2013). "Why the youth movement matters," *Taipei Times*, May 7.

Cole, J. M. (2014). "Debunking the myths about Taiwan's Sunflower Movement," *China Policy Institute Blog*, April 4. Available at: http://blogs.nottingham.ac.uk/chinapolicy institute/2014/04/04/debunking-the-myths-about-taiwans-sunflower-movement/

CommonWealth Magazine (2009). "2010 State of the Nation Survey," *CommonWealth Magazine*, 437, December 15. Available at: http://english.cw.com.tw/article.do?action =show&id=11589

Connor, W. (1978). "A nation is a nation, is a state, is an ethnic group, is a, …," *Ethnic and Racial Studies*, 1(4): 377–400.

Council for Hakka Affairs, Executive Yuan (2008.) 行政院客家委員會委託研究報告97年度全國客家人口基礎資料調查研究 [Research Report on 2008 National Research Survey on Hakka Population]. Taipei: Council for Hakka Affairs Press.

Dzur, A. W. (2002). "Nationalism, liberalism, and democracy," *Political Research Quarterly*, 55(1): 191–211.

Election Study Center, NCCU (2009). "Important political attitude trend distribution." Available at: http://esc.nccu.edu.tw (accessed July 2009).

Election Study Center, NCCU (2012). "Important political attitude trend distribution." Available at: http://esc.nccu.edu.tw (accessed July 2012).

Election Study Center, NCCU (2016). "Important political attitude trend distribution." Available at: http://esc.nccu.edu.tw (accessed January 12, 2017).

Fell, D. (2011). *Government and Politics in Taiwan*, London: Routledge.

Fell, D. (2012). *Party Politics in Taiwan: Party Change and the Democratic Evolution of Taiwan, 1991–2004*, London: Routledge.

Gellner, E. (1983). *Nations and Nationalism*, Oxford: Blackwell.

GVRSC (Global Views Survey Research Center) (2011). "Survey on President Ma Ying-jeou's approval rating and people's views on the unification-independence issue," Global Views Survey Research Center, April 25.

GVRSC (Global Views Survey Research Center) (2014). "Survey on Taiwanese views on independence and unification, March 2014," Global Views Survey Research Center, April 2014. Press release.

Helbling, M. (2009). "Nationalism and democracy: Competing or complementary logics?" *Living Reviews of Democracy*, 1. Available at: http://lrd.ethz.ch/index.php/lrd/article/view/lrd-2009-7/20

Ho, S. Y. and Liu, I. C. (2003). "The Taiwanese/Chinese identity of the Taiwan people in the 1990s," in Lee, W. C. and Wang, T. Y. (eds.) *Sayonara to the Lee Teng-hui Era: Politics in Taiwan, 1988–2000*, Lanham, MD: University Press of America, pp. 149–183.

Hobsbawm, E. J. (1990). *Nations and Nationalism since 1780: Programme, Myth, Reality*, Cambridge: Cambridge University Press.

Hsiau, A. C. (2000). *Contemporary Taiwanese Cultural Nationalism*, London: Routledge.

Jacobs, J. B. (2012). *Democratizing Taiwan*, Leiden: Brill Academic.

Laitin, D. (2007). *Nations, States, and Violence*, Oxford: Oxford University Press.

Lee, W. C. and Wang, T. Y. (eds.) (2003). *Sayonara to the Lee Teng-hui Era: Politics in Taiwan, 1988–2000*, Lanham, MD: University Press of America.

Le Pesant, T. (2011). "Generational change and ethnicity among 1980s-born Taiwanese," *Journal of Current Chinese Affairs*, 40(1): 133–157.

Le Pesant, T. (2012). "A new generation of Taiwanese at the ballot box: Young voters and the presidential election of January 2012," *China Perspectives*, 2: 71–79.

Le Pesant, T. (2014). "Processus de construction nationale et génération post-réformes à Taiwan," *Sociétés et politiques comparées*, 36: 91–133.

Liberty Times (2006). Poll issued on February 16.

Lin, T. H. 林宗弘, (2013). "再探台灣的世代政治: 交叉分類隨機效應模型的應用 1995–2010" [Generational politics in Taiwan revisited: The application of cross-classified random effects model, 1995–2010], paper presented at the 2013 Annual Conference of Taiwan Sociology Association, National Chengchi University, Taipei, November 30–December 1.

Lin, T. H. 林宗弘, (2014). "台灣的民主轉型與世代政治1995–2010", 趙永佳, 蕭新煌, 尹寶珊編, 一衣帶水: 台港社會議題縱橫談 [Taiwan's democratic turn and genera-tional politics, 1995–2010], in Wing-kai Chiu, S., Hsin-huang Hsiao M., and Wan, P. S. S. (eds.) *Only Separated by a Strip of Water: Discussing Taiwan and Hong Kong Social Issues*, Hong Kong: Hong Kong Institute of Asia-Pacific Studies, Chinese University of Hong Kong, pp. 171–214.

Liu, I.-C. and Ho, S. Y. (1999). "The Taiwanese/Chinese identity of the Taiwan people," *Issues and Studies*, 35(3): 1–34.

Lynch, D. (2002). "Taiwan's democratization and the rise of Taiwanese nationalism as socialization to global culture," *Pacific Affairs*, 75(4): 557–74.

Ma, Y. J. (2008). "Taiwan's renaissance," President Ma's inaugural address, May. Available at: http://english.president.gov.tw/Portals/4/FeaturesSection/Other-feature-articles/20080520_PRESIDENT_INAUGURAL/e_speech.html.

Muyard, F. (2012). "The formation of Taiwan's new national identity since the end of the 1980s," in Blundell, D. (ed.), *Taiwan Since Martial Law: Society, Culture, Politics, Economy*, Taipei: National Taiwan University Press, pp. 297–366.

Muyard, F. (2015). "Voting shift in the November 2014 local elections in Taiwan," *China Perspectives*, 1: 55–61.

Nielsen, K. (1999). "Cultural nationalism, neither ethnic nor civic," in Beiner, R. (ed.), *Theorizing Nationalism*, Albany, NY: SUNY Press, pp. 119–130.

Nodia, G. (1992). "Nationalism and democracy," *Journal of Democracy*, 3(4): 3–22.

Noiriel, G. (1991). "La question nationale comme objet de l'histoire sociale," *Genèses*, 4: 72–94.

Rigger, S. (2006). *Taiwan's Rising Rationalism: Generations, Politics, and Taiwanese Nationalism*. Washington, DC: East-West Center Washington Policy Studies, 26.

Rigger, S. (2007). "Strawberry jam: National identity, cross-Strait relations and Taiwan's youth," in Yuan, I. (ed.) *Is There a Greater China Identity? Security and Economic Dilemma*, Taipei: Institute of International Relations, pp. 115–135.

Schubert, G. (2006). "Towards the end of a long journey: Assessing the debate on Taiwanese nationalism and national identity in the democratic era," *ASIEN*, 98: 26–44.

Shen, S. C. and Wu, N. T. (2008). "Ethnic and civic nationalisms: Two roads to the formation of a Taiwanese nation," in Chow, P. C. Y. (ed.) *The "One China" Dilemma*. New York: Palgrave Macmillan, pp. 117–143.

TBT (2014). Taiwan Brain Trust Survey, June. Available at: www.braintrust.tw/

TBT (2015a). Taiwan Brain Trust Survey, March 18. Available at: www.braintrust.tw/

TBT (2015b). Taiwan Brain Trust Survey, July 17. Available at: www.braintrust.tw/

Thiesse, A. M. (1999). *La Création des identités nationales. Europe, 18ᵉ–20ᵉ siècles*, Paris: Seuil.

TISR (2014). "Taiwan Mood Barometer Survey and Survey on cross-Strait relations and Double Ten National Day," September 30. Available at: www.tisr.com.tw/?p= 4613#more-4613.

TISR (2016). "Taiwan Mood Barometer Survey and survey on the new government and the cross-Strait divisions," May 30. Available at: www.tisr.com.tw/?p=6812#more-6812.

TVBS Poll Center (2012). "Opinion poll on Hsieh Chang-ting's trip to Mainland China, independence and unification, and national identity," October 18. Available at: www.tvbs.com.tw/export/sites/tvbs/file/other/poll-center/0p4v11j38l.pdf.

TVBS Poll Center (2013). "Opinion poll on Ma-Xi meeting and national identity," October 28. Available at: www.tvbs.com.tw/export/sites/tvbs/file/other/poll-center/20131106112520608.pdf.

Wang, F. C. 王甫昌 (2008). "族群政治議題在臺灣民主化轉型中的角色" [The role of ethnic politics issues in Taiwan's democratization transition], *Taiwan Democracy Quarterly*, 5(2): 89–140.

Wang, F. C. (2013a). "A prolonged exile: National imagination of the KMT regime in postwar Taiwan," *Oriens Extremus*, 52: 137–172.

Wang, F. C. (2013b). "Ethnic politics and democratic transition in Taiwan," *Oriental Institute Journal*, 22(2): 81–107.

Wang, F. C. (2014). "A reluctant identity: The development of Holo identity in contemporary Taiwan," *Taiwan in Comparative Perspective*, 5: 79–119.

Wang, H. L. (2000). "Rethinking the global and the national: Reflections on national imaginations in Taiwan," *Theory, Culture & Society*, 17(4): 93–117.

62 *Frank Muyard*

Wu, N. T. (2012). "Trend of national identities in Taiwan, 1992–2005," in Chang, M.-K. et al. (eds.) *Social Change in Taiwan 1985–2005*, Series 3, Vol. 4, pp. 93–128 (in Chinese).

Wu, N. T. (2013). "Will economic integration lead to political assimilation?" in Chow, P. C. Y. (ed.) *National Identity and Economic Interest: Taiwan's Competing Options and Its Implication for Regional Stability*, New York: Palgrave Macmillan, pp. 187–202.

Wu, N. T. 吳乃德 (2014). "誰愛中華民國?「民族」和「國家」的糾葛" [Who loves the Republic of China? The entanglement of 'ethnie' and 'nation'], paper presented at the 23rd Taiwan Social Change Survey Conference: National Identity, Institute of Sociology, Academia Sinica, December 5.

Wu, N. T. and Cheng, T. J. (2011). "Democratization as a legitimacy formula: The KMT and political change in Taiwan," in Kane, J., Loy, H. and Patapan, H. (eds.) *Political Legitimacy in Asia New Leadership Challenges*, New York: Palgrave Macmillan, pp. 239–260.

Yack, B. (1999). "The myth of the civic nation," in Beiner, R. (ed.) *Theorizing Nationalism*, Albany, NY: SUNY Press, pp. 103–118.

4 Taiwan's political parties in the aftermath of the 2016 elections

Dafydd Fell

Political parties are an essential feature of modern democracies. They play a central role in political recruitment, setting policy direction for governments, simplifying politics for voters, and linking state with society. One way we can assess the health of a democracy is whether it has strong parties and a relatively stable party system. On the surface, Taiwan has one of the most stable party systems among Asian democracies. In Taiwan's first multi-party election held in 1986, the Kuomintang (KMT) and Democratic Progressive Party (DPP) won the majority of contested seats. Over the subsequent three decades, although other parties have entered the party system, they have almost never threatened the domination of the DPP and KMT. In the most recent national elections in January 2016, the same two parties dominated the parliamentary and presidential votes. Despite the continuity in actors, I argue in this chapter that since 2014 we have witnessed monumental changes in the party system.

This chapter dissects Taiwan's changing party scene in the build-up to and aftermath of the 2016 elections. An understanding of the party scene requires us to examine both the development of key individual parties and the overall party system. Alan Ware defines the party system as 'patterns of competition and co-operation between the different parties in that system' (1996: 7). Thus, studies of the party system consider fragmentation, ideological positioning, the openness of the system to new entrants and the relationship between the relevant political parties. Party system fragmentation can have important implications for the way a democracy operates. A democratic but one-party dominant system can operate in a similar way to an authoritarian state, as there are no genuine checks on the ruling party. However, where a party system is too fragmented, it may lead to political instability and frequent government coalition breakdowns. Ideological positioning has similar ramifications. Where parties are too convergent, voters may complain that there is little to choose from between the main competitors. However, when parties are concentrated at the poles, there is the possibility that more extremist anti-system parties may undermine the democratic system.

Party and party system change are huge topics, so my analysis focuses on a more limited number of aspects to the changing party scene. In the first section, I briefly discuss changes in party strength and fragmentation by looking at both election results but also campaign spending data. The second section considers change in terms of the parties' treatment of political issues during the campaign. This allows us to get a sense of whether the main parties are converging or becoming more polarised. I have done this by examining how the parties' address the most salient issues in their election advertising. The three broad issue areas that have been especially salient in recent years are: (1) national identity; (2) Taiwan's economic relationship with China; and (3) social movements. Any study of Taiwanese party positioning needs to take into account questions of national identification, as it is widely regarded as having been the central political cleavage in Taiwan since democratisation. The second two issue areas have grown in salience over the last decade, as Taiwan has become increasingly economically integrated with China, there have been concerns that this process could undermine Taiwan's freedom and democracy. Such concerns led to the emergence of the Sunflower Movement against the Cross-Strait Service Trade Agreement (CSSTA) in the spring of 2014. Although the China factor does feature in many of Taiwan's social movements, the growing protest scene is much more diverse, thus I have chosen to examine party treatment of this topic separately. In each case the issues are framed as left-right spectrums and advertising analysis is used as evidence to plot the parties' positions on these spectrums.

Party system fragmentation

Examinations of party system fragmentation particularly focus on the number of relevant parties and their relative size and strength. The first place to get a sense of the degree of change in this dimension of the party system is elections results. During Taiwan's democratic transition period it seemed to be holding at least one major election each year. In recent years there has been a consolidation of the election calendar, so that every four years all national elections are held on the same day and there has been a similar concentration of local elections. Thus, during the second Ma Ying-jeou (馬英九) term, all the local elections were held on November 29, 2014, just over six months after the end of the Sunflower Occupation. Local elections can often serve as warnings for subsequent national elections. Just over two and a half years before the KMT lost power in 2000, the DPP's vote and seat share exceeded those of the KMT's for the first time in 1997. The KMT's decisive election victories in 2008 were preceded by similar landslide local victories in 2005. The local elections in November 2014 also saw landslide victories for the DPP, as the party enjoyed its best ever local executive results. That year the DPP won 13 out of the 22 local executive seats, with the KMT winning just six. Thus, the KMT had suffered its worst ever local elections results. These elections meant that at the local level the DPP was the dominant party for the first time and served as an ominous warning for the ruling KMT.

The DPP gained similar domination of the party system at the national level just over a year later. Tables 4.1–4.3 give a picture of continuity and change since democratization began in the mid-1980s. Table 4.1 shows the party vote shares in parliamentary elections, Table 4.2 shows seat shares in parliamentary

Table 4.1 Vote shares in national parliamentary (legislative Yuan and national assembly) elections

	1986	1989	1991	1992	1995	1996	1998	2001	2004	2008	2012	2016
KMT	69.2	60.2	71.2	53	46.1	49.7	46.4	28.6	32.8	51.2	44.5	26.9
DPP	22.2	28.3	23.9	31	33.2	29.9	29.6	33.4	35.7	36.9	34.6	44.1
NP					13.0	13.7	7.1	2.9	0.1	4.0	1.5	4.2
PFP								18.6	13.9		5.5	6.5
TSU								8.5	7.8	3.5	9.0	2.5
GPT											1.7	2.5
NPP												6.1

Source: Central Election Commission Database: http://db.cec.gov.tw/histMain.jsp.

Notes

These figures show the vote shares for the main political parties in legislative and National Assembly elections.

KMT: Kuomintang; DPP: Democratic Progressive Party; NP: New Party; PFP: People First Party; TSU: Taiwan Solidarity Union, GPT: Green Party Taiwan, New Power Party (NPP).

1 The PFP won one seat out of its three official candidates in 2008. The PFP only had one (unsuccessful) district-level candidate in 2008, who won 47.04 per cent of the vote in Lienchiang County. This only amounted to 2064 votes and represents 0.02 per cent of the national vote share. The successful PFP candidate won an aboriginal constituency seat with 11,925 votes; however, votes for the aboriginal constituencies were not included in the Central Election Commission's party vote share figures.

2 The party vote share figures for the 2008, 2012 and 2016 legislative elections are from the party list votes.

3 Figures for 1986, 1989 and 1992 from Hsieh, 'Continuity and Change in Taiwan's Electoral Politics', 37.

4 Figures for 1991 from *Lianhebao* 12 December 1991, 1.

Table 4.2 Seat shares in national parliamentary (legislative Yuan and national assembly) elections

	1986	1989	1991	1992	1995	1996	1998	2001	2004	2008	2012	2016
KMT	80.8	68.6	78.2	59.0	51.8	55	54.7	30.2	35.1	71.7	56.6	30
DPP	16.7	20.6	18.6	31.7	32.9	30	31.1	38.7	39.6	24	35.4	60
NP					12.8	14	4.9	0.4	0.4	0	0	0
PFP								20.2	15.1	0.9	2.7	2.7
TSU								5.8	5.3	0	2.7	0
NPP												4.4

Source: Central Election Commission Database: http://db.cec.gov.tw/histMain.jsp.

Notes

These figures show the seat shares for the main political parties in national parliamentary elections.

1 Figures for 1986 Chao and Myers, *First Chinese Democracy*, 139.

2 The seat share for 1989 is based on my own calculations from *China Times* 3 December 1989, p. 1.

3 Figures for seat shares in 1991 were from Chao and Myers, *First Chinese Democracy*, 237 and for 1996 Chao and Myers *First Chinese Democracy*, 285.

Table 4.3 Vote shares in presidential elections

	1996	2000	2004	2008	2012	2016
KMT	54.0	23.1	49.9	58.45	51.6	31.0
DPP	21.1	39.3	50.1	41.55	45.6	56.0
NP	14.9	0.1				
PFP		36.8			2.7	12.8

Source: Central Election Commission Database: http://db.cec.gov.tw/histMain.jsp.

Notes
1 The vote share for the NP in 1996 refers to the Lin Yang-kang ticket, which was supported by the NP but not officially a nominated NP candidate.
2 The PFP vote share in 2000 refers to Soong Chu-yu's independent candidacy. Soong went on to form the party in the aftermath of his narrow defeat in 2000.

elections and Table 4.3 shows presidential vote share. Taken together, we can see that although the number of relevant parties remained at four, there has been radical change in the make-up of the party system in 2016. First, the elections left the DPP with unprecedented majorities and thus control of both local and national government. In the presidential election Tsai enjoyed the biggest margin of victory since Lee Teng-hui's (李登輝) in 1996. In the parliamentary election the DPP had its best-ever performance, both in terms of vote and especially seat share. For the first time ever, the DPP has a majority in parliament. In contrast, this was the KMT's worst-ever national election result. It is true that Eric Chu's (朱立倫) vote share was higher than Lien Chan's (連戰) in 2000 and the KMT's seat share in 2016 (30 per cent) is almost the same as its earlier low point in 2001's legislative election. However, in 2000, the combined score of the official and rebel KMT presidential candidates was 60 per cent and in both 2001 and 2004 the KMT together with its ally, the People First Party (PFP), retained a parliamentary majority. We see a similar picture of change in the party system in party identification trends. Almost as soon as the KMT had won re-election in 2012, its support rate began to decline drastically, while the DPP's support rate grew gradually. By the time of the 2014 election the DPP had a clear lead over the KMT for the first time since the early 2000s. In the most recent survey the DPP enjoyed its highest-ever party identification figure of 31 per cent and its widest-ever lead over the KMT.[1] Thus the party identification trends mirror those seen in the 2014 and 2016 election results of the DPP as the dominant party in a two-party system.

Another way we can get a sense of the relative strength of the main parties is in the resources employed during the election campaign. The KMT has the reputation as being one of the richest parties in the world and this has allowed it to vastly outspend its rivals in the majority of election campaigns.[2] Chen and Fell's (2014) study showed that in 2012 the KMT purchased significantly more election advertisements compared to the DPP. Table 4.4 summarises campaign advertising spending for the presidential and party headquarters in the 2012 and 2016 campaigns. The first change that catches the eye is the fact that campaign

Table 4.4 Campaign spending items in 2015–2016

	Party spending in 2015–16 (unit NT$1,000)	Presidential campaign spending 2015–2016	Party spending in 2011–2012 (unit NT$1,000)	Presidential campaign spending 2012
KMT	38,654	31,526	92,180	166,421
DPP	28,288	32,677	84,921	133,694
NP	14,730		6,766	
PFP	7,774	10,750	5,715	8,503
TSU	7,186		4,495	
CUPP	12,578			
NPSU	4,757			
NPP	3,013			
MKT	9,602			
FHA	4,334			
GPT/SDP	149			

Source: Data supplied by Rainmaker XFM.

spending by both the major parties drastically declined in 2016 compared to 2012. It should be noted here that these figures only include spending on TV, newspaper, magazine and radio advertising. Thus, one possibility is that parties have shifted their spending to the internet and social media. Nevertheless, we can see how the gap between the parties has narrowed significantly. Although the KMT's total spending on advertising exceeded the DPP's in the campaign, at least in terms of presidential advertising spending, the DPP spent slightly more.

Despite high levels of distrust of Taiwan's mainstream parties and much talk of the arrival of a third force in Taiwanese politics, Tables 4.1–4.3 suggest limited change in party system openness. On the back of James Soong's improved 2016 presidential campaign, the KMT splinter party, the PFP, was able to increase its vote share and match its 2012 achievement of wining three seats. Given that the PFP caucus did not play a particularly prominent role in the second Ma term, it is uncertain whether they will be more visible in the first Tsai term. In 2012, the Taiwan Solidarity Union (TSU) surprised many observers by winning almost 9 per cent of the party list vote and three parliamentary seats. Four years later the TSU vote collapsed, gaining only 2.5 per cent and it failed to win any seats.

Nevertheless, there are a number of reasons why the campaigns of Taiwan's smaller parties since 2014 are worthy of attention for our understanding of the new party system. First, the TSU was replaced by the newly formed New Power Party (NPP), winning five seats. The NPP is likely to have a greater impact on the new party system than the TSU (or the PFP). A sign of its potential is that the NPP was able to win three single member districts. Naturally the fact that the DPP did not nominate in these districts played a role, but these were relatively safe KMT seats. A key factor in the NPP's breakthrough is that it has much better-known candidates than the other small parties. For example, the Sunflower Movement leader Huang Kuo-chang (黃國昌) and rock musician Freddy Lim were able to defeat veteran incumbent KMT legislators. Well-known politicians also tend to bring greater levels of media attention. Moreover, the NPP's leaders and newly elected politicians are not traditional politicians. In other words, unlike most other small splinter party politicians, the NPP's legislators are not defectors from mainstream parties. The fact that the NPP was able to make a breakthrough despite very low levels of advertising spending reveals the party's potential and suggests it has relied heavily on new technology to reach voters. One challenge created by the NPP is how best to categorise the party. Should we view it as a Pan Green party, like the TSU? Or should it be seen as an alternative party? This is a topic I will return to in the section on ideological positioning later in the chapter.

A second noteworthy element of the campaign was that while support for smaller parties was higher than the previous two elections under the new system, competition was very intense for those votes. In fact, in 2016, there was a record 18 parties contesting the party list. The vote shares of the party list section is shown in Table 4.5. Moreover, a larger number than ever of these actually ran serious campaigns. We can see this for instance in the advertising spending figures shown on Table 4.4. For instance, the Chinese Unification Promotion Party (CUPP) and Min Kuo Tang (MKT) were among the highest spenders on traditional advertising. While in earlier campaigns many of the smaller parties on the party list were really just making up the numbers, in 2016, a number of these parties made serious attempts to break into the party system and break the DPP/KMT domination. For example, the MKT made a massive membership recruitment drive, claiming within months to be the third largest party and aiming to become the largest (Fang 2015). Another example was the attempt by the Green Party (GPT) to create an alliance with trade union groups and to establish active local party branches.

Table 4.5 Party list vote shares for 2008, 2012 and 2016

	2008 party list vote share	2012 party list vote share	2016 party list vote share
KMT	51.2	44.5	26.9
DPP	36.9	34.6	44.1
NP	4.0	1.5	4.1
PFP		5.8	6.5
TSU	3.5	9.0	2.5
NPP			6.1
MKT			1.6
GPT/SDP	0.6	1.7	2.52
FHA			1.69
NPSU	0.7		0.63
CUPP			0.46
NHSU		1.24	0.41

Source: Central Election Commission Database: http://db.cec.gov.tw/histMain.jsp.

Note

Abbreviations not previously used: NHSU: National Health System Union.

The third noteworthy element of the smaller parties has been how their political projects have become more diverse. For the first time Taiwan had an openly pro-PRC political party in the CUPP. The GPT/SDP campaign represents the most serious left-wing campaign since the late 1980s. Another interesting case was the Faith and Hope Alliance (FHA) which was widely viewed as a single issue grouping motivated by the desire to block legislation on same sex marriage and adoption. Naturally there were also attempts to establish new purifier parties on both sides of the political spectrum, for example, there were two new pro-independence parties. However, despite the growing support for non-mainstream parties and their improved campaigns, the fact that only the NPP and PFP among the smaller parties were able to win seats reveals the challenges faced by challengers to enter the party system.

Ideological movements

In this section I examine how the main parties have dealt with three key issue areas that have been salient since 2014. As mentioned earlier, the three broad issue areas I have selected to focus on are debates over national identification, Taiwan's economic relations with China, and debates over social movements. In each case I have tried to place the parties on issue spectrums. Thus, I attempt to show whether the parties are taking centrist or polarised positions, and at least where parties had joined earlier elections, I also identify whether parties are shifting towards the centre or towards the poles.

Competing national identities

The main issue spectrum used to examine party positions in Taiwan revolves around the national identification debates. One of the most common methods has been to use surveys to ask voters to locate themselves and the main parties on a spectrum in which one end calls for rapid unification with China and the other end for immediate declaration of independence.[3] An alternative method that I have used over the last decade has been to use parties' advertising material as the basis for plotting their positions on a range of issues, including national identification. There are two main survey questions that address national identity in Taiwan. These are (1) whether respondents prefer unification or independence, and (2) whether respondents see themselves as Taiwanese, Chinese or both. I have tried to use the way parties' political advertising address both the political relationship with China question and the more symbolic identification appeals to plot their positions. The spectrum I use consists of five broad types. At the far right is what I call *Greater Chinese* or *PRC Chinese nationalism* and includes positive references to unification, including the PRC's proposal for One Country, Two Systems. In addition, this also includes symbolic appeals associated with unification such as the PRC flag or Chiang Kai-shek. At the centre right is *ROC-style Chinese nationalism*. Here, though we will see opposition to Taiwan independence, there will not be positive references for unification. Instead the focus is on protecting the ROC and use of ROC symbols. In the middle of the spectrum are references to maintaining the status quo of neither full independence nor unification, as well as appeals to dual Chinese and Taiwanese identity. Next we come to the centre left position I have termed *civic Taiwanese nationalism*. This will feature opposition to unification but not support for an outright declaration of independence. Instead it features softer appeals such as self-determination or the idea that there is no need to declare independence as Taiwan is already independent. The symbolic appeals tend also to be more inclusive of all Taiwan's ethnic groups. Lastly, at the far left is what I term *ethnic Taiwanese nationalism*. Here we see calls for declaring a Republic of Taiwan but also exclusive ethnic appeals, such as anti-Mainlander messages.

Although the national identity debates were perhaps not as intense as some of those seen in the 1990s, the main parties appealed to voters with a diverse range of appeals from extreme Chinese nationalism at one end of the spectrum to calls for de jure independence at the other. The appearance for the first time in a national election by the CUPP was significant for a number of reasons. First, as we saw earlier, it was one of the heaviest spenders on advertising in the election, thus in contrast to earlier pro-unification new parties, it was running a serious campaign. Equally important though was its positioning at the far right on the unification versus independence spectrum. The CUPP was the first serious party to openly advocate unification under the PRC's preferred formula of One Country, Two Systems (OCTS).[4] Therefore, the election allowed a test of the suitability of the PRC's nationalist message for Taiwan's population. The CUPP's first TV ad released on 26 December was narrated by its party leader, Chang An-lo (張安樂). Chang argued that now was the right time to negotiate Taiwan's unification under OCTS and warned that this was much better than waiting to be unified in war. A number of the CUPP's newspaper ads offered further detail on the thinking behind its unification proposals. One such ad noted:

> Many friends that care about the CUPP have told us for the sake of votes do not emphasize the word unification; otherwise you will be labelled red. However, the red proposal for peaceful unification, one country, two systems, is the best guarantee for the well-being of Taiwan's people.[5]

The CUPP's proximity to the PRC was seen in the same ad where it states, 'We are the real orthodox red flag' (我們是真正的正紅旗). Therefore we can safely place the CUPP at the far right of our national identity spectrum.

Previously, the NP had dominated the far right of the national identity spectrum, but the arrival of the CUPP meant it had a competitor. Protecting the Republic of China (ROC) and opposition to Taiwan independence have been constant themes for the NP. However, the party became increasingly extreme and narrowly focused from 1998, contributing to its subsequent electoral decline.[6] In recent years the party has continued this shift towards the extreme end of the national identity spectrum. The party's appeal is clear from its website which describes itself as 'the political party for Chinese' and lists unification as one of its four core appeals.[7] In the NP's advertising it did not mention unification in 2016. Its only reference to future political relations with China was a call to sign a peace agreement (with China).[8] Naturally the party's highlighting of its party leader Yu Mu-ming (郁慕明), PR candidates Chiu Yi (邱毅) and Wang Bing-zhong (王炳忠), who are all well known for their pro-China positions, did reinforce the party's image. As in earlier elections, the ROC flag featured prominently and its first TV ad did use its old slogan 'Protect the ROC.'[9] However, while the CUPP called itself the true red party, the NP emphasized itself as being the 'true Blue party', thus it should be placed slightly to the left of the CUPP.

One of the challenges for plotting the KMT's position on national identity in the 2016 election was the fact that it had changed presidential candidates so late in the campaign and one of the justifications for replacing Hung was that her identity positions were out of step with mainstream Taiwanese public opinion. Chu tried to project an image as someone more moderate than Hung, and his advertising appeals on national identity overlapped heavily with those used by Ma in 2012. While Ma's core slogan was台灣加油 ('Go Taiwan'), Chu selected 'One Taiwan' and 台灣就是力量 ('Taiwan is the force'). In a number of ads Chu tried to elaborate on his concept of One Taiwan. For instance, in his 25 November TV ad, he distinguishes between two Taiwans, 'One is where we argue with each other, one is a Taiwan where we embrace each other.' He goes on to accuse the DPP of being divisive, noting how 'Although some people can divide Taiwan into four or eight, but I would rather work hard to make the two opposed Taiwans return to that warm and mutually trusting Taiwan.' This is something Chu returned to in his 27 December TV ad. This ad again stressed the inclusive appeal by using multiple languages and multiple ethnicities. The first speaker tells us: 'There used to be a Taiwan where you would not be suspected and rejected because you have different points of view.' Since we are told that was when Taiwan created a miracle, we can surmise that this golden era refers to the Chiang Ching-kuo soft authoritarian years that are most associated with Taiwan's economic miracle. Then we are told that: 'At that time we all believed we were part of each other' (那個時候我們都相信彼此是彼此的一部分). Chu ends the ad by saying, 'From today let us reject being divisive and oppositional. Let us rediscover that Taiwan that belongs to us' (從今天起, 讓我們拒絕分割對立, 找回屬於我們的台灣). This ad's message is thus very similar to that used by Ma in his often recycled Happy Gathering Song (歡聚歌) ads, that stress how all Taiwanese are one happy family, but in doing so these ads also insinuate that the DPP is inciting ethnic divisions. The difference between Ma and Chu, however, was that while for Ma this ethnic harmony was something he had helped to create, for Chu, that utopia lay in Taiwan's past. It is rather ironic that most of those talking of that golden past in Chu's ad could not have been alive at the time of Chiang Ching-kuo's presidency.

In addition to this inclusive Taiwan message, Chu needed to appeal to those traditional supporters with ROC identities, including those who had originally supported Hung's aborted presidential campaign. The ROC flag became more prominent in KMT ads in the final two weeks of the campaign. Its prime pre-election weekend rally was entitled 'National Flag Party' (國旗 Party) and participants were encouraged to wear anything with an ROC flag on it.[10] Again this was something seen in Ma's 2012 campaign, not only in Ma's ads but also his micro-film *National Flag Girl* (國旗的女孩).[11] Both were attempting to make ROC nationalism young and cool. To a certain extent, party unity meant that Chu needed to reach out to dark blue supporters, or risk them defecting to the NP or even CUPP. We saw this in the advertisements featuring Hung in an exhibition room about the KMT and ROC's history.[12] The camera shows images of Chiang Ching-kuo, Sun Yat Sen, the KMT and ROC flags, and the ROC Constitution. She explains why she has remained in the KMT, because 'Some people want to change our passports, to put an end to our country' (有些人想換掉你我的護照, 想終結這個國家). She ends the ad saying, 'I am Hung Hsiu-chu, I love my country, the ROC' (我是洪秀柱我愛我的國家, 中華民國). Then hear her rally location call 'Let us come together to support Eric Chu' (讓我們一起支持朱立倫).

I have located the two other KMT splinter parties, the PFP and MKT, closer to the centre than the KMT. Although in the past the PFP had been associated with the Dark Blue side of Taiwanese politics for much of the Chen Shui-bian (陳水扁) (2000–2008) era, it had become much more Taiwan-focused since the 2012 campaign. It proposes setting aside the unification versus independence dispute and insists that any future changes to Taiwan's status need the approval of the Taiwanese people.[13] Its 2016 ads did not feature the ROC flag or references to protecting the ROC. The political platform adopted by the newly established MKT appeared quite similar to the PFP. Its selection of the ROC emblem (with a yellow background) as its party badge is further evidence it should be regarded as a Pan Blue party. At the party's opening ceremony, the party flag and the ROC flag were placed to the left and right of a portrait of Sun Yat Sen. The similarly moderate positioning compared with the PFP on the national identity spectrum can be seen in the first few lines of its party song, 'Republic of China MKT, Love the People, Love Taiwan.'[14]

The DPP was especially cautious in this election in its references to national identity. For some of Tsai's supporters, her emphasis on maintaining the status quo of neither independence nor unification was seen as a betrayal of the DPP's values. Her 2016 core election slogan was the rather vague: 'Light Up Taiwan' (點亮台灣) and like Ma in 2012 a number of ads featured the slogan 'Go Taiwan' (台灣加油). Unlike many earlier DPP campaigns there were no anti-unification appeals or even attacks on the KMT's China policy. Instead Tsai attempted to project an inclusive identity message to counteract the common KMT accusation that the DPP was stirring up ethnic tensions and was biased against non-Hokklo ethnic groups. For example, one line in her 29 December 2015 and 6 January 2016 TV ads notes that 'maybe we do not understand each other enough; maybe we are not tolerant enough of each other'. Her inclusive message was also clear in the multiple languages used in her advertising. In Tsai's first TV ad on 17 September 2015 she mixed Taiwanese, Hakka and

Mandarin, while in her 15 December 2015 one-minute ad she talks almost all in Hakka. She was also supported in a number of campaign events by the award-winning Hakka language singer Lin Sheng-hsiang (林生祥). We also see this inclusive identity message in the way an ultimate symbol of Chinese national-ism, a statue of Chiang Kai-shek, is shown followed immediately by a clip of a Taiwan independence flag, while the narrator notes, 'What has passed has passed' (所有過去的已經過去了).[15] Overall then, we can take the DPP as de-emphasising national identity but also moving slightly further towards the centre compared to 2012.

In recent elections the TSU had been able to dominate the issue space to the left of the DPP on the unification versus independence debates. However, as was the case at the far right of the spectrum, the far left also became more com-petitive. The NPP adopted a position to the left of the DPP but quite similar to the DPP of the 2008 election. Among the NPP's three basic advocacies, the first is, 'The NPP advocates normalising the country's status.'[16] Similarly, in the NPP's Party List TV ad we see it protesting against the Ma-Xi meeting in Singa-pore. However, though the NPP was competing for voters supporting independ-ence with the TSU, this was just one of a variety of its social movement appeals.

In contrast, the TSU had a much greater focus on opposition to China. For example, one of its TV ads showed a university student throwing the book *Formosa Betrayed* at President Ma and as he was being held to the ground by security agents shouting 'Taiwan and China, one country on each side.' A number of its TV ads used the case of Hong Kong to discredit the PRC's (and the CUPP's) OCTS unification formula. The ad featured images of violent police handling of Hong Kong's Umbrella Movement and the narrator (speaking in Cantonese or Mandarin with a Cantonese accent) telling viewers, 'Taiwan's friends, you still have the chance, you must stand firm, don't let today's Hong Kong become tomorrow's Taiwan.' One way that its anti China message was visualised was in the form of weighing scales. The viewer is told how the KMT and PFP are so pro-China, the scales are tipping in China's favour. The narrator explains how the DPP will be constrained because it will need to look after different views (once in power) and so Taiwan needs the TSU to keep the scales balanced. Almost all the TSU's ads featured TSU protests against either political or economic ties with China. Unsurprisingly the TSU brands itself as 'Number One Anti China Brand' (抗中第一品牌). However, unlike earlier elections, the TSU did not talk of declaring independence, thus it should not be placed as far left as another new party, the Free Taiwan Party led by Tsai Ting-kuei (蔡丁貴), which has attempted to claim that spot. Its TV ad stated: 'Taiwan is Taiwan, not China, it is not Chinese Taipei' (台灣就是台灣不是中國, 不是中華台北). Among its demands, it called for scrapping the ROC Constitution and for inde-pendence by 2020. Thus the Free Taiwan Party's position is quite similar to the DPP's at its most extreme in 1991.

Economic ties with China

Despite Taiwan's growing economic integration with China, it was not until well into the DPP era that it became a salient electoral issue. For example, from the mid-1990s through until early in the DPP era, the only party that really tried to win votes on this issue was the NP. It forcefully argued for trade and investment liberalisation with China at the time.[17] Towards the end of the DPP era, the picture changed as the TSU began warning of the risks of integration, while the KMT adopted the NP's cross-Strait blueprint with the clear message that economic integration with China offered a solution to Taiwan's economic woes. In the 2008 campaign the DPP joined the TSU in warning of the dangers of the KMT's plans on economic integration. It warned how the KMT planned what it called the One China Common Market (一中市場) and in particular the threat of Chinese labour. The issue would remain highly salient throughout the Ma era. Once it came to power, the KMT began to implement its blueprint of integration with a series of cross-Strait economic agreements, with ECFA the most significant in the summer of 2010.[18] While in 2008 the parties debated about what would or could happen if Taiwan became economically integrated with China, in 2012, the parties debated what had actually happened. Thus, much of the KMT propaganda stressed the positive economic benefits of integration, particularly for Taiwanese farmers, as well as the tourist industry.[19] A number of KMT ads compared these economic developments with the bleak picture under the DPP. The KMT did also attack the DPP on this issue, warning how the fruits of cross-Strait relations would be destroyed if the DPP were to come back to power.[20] In contrast to earlier elections, the DPP was quiet on the issue, no longer opposing ECFA or the agreements signed, instead it preferred to focus its attention on domestic issues. There was an overall consensus that in 2012 the cross-strait economic issue was a key factor in the KMT's ability to win re-election (Schubert 2012).

Two years later, with the advent of the Sunflower Movement, the atmosphere had radically changed. The pausing of cross-Strait agreements and the clear shift towards a more cautious public opinion set the scene for the debates over this issue in the 2014 and 2016 elections. In 2014, the KMT made a concerted attempt to attack the DPP (and its social movement allies) on this issue in its advertising. For example in its 21 November 2014 ad entitled 'On November 29 make a correct choice' (11月29日, 做一個對的選擇!), we see contrasting images of cheerful-looking young business people with the chaotic scenes in the Legislative Yuan where the DPP was trying to block KMT legislation. Although cross-Strait agreements are never mentioned, viewers will immediately guess these protests must be related to cross-Strait agreements. The viewer is asked whether this is progress or locking up the country (進步? 鎖國). The ad ends with the plea: 'Don't let them destroy our happiness' (別讓他們拖垮我們的幸福).[21] The KMT was also willing to broaden this attack with a comparative international angle in the campaign. A much discussed case was its TV ad entitled 'Who was it that allowed Korea to snigger at us?' (是誰, 讓韓國在竊笑?).[22]

The ad showed Korea represented by a lady in traditional Korean dress at a card table. The narrator tells us that Korea says thank you to the DPP for blocking legislation. We are told how Korea has just signed a free trade agreement with China and how this gives Korea a major economic advantage over Taiwan and that Taiwan has 'officially become Asia's economic orphan' (正式成為亞洲的經濟孤兒). The ad ends with the questions, 'Will the DPP be able to continue its rough blocking of the next generation? Will Taiwan choose to go forward or go backwards?' As the Korean lady looks at the viewer, we are told, 'Korea is watching.'

In 2016, the pattern of party emphasis on cross-strait economic relations showed both continuity and change. Overall the issue received far less political attention than in either 2008 or 2012. At opposite ends of this spectrum lay the CUPP and TSU, with both framing the economic consequences of integration through their own nationalist lenses. The CUPP argued, for instance, that unification under OCTS would allow Taiwan to enjoy a peace dividend, as it would save on military spending and be able to take full advantage of the mainland's resources and huge market.[23] Perhaps sensing the shift in public opinion, the KMT gave far less emphasis to economic ties compared to 2012 or even 2014. Often where the KMT did touch upon the issue, it was in a more indirect style. For instance, in a 25 November 2015 TV ad, Chu comments, 'These last few years I often see two Taiwans. One is a Taiwan that needs to be careful and protection, one Taiwan needs to go out and take risks.' Its newspaper ad warned that 'Only if the KMT holds on to a majority in the Legislative Yuan can cross-Strait risks be reduced.'[24] The ad went on to remind voters about the different formats of cross-Strait relations following the two changes of ruling parties and how they can no longer take risks with Taiwan's peace and stable development. This was thus a softer variation of the KMT's terror message that it had adopted so frequently since 1991.[25] I only located a single KMT TV ad that stressed the substance of the KMT's cross-Strait economic integration since 2008. Moreover, this was only broadcast on 12 January 2016, just before voting day. First, we see tour buses and hear a tour bus owner stating we never realised how many people's lives could be changed by tourism, then we hear from fishery industry farmers. One notes how ECFA has saved his livelihood and another says if cross-Strait relations are not good, then there will be no market for his (午仔魚) fish. The ad ends with a clip of mango trees and the head of the Yujing Farmers Association (Yujing is known for its mangoes) talking about how if there is uncertainty about the future, rich people will not invest (in agriculture). However, while there were dozens of such ads issued by the KMT in 2012, this was the only one in 2016. It appeared the KMT was no longer confident about campaigning on its record of cross-Strait economic achievements. Another similar absence was newspaper ads supporting the KMT and its cross-Strait policy sponsored by Taishang associations in China, something that featured very heavily in 2012.

Most other parties either ignored the issue or only dealt with it in passing. In one PFP TV ad, Soong stressed that he had the 'Cross-strait wisdom that people could trust' (人民放心的兩岸智慧).[26] The MKT's Party Song (黨歌篇) ad included the vague line 'Cross-Strait peace needs to be developed' (兩岸和平要發展). The DPP, as in 2012, largely steered clear of the issue in its propaganda. One of the few exceptions came in its 11 January 2016 TV ad. As with many ads, it was a critique of the Ma era. It first asks the viewer whether they care about key concerns such as environmental pollution, food safety and the black box. The latter term, with the visual of the Legislative Yuan, is a clear critique of the CSSTA procedure. The narrator then goes on to explain that what the DPP will do is to turn issues voters care about into legislation and to supervise the government on these matters.

Unsurprisingly the parties that had the reputation for being the most opposed to economic integration were the NPP and TSU, but they took a different approach in making such appeals. In the NPP's PR list TV ad we see clips from a wide range of mass social movement protests. The ad starts with the slogan 'Reject the CSSTA' (退回服貿) and later clips of Sunflower protestors both inside and outside the parliament, including shots of NPP candidates. In addition, we see NPP candidate Cheng Hsiu-ling (鄭秀玲), a National Taiwan University economist, who has been influential in public debates on the dangers of Chinese influence on media monopoly and also over CSSTA. Thus the NPP framed its opposition to economic integration with China in terms of its place in mass social movements.

While the NPP only issued one TV ad, the TSU spent much more freely with 20 separate TV ads and numerous newspaper ads. One of the most common TSU themes was the danger of integration with China and how the TSU had consistently protested against such trends. For instance, its 8 January 2016 TV ad contained a long list of areas where it has tried to block integration, including its repeated attempts to allow a referendum on ECFA. The ad described the TSU as the 'boldest at opposing China' (抗中第一勇).[27] Unlike the NPP ads, however, the TSU tended to focus on its own TSU anti China protests and only later showed brief follow-up clips of the Sunflower protests, implying that the Sunflowers were a consequence of the TSU actions. For instance, in the TSU's 18 December and 26 December 2015 ads we see clips of TSU anti CSSTA demonstrations with the party chair discussing how Chinese immigration to Taiwan is taking away Taiwanese jobs. In fact, this was a message that the DPP had used quite frequently in 2008–2010. In addition to the spectre of Chinese labour, the TSU also openly made clear its opposition to including Chinese students in Taiwan into the National Health Insurance system. A similar ad on 9 January 2016 followed this migration threat with the warning of how Chinese business people were opening retail chains in Taiwan but only selling Chinese products. Another ad placed on 9 January 2016 appealed to exactly the same people as those of the KMT's 12 January TV ad, Taiwan's farmers. The ad tells us the TSU is the one 'really fighting for Taiwan's farmers' (真正為台灣的農民) and the one 'really fighting for Taiwan's traditional industries' (真正為台灣的傳統產業). We see images of TSU-led protests for protecting both these sectors and it is clearly implied that they are the victims of cross-Strait integration.

Social movements

Questions of protests and social movements have often featured in Taiwan's election campaigns. For example, during the 1990s, the DPP stressed its role in leading Taiwan's democratic transition through protests. In contrast, the KMT painted democratisation as a top-down process in which it had played the leading role and its advertising tended to highlight the message that the DPP was a violent party. When the DPP was in power, it was faced by KMT protests against the controversial 2004 presidential election and Red Shirts anti-corruption movement. It even attempted to poke fun at the KMT and paint it as the violent party damaging the stock market and unable to accept democracy. Given the salience of social movements in the build-up and aftermath of the Sunflower occupation of parliament, it is not surprising that this was something that featured prominently in the main parties' advertising and was also reflected in their patterns of nomination.

At one end of the political spectrum were the KMT's splinter and allied parties, such as the CUPP, Faith and Hope Alliance (FHA) and the NP. These parties appealed to voters with anti-social movement appeals or adopted positions opposed to those advocated by the mainstream social movement groups. This was especially clear in the case of the NP. Its 2 January 2016 TV ad opened with a cartoon scene of demonstrators holding placards showing the word 'protest' (抗議). The protestors are demonized by giving them demon's eyes. They are then contrasted with social elites who will stand up to this evil force (邪惡勢力). These are then shown in the form of the NP's top ranked PR candidates Chiu Yi and Ye Yu-lan (葉毓蘭) who are holding *Star Wars*-style lightsabres. The NP's 17 December 2015 newspaper ad revealed its opposition to key social movement demands. For instance, one of its candidates is listed as opposing lifting the death sentence, while another opposes 'Taiwan Independence School curriculums' (台獨課綱).[28] The latter appeal placed the NP in direct opposition to the high school student-led movement that had opposed controversial proposed changes to school curriculums in 2015 and had featured the occupation of the Ministry of Education. Another theme addressed by these Pan Blue parties was the protection of the family, something widely understood as code for opposing LGBT rights. The NP's Su Heng (蘇恆) was listed as protecting family values.[29] However, the conservative counter-movement against gay marriage was most associated with the FHA. The party had only been formed in early 2015 by a number of conservative evangelical churches with the sole objective of preventing the passage of Same Sex Marriage Legislation. As we saw in Tables 4.1 and 4.4, the FHA had spent quite heavily and scored a respectable 1.69 per cent in its first election. It is also noteworthy that the FHA had concentrated its advertising on the radio and in fact in January 2016 it was the highest spender on radio ads. The FHA's first TV ad on 7 January listed protecting the family and youth among a number of its other core policies, but the anti-LGBT focus was made clearer in its 11 January TV ad that called for a 'Million People Petition for a Referendum on Protecting the Family' (百萬公投連署保

護家庭). The anti-social movement appeal was also apparent in the nomination of candidates by these parties. The public face of the CUPP was Chang An-lo in the campaign, and he became a household name when he led a group of his supporters in a counter-protest against the Sunflower Movement in April 2014 (Hsiao 2014: 1). The NP's nomination of Chiu Yi on its PR list was a similar anti-social movement statement. Chiu had been a KMT legislator during the Ma era and a regular on Taiwan's political talk shows since the early 2000s. He had been a frequent critic of many of the Ma era social movements. While appearing on Chinese state TV he famously accused the DPP of supporting the Sunflower Movement by supplying them with bananas. After not being nominated by the KMT, he stood for the NP in 2016 and his ads featured for much of the campaign on the front page of the *United Daily News* and *China Times*.

What about the ruling party, the KMT? How did it handle the social movement topic? A number of its advertisements in both 2014 and 2016 attempted to appeal to voters uncomfortable with the rise of social movements. A good example of this was the KMT's 2014 campaign ad 'Let Us Quietly, Speak Loudly' ad (讓我們靜靜地, 大聲說話). The ad shows a middle-aged man in a classroom and a narrator offering a critique of recent developments. The narrator explains that in the current climate: 'Because *you don't go* on the street to protest, you are wrong. Because you quietly work hard, you can't snatch the microphone' (因為你不上街抗議, 所以你是錯的, 因為你只會靜靜努力, 你搶不到麥克風). The ad ends with the man going to the voting booth with the narrator explaining, 'This is Taiwan, those that do not argue have huge power. On November 29, hold your ballot paper tightly and let us quietly speak loudly' (這裡是台灣, 不吵架的人也有巨大力量, 握緊手上的選票, 11月29日, 讓我們靜靜地, 大聲說話).[30] The KMT made a similar but more direct attack on social movements in their 2016 advertisement known as 'I'm the Fifth generation' ad (我是五年級生). The narrator explains how 'They forbid me from using the word justice, because justice is theirs exclusively, court justice is theirs, residential justice is theirs [at this point we see protest banners behind the protagonist], economic justice is theirs, I have no justice.'[31] The 'they' here can be taken as broadly referring to both the DPP and its social movement allies. We see a similar critique in the KMT's 1 January 2016 TV ad. In this advertisement former presidential candidate Hung is explaining her decision to stay in the KMT and support Chu. As she is talking, we see protest placards in the background, however, these were protests banners used in the Legislative Yuan by the KMT against the DPP and the Sunflower Movement. Here the banners read: 'Oppose Locking up the Country, Oppose wasteful internal struggle, Fight for the Economy,'(反鎖過, 要開放, 反內耗,拚經濟).

The DPP tried to handle the social movement topic in a relatively cautious manner. The party had benefitted greatly from the Sunflower effect in November 2014 and beyond. However, the party had struggled in the past with the reputation of being violent and anti-business, and thus Tsai naturally took quite a different approach compared to the GPT and NPP whom I locate at the far end of this issue spectrum. First, the DPP appealed to those who supported social movements by nominating key social movement activists, especially on its PR list. Most noteworthy were figures, such as Frida Tsai (蔡培慧), who had been the leader of the Taiwan Rural Front and was associated with numerous land justice disputes, Yu Wan-ju (余婉如), who is a leading figure in Taiwan's Fair Trade movement, as well as the feminist leader, Chen Man-li (陳曼麗). In fact, both Yu and Chen were former leaders of Taiwan's Green Party. Moreover, the DPP stressed this nomination especially heavily in the final week of the campaign in its newspaper, TV and social media ads. Half-page ads featuring these social movement-linked candidates appeared on the front page of newspapers between 8–10 January,[32] and a number of these candidates also featured in their own short ads that were used only on social media.

The DPP ads also included images of protest that were being used to critique the KMT. In Tsai's 17 September 2015 TV ad we see images of water cannon being used against Sunflower protestors and then police forcefully removing protesters from a protest scene. For these scenes Tsai narrates that 'While the people are looking for a government that can solve problems, the government is solving people who are looking for problems' (人們在找可解決問題的政府，而政府在解決找問題的人們). Tsai's TV ads also alluded to a number of key issues driving the social movement scene. For instance, in Tsai's 29 December 2015 TV ad that offers a critique of Taiwan in recent years, we see a clip of the Dapu residence that was at the centre and became a symbol of the struggle for land justice. At this point the narrator tells us that 'fairness and justice have come to a halt' (公平正義停滯了). Later in this ad we see youngsters holding the LGBT flag and a legalize gay marriage flag. The party also made gestures towards the environmental movement, for instance, Chen Man-li is called an environmental protection specialist[33] and a number of the TV ads showed the third nuclear power station at Kenting, a clear reference to the party's anti-nuclear stance.

In addition to the DPP, however, there was intense competition among other non-Pan Blue parties for the support of those sympathetic to social movements. This time in addition to the TSU, the GPT SDP alliance, NPP, the Free Taiwan Party and the Tree Party all appealed on social movement themes. Although as discussed earlier, the Free Taiwan Party's main appeal was Taiwan independence, its party leader did label himself the 'Mastermind behind the Sunflowers' (太陽花首謀).[34] The party that had the most positive representations of protests in its advertising in the election was the TSU, however, since these protests dealt almost exclusively with issues related to Taiwan's political and economic relations with China, they were discussed in the previous two sections. It is ironic that the most openly pro-protest party was the one swept away by its new rival as the DPP's allied party, the NPP, a social movement-inspired party.

Nevertheless, the two parties that had the best claim to be social movement parties were the GPT-SDP Alliance and the NPP. In fact, there was clear competition between these two over which would be the party that best represented Taiwan's civil society. For both parties, the majority of their nominated candidates had clear social movement backgrounds. Unsurprisingly the GPT stressed its environmental credentials by nominating its co-convenor, Li Gen-zheng (李根政), who also headed environmental NGO Citizens of the Earth on its PR list. Another noteworthy element in the GPT's attempt to reach new voters was to focus on labour-related issues. The nomination of Chang Li-fen (張麗芬), the Secretary General of the China Telecom Union, at the top of its party list signified this new approach. One particularly notable GPT appeal has been over gay and lesbian rights, an issue on which the mainstream parties have tended to either ignore or take divided or ambiguous stances. The GPT was the first party to nominate openly gay candidates in local and national elections. This emphasis was also apparent in the nomination of Hsu Hsiu-wen (許秀文), a leading figure in the Taiwan Partners Rights Promotion Alliance on its party list.

The key themes for the GPT-SDP Alliance in 2016 were visible in its Change TV ad.[35] We first see images of before and after at the controversial Miramar Resort, then before and after the Dapu land dispute case, we are reminded of the growing gap between GDP and wages, images of melamine milk to remind voters about food safety scandals, and it ends with the image of a couple kissing at a lesbian wedding ceremony. Thus the party was reminding voters of key issues of concern to social movements. In short, the GPT/SDP attempted to play the role of a genuinely alternative party in its political project. The fact the party failed to reach 5 per cent shows the challenges of such an alternative political project strategy.

Like the GPT, the NPP also markets itself as the representative of the new Taiwanese civil society. Party founder and district candidate, Huang Kuo-chang (黃國昌) was one of the three most prominent leaders of the Sunflower Move-ment. An examination of the NPP's party list TV advertisement reveals the movement appeals adopted by the party. The ad showed images of its candidates and supporters at a variety of protests such as the Sunflower occupation, anti-nuclear demonstrations, protesting against the Ma-Xi meeting and at gay pride parades. And towards the end of the ad we see a rally scene showing the NPP's Huang with Tsai Ing-wen. Thus a major difference between the GPT/SDP and the NPP was that the latter had a closer working relationship with the DPP. For instance, the parties cooperated in a number of districts, with the DPP leaving three districts for the NPP to stand against the KMT. Overall it appears the NPP's combination of social movement appeals, more famous candidates, cooperation with the DPP, and a clearer national identity position gave it a deci-sive advantage over its social movement rival the GPT.

Conclusion

This chapter has revealed a number of important trends of continuity and change in Taiwan's party scene. While it is true that the challenger parties only made a limited breakthrough and the same two parties remain dominant, 2016 saw major changes in the party system that are likely to have long-term implications. First, it saw the DPP winning a clear national election victory over the KMT and its allies for the first time. It also has left the KMT looking deeply divided, demoralised and led by a leader clearly out of step with mainstream public opinion, its prospects of recovery in the short to medium term look bleak. The arrival of the NPP into parliament is also significant, as it is the first non-splinter party to break into the party system and because its hybrid issue appeals are quite distinct from earlier challenger parties. The NPP's performance since entering parliament suggests that it will continue to expand in the next round of local elections in 2018. The election also suggests we are witnessing the demise of the traditional splinter parties, with the failure of the TSU, NP and MKT. Although the PFP managed to survive in parliament, it is unclear whether it will be able to find a role once Soong eventually retires. The election has again shown that Taiwanese voters tend to punish extremism on both sides of the main issue spectrum. Despite heavy spending, the CUPP and NP performed disastrously. We have seen how public opinion can shift over a short time period. Only four years earlier the KMT had won a comfortable re-election on its record of promoting cross-Strait economic integration, but in 2016 this appeal had become a serious electoral liability. In terms of the issue agenda, the election has shown how Taiwan's politics should not be simply understood as referenda on political relations with China. Instead we have seen how parties need to take broad issue approaches and how a range of social issues became highly salient in this campaign. This means that the new Tsai administration will have significant pressure to address a wide range of domestic reforms or face a similar set of protest movements to those that dogged the Ma government.

Notes

1 It is true the DPP had similar leads in party identification over the KMT in 2001 and 2002. However, if the KMT and PFP support levels were combined, they still exceeded those of the DPP.
2 For more on KMT party assets, see Xu (1997).
3 For instance, Hsieh (2002: 38–40).
4 The only other case I have come across was when NP legislator Elmer Feng also used One Country, Two Systems in his 2001 bus advertisements. At the time the NP officially talked of One Country, Three Systems.
5 *China Times*, 25 December 2015, A1.
6 For a discussion of the rise and decline of the NP, see Fell (2006).
7 See www.np.org.tw/
8 *China Times*, 17 December, A5.
9 Broadcast on 30 December 2015.
10 *China Times*, 7 January, A7.
11 See www.youtube.com/watch?v=OatkmnEiBz0
12 Broadcast on 1 January 2016.
13 See www.pfp.org.tw/Party_Show.asp?id=3
14 See www.mkt.org.tw/Home
15 Broadcast on 29 December 2015.
16 See www.newpowerparty.tw/proposal
17 For a discussion of the development of this topic as an electoral issue from the 1990s through to 2012, see Fell (2015).
18 For a comprehensive discussion of cross-Strait integration through to 2015, see Lee Pei-shan and Chu Yun-han (2016).

19 For a detailed discussion of the 2012 ads on this issue, see Fell (2015).
20 *China Times*, KMT support advertisement, 22 December 2011, A1.
21 See www.youtube.com/watch?v=RJRvX5D7zW4
22 See www.youtube.com/watch?v=fmjTBggNGyI
23 *United Daily News*, 27 Nov. 2016, A1.
24 *China Times*, 8 January, A3.
25 That terror message was DPP = Taiwan Independence = War. It was used repeatedly until 2000.
26 Broadcast on 11 January 2016.
27 *Liberty Times*, 8 January 2016, A5.
28 *China Times*, 17 Dec. 2015, A5.
29 Ibid.
30 See www.youtube.com/watch?v=CLYThf2PkwM
31 Although this ad was made by the Council for Industrial and Commercial Development (CDIC), it was shown on the KMT's Facebook pages and was probably the most widely discussed KMT ad of the 2016 campaign.
32 *Liberty Times*, 8 January, A1.
33 Ibid.
34 *Liberty Times*, 15 January, A5.
35 See www.youtube.com/watch?v=C9z6iaXqNao

References

Chen, I. H. C. and Fell, D. (2014). Lessons of Defeat and Success: Taiwan's 2012 Elections in Comparative Perspective. *Journal of Current Chinese Affairs*, 43(3): 13–43.

Fang, B. C. (2015). Aiming to Exceed the Second Largest Party, the MKT Will Nominate a Presidential Candidate, *Storm Media*, 23 June 2015. Available at: www.storm.mg/article/54329

Fell, D. (2006). The Rise and Decline of the New Party: Ideology, Resources and the Political Opportunity Structure, *East Asia: An International Quarterly*, 23(1): 47–67.

Fell, D. (2015). The China Impact on Taiwan's Elections: Cross-Strait Economic Integration through the Lens of Election Advertising, in Schubert, G. (ed.) *Taiwan and the 'China Impact': Challenges and Opportunities*. London: Routledge, pp. 53–69.

Hsiao, A. (2014). White Wolf leads pro-pact rally, *Taipei Times*, 2 April 2014, 1.

Hsieh, J. (2002). Continuity and Change in Taiwan's Electoral Politics, in Hsieh, J. and Newman, D. (eds) *How Asia Votes*, New York: Chatham House Publishing, pp. 32–49.

Lee, P. S. and Chu, Y. H. (2016). Cross-Strait Economic Integration (1992–2015), in Schubert, G. (ed.) *Routledge Handbook of Contemporary Taiwan*, London: Routledge, pp. 410–425.

Lee Pei-shan and Chu Yun-han (2016). Cross-Strait Economic Integration (1992–2015), in Gunter Schubert (ed.), *Routledge Handbook of Contemporary Taiwan*. London: Routledge, pp. 410–425.

Schubert, G. (2012). No Winds of Change: Taiwan's 2012 National Elections and the Post Election Fallout, *Journal of Current Chinese Affairs*, 41(3): 143–161.

Ware, A. (1996). *Political Parties and Party Systems*, Oxford: Oxford University Press.

Xu, D. (1997) The KMT Party's Enterprises in Taiwan, *Modern Asian Studies*, 31(2*): 399–413.

5 From protest to electioneering

Electoral and party politics after the Sunflower Movement

Ming-sho Ho

Democracy disrupted or regeneration?

Reflecting on the contemporary global explosion of social protests, Krastev (2014) provides a gloomy picture. Massive, spontaneous, and largely non-violent protests have taken place in major cities throughout the world in the past decade, and yet they have departed from the classical tradition of revolution which aims to establish a progressive agenda or program. While these dramatic acts of collective defiance are more or less capable of overthrowing unpopular rulers or derailing detested policies, they usually fail to bring about meaningful changes. The contemporary protests are propelled by a decidedly "rejectionist ethics" that stops short of proposing an alternative (ibid.: 59). With the absence of a concrete program or a guiding ideology, street occupation has become "a kind of performance art" for itself (ibid.: 20). These protests leave behind a profoundly disruptive effect on democracy; since few incumbents can meet the growing demands from their citizens, elections are losing their political function of creating a legitimate majority. As such, the urge to express discontentment takes precedence over offering a viable solution, and "protesting itself seems to be the strategic goal of many of the protests" (ibid.: 3).

A number of contemporary observers of different political persuasions echo Krastev's diagnosis. The uprisings in the Arabic countries in 2010–2011 were "successful by what they did not want – a specific ruler, his party, his family, his policies that enriched his elites and impoverished the people." And the visible lack of "a clear program, a hierarchical organization with figureheads and followers" turned out to be the very source of their strength (Noueihed and Warren 2012: 6). Mason (2012: 3, 187) maintains that protest activists in the West are "hostile to the very idea of a unifying theory, a set of bullet-point demands, a guru or a teleology." Even these protests appear ideologically akin to the left, the mainstream left-wing politicians, including American liberals and European socialists and social democrats, are equally at a loss about how to deal with these explosions of discontent. In his global survey, Castells (2012: 227) also concludes that these movements are rarely programmatic and their leaderless structure makes it nearly impossible to "be co-opted by political parties."

In the case of Occupy Wall Street, Graeber (2012) spoke positively about the principled rejection of hierarchical leadership that made possible spontaneous collaboration from the grassroots. He maintained the refusal to raise demands and to negotiate with the authorities constituted the strength as well as the global appeal of this movement. However, there existed contrasting appraisals in that the excessive pure display of playfulness and spontaneity might amount to a "moment rather than movement" (Gitlin 2013), or "more performance than program" (Calhoun 2013).

There appears to be a rather consensual understanding of these large-scale anti-government movements. For their admirers, these spontaneous and creative protests promise to herald a fundamental restructuring of contemporary politics, while the detractors point to the corrosion of political institutions that is likely to precipitate a crisis of governability. That these protests emerge in extra-institutional fashion, such as nonviolent occupation of urban space, seems to imply their inherently anti-institutional characteristics. There exists a rarely asked question whether these explosions of protest activism might generate a positive feedback to the existing political institutions in the long run in spite of their "unlawful" disturbance of public order. Could the chaotic disruption of democracy ultimately lead to its regeneration? To be sure, ailing political institutions generate mass dissatisfaction that ignites these large-scale acts of occupation in the first place. However, is it possible that the massive outpouring of grassroots activism might provide the remedy for the pre-existing illness?

This chapter will look at the evolution of Taiwan's electoral politics after the Sunflower Movement to understand how this unprecedented protest helps to usher in a new political generation, whose activism has resulted in significant changes. In contrast to the above-mentioned view, quite a number of Taiwan's young protest participants turn out to be pragmatic by taking the route of electioneering to continue their activism. In particular, I will examine the Sunflower activists' participation in the 2014 local election and the 2016 legislative election. Second, this chapter analyses the adaptive strategy by the Democratic Progressive Party (DPP), which has scored landslide victories in the two consecutive elections. That the DPP skillfully harnessed this unexpected surge of protest activism contributed to their electoral triumph.

Social movements in Taiwan's democratization

Before turning to a closer examination of the Sunflower Movement, it will be useful to look at the preceding developments in Taiwan. Social movements, viewed as the sustained and collective efforts to promote social changes from below, emerged in the early 1980s as the authoritarian rule waned in the face of a growing civil society. Intellectuals and liberal professionals (lawyers, journalists, and professors) spearheaded a number of advocacy campaigns in human rights, environmental protection, and gender equity, while grassroots groups mounted disruptive protests to protect their jobs and livelihoods. The termination of martial law in 1987 opened the floodgates of public discontent, as more and more social movements came into place and adopted increasingly militant tactics (Hsiao 1992).

The simultaneous explosion of social movements and the rise of the DPP (in 1986) left an enduring legacy on the subsequent trajectory. The nascent opposition party adopted a number of movement demands, most notably the opposition to nuclear energy, and thereby cemented a movement-party alliance. The advent of social movements eroded the Kuomintang (KMT) regime's control (e.g. student movement and campus conformism) as well as its social basis (e.g., the farmer movement and anti-pollution protests in the rural society), which drew the DPP and social movements closer. While the government suppressed some radical protests, it also expanded and upgraded its administrative apparatus to meet the growing expectations from civil society, as evidenced by the establishment of the Environmental Protection Agency and the Council of Labor Affairs, both in 1988, as well as the absorption of the movement demands into state policies, such as education reform and community building in the mid-1990s.

Until the first power turnover in 2000, the DPP's growth facilitated social movements to generate political impacts, as its local executives were more willing to adopt reforms and its seats in the legislature were instrumental in securing more progressive laws and policies (Lee 2017). However, as the DPP became a would-be ruling party, it also took on a more moderate approach around the mid-1990s. This reorientation certainly frustrated its erstwhile movement allies; however, with unsuccessful attempt of movement parties, Workers' Party (1987), Labor Party (1989), and Taiwan Green Party (1996), the DPP-movement nexus remained largely intact.

During the first DPP government (2000–2008), its relationship with social movements underwent a profound change. Chen Shui-bian's government backtracked on a number of reform promises that had disappointed their movement allies. While the DPP in power gravitated to a development-first outlook, it also made possible broader and deeper policy participation for movement leaders (Ho 2005). The result of this was that Taiwan's movement communities were split into a pragmatist wing that believed it was possible to generate some changes by collaborating with the DPP and a fundamentalist wing that thought the two main parties were virtually indistinguishable in ideology (Chu 2011; Wei 2016). Second, the first DPP government did not enjoy a legislative majority, and the vulnerability of a minority government tended to invite counter-movement from the conservative camp. As such, conservative movements, such as the church-based anti-abortion movement and anti-homosexual movement, came to the surface in this period (Huang 2017). Also related to this was the fact that political protests mobilized by politicians and political parties also reappeared in Taiwan during this period after the DPP gradually ceased to mobilize its supporters in the early 1990s. The KMT protest against the 2004 presidential election result and the Red Shirt Army protest against Chen's financial irregularities as well as pro-Chen mobilization in 2006 were the most notable cases here (Lin 2015).

With the KMT's return to power in 2008, Taiwan's social movements resurged. Ma Ying-jeou's government was not only more conservative in policy orientation, but also shut down the policy avenues opened up in the preceding DPP government. As a result, social movements that had long since been in a period of dormancy revived after 2008, such as the student movement, the antinuclear movement, and the farmers movement (Hsiao and Ku 2010; Fell 2017). The re-emergence of student activism, in particular, generated spillover effects, because they injected new blood into protests related to labor, environmental, and other issues. Learning from the previous lesson, movement activism in this period attempted to navigate a more politically independent course (Ho 2016). Hence the term "citizen movement" (*kungmin yüntung gongmin yundong*) almost came to replace "social movement" in public discourse for its implications of idealism and non-partisanship. Newer activists were willing to adopt confrontational tactics (Grano 2015; Ho forthcoming), as the discussion on civil disobedience became more prevalent. Finally, reflecting the fact of the growing influence of China, Taiwan's civil society has launched a series of defensive resistances against its pernicious effects (Schubert 2016; Wu, Tsai and Cheng 2017). As such, the term "China factor" has become popular in movement circles. Needless to say, the combination of a reactivated civil society, a conservative government, and the encroachment from China planted the seed for the Sunflower Movement, arguably the largest episode of non-violent protest in post-war Taiwan.

In sum, Taiwan's social movements have demonstrated remarkable resilience for their continuing agitation for progressive reforms. By the time that Ma Ying-jeou led his KMT to regain national power, Taiwan had witnessed two peaceful regime changes and thus can be fully qualified as a consolidated democratic regime. Nevertheless, social movements retained their momentum and were capable of mounting a frontal challenge to the regime incumbents. In hindsight, the Sunflower Movement generated a long-lasting political impact comparable to the 2006 Red Shirt Army Movement, both taking place in the second tenure of sitting presidents (Chen Shui-bian and Ma Ying-jeou) who had become unpopular among voters. However, the two protests were in polar difference: the Red Shirt Army Movement was led by politicians with minimal participation from NGOs, whereas the Sunflower Movement was organized by students and their NGO allies and the politicians only played an auxiliary role. In other words, the Sunflower Movement was solidly based on Taiwan's civil society, but the anti-Chen protest remained an outgrowth of partisan rivalry, which has re-energized the KMT politicians and their supporters and thus facilitated them to win national power from the discredited DPP. In spite of these far-reaching consequences, the protests by the Reds failed to engender movement activism and party formation as the Sunflower Movement did.

The Sunflower Movement

To oppose a sweeping trade liberalization agreement with China (the Cross-strait Service Trade Agreement, hence the CSSTA), Taiwan's university students launched a sit-in protest by breaking into the national legislature on the evening of March 18, 2014, unexpectedly giving rise to a 24-day occupation. The student-led occupation engendered a political confrontation between protestors who enjoyed support from opposition parties, chiefly the DPP, to challenge the ostensibly divided KMT government. The so-called Sunflower Movement argu-ably amounted to the largest and longest episode of collective contention in Taiwan, and its culmination came with the mass rally on March 30, which pur-portedly attracted half a million participants. In the end, the Sunflower Move-ment was peacefully concluded, with the disputed CSSTA mired in the legislative process (Green 2016; Ho 2015; Lee 2015; Rowen 2015).

Taiwan's Sunflower Movement shared many similar features with the con-temporary large-scale anti-government protests elsewhere in the world. Tech-savvy young people made up the main contingent as well as the core leadership of this movement. The young generation's economic plight provided the main impetus for their protest participation, and their mastery over digital communi-cation facilitated instant mobilization in seizing the national legislature and sub-sequent resistance against the police eviction. The Sunflower Movement emerged through the strength of the unpremeditated collaboration of particip-ants. Although Taiwan witnessed an escalating protest wave since the KMT had returned to power in 2008 (Ho 2014a), there were no strong or overarching social movement organizations that were capable of coordinating protest activ-ities of such magnitude. Instead, what existed were but a motley crew of small ad-hoc protest organizations and interpersonal networks, whose swift response and creative cooperation turned out to generate a powerful political impact. Protestors were unified by their determined opposition to the CSSTA, but their participation was motivated by a variety of reasons, including the rejection of closer political and economic integration with China, skepticism over free trade and neo-liberalism, as well as the defense of procedural justice.

Although the protest movement against trade liberalization with China relied on the help of friendly DPP politicians, who provided the logistical support for occupiers, the opposition party did not oppose the CSSTA officially until the stu-dents stormed the legislative complex. Nor did the DPP take part in the strategic decision-making of the Sunflower Movement, which maintained an autonomous core of leadership. Similar to other major protests world-wide, the Sunflower Movement forced the reluctant incumbents to open the door for negotiation pre-cisely because of its proven capacity to disrupt the public order. Yet, in compari-son, Taiwan's activists seemed to possess the tactical advantage in their bargaining with the authorities. They created huge political pressure on the incumbents because they had paralyzed the normal functioning of a vital govern-ment branch, not just occupying a city square. Their political leverage came without incurring destructive social polarization, economic disturbances, or massive inconveniences for urban residents. The Sunflower Movement only affected a small area around the national legislature, and outside the protest zone, the city's daily routines went on as usual, as if completely undisturbed by the ongoing political crisis.

As the occupation entered the third week in early April, the movement leaders made a strategic decision to evacuate the legislature voluntarily since it had become increasingly difficult to extract more concessions from the KMT government and the public support and participants' morale were visibly waning. As fatigue set in, the decline in protest participation rendered the movement vulnerable to government crackdown. It appeared a rational choice to terminate the legislature occupation quickly before the movement ran out of steam.

Evidently the movement leadership understood the vital need to strike a balance between the tactical necessity of a timely retreat and the imperative of maintaining morale among the participants. In its official statement "Turning Defensive to Offensive by Leaving the Fortress to Plant the Seeds" (*chuan shou wei kung ch'ukuan pochung zhuanshou weigong chuguan bozhong*), released on April 8, two days before the eventual evacuation, the Sunflower leaders rhetorically contended that the movement had "fulfilled the preliminary tasks and obtained significant achievements." They called for the continuing vigilance on the government and the cross-Strait negotiation, and encouraged the youthful participants to venture into "every place in the country" in the attempt to "transform the accumulated energy of a student movement into an all-citizen movement (*ch'üanmin yungtung quanmin yundong*)."[1]

The post-Sunflower activisms

After the conclusion of the legislature occupation, there indeed emerged a new wave of political activism that focused on a number of reform issues. Most of these participants had received their first political enlightenment during the Sunflower Movement, and they sought to sustain their movement commitment elsewhere.

As the CSSTA remained a pending issue after the withdrawal of the occupiers, there emerged several efforts to promote the awareness of potentially harmful free trade with China in a number of professions. Activist students in the medical school had been protesting against the deterioration of their working conditions since 2011, and the unprecedented participation of medical professionals during the Sunflower Movement further heightened their public concerns. Afterwards, a nation-wide speaking tour around Taiwan's medical schools took place to promote awareness of the impacts of free trade upon the medical profession.[2] The Taiwan Publishing Freedom Front (*taiwan chupan chenhsien taiwan chuban ziyou zhenxian*) came into being because a number of press editors were galvanized into action after the legislature was occupied. That the CSSTA allowed Chinese investment in the printing industry would have chipped away an integral link in Taiwan's publishing trade. As such, professional editors mobilized to protest the CSSTA, and afterwards, their collective action continued through negotiation with the officials of the Ministry of Culture on the issue of how to promote domestic book publishing.[3] In addition, there were similar protest activisms in the professions of ICT (information and communication technology)[4] and social work.[5] Finally, it was due to the consideration of economic grievances, that the first anti-CSSTA organization, the Democratic Front against Cross-Strait Trade in Services Agreement, renamed itself the Economic Democracy Union in September 2014.

Aside from these subsequent economic protests, there emerged other movements for political reform. Before the 2016 historical election that awarded presidency and legislative majority to the DPP, there were at least five related, but distinct political campaigns that explicitly carried on the spirit of the Sunflower Movement.

1 The campaign to revise the referendum law

The 2003 Referendum Act adopted very restrictive regulations on proposing and validating questions to put to the vote, so that Taiwan had never produced a legally binding referendum since its enactment. Since the KMT-dominated legislature was unlikely to allow a revision, some Sunflower core leaders organized a Taiwan March Foundation, which initiated a campaign to put the Referendum Act to a referendum. They launched a nation-wide signature-collecting movement for half a year, which in the end enlisted the endorsement of more than 130,000 citizens, but still fell short of the required threshold.[6] Despite the failure, the campaign evolved into the New Power Party, the third largest party in the national legislature after 2016.

2 The re-call and blacklisting campaign

Some activists took part in a movement to remove those KMT politicians who appeared particularly hostile to the Sunflower Movement from their elected positions. Due to their effort in collecting enough signatures, an official re-call vote took place against a KMT lawmaker in February 2015. Although the result generated an overwhelming percentage in favor of the re-call (97.2 percent), the turnout rate failed to meet the legally required 50 percent threshold (only 25.0 percent of the electorate showed up at the poll stations). Nevertheless, this group of activists, the so-called "Appendectomy Project" (*kolanwei gelanwei*, or "removing the bad/blue lawmakers"), mounted a blacklisting campaign in the 2016 legislative election. In the end, all three targeted KMT incumbent lawmakers lost their seats to the DPP challengers.

3 The campaign to lower the voting age to 18

The eruption of the Sunflower Movement accentuated a glaring problem in that many youthful participants in the occupied legislature were not allowed to cast their ballots because they were under 20. A subsequent campaign to revise the constitutional requirement emerged, initially by some Sunflower activists and then continued by a NGO coalition.[7] In early 2015, there arose a window of opportunity in that both the KMT and the DPP agreed on the need for a constitutional revision and the lowering of the voting age was among the bipartisan consensual list. However, the two major parties decided to part ways at the last minute so that the demand failed to materialize.

4 The campaign for legislature monitoring

Immediately before the student occupation, the attempt to strengthen public supervision of lawmakers with the use of digital communication was under way. Afterwards, the newly-founded watchdog organization Watchout (*wo ts'ao wo cao*), set up as a social enterprise, launched its operation. Unlike the previous legislature-monitoring movement, Watchout demonstrated more technological sophistication, which allowed it to access more young *netizens*.

5 The campaign too bus young citizens to go home for voting

For the 2014 local election, the Taiwan Citizen Union (TCU), a movement-oriented political party formed immediately before the Sunflower Movement, joined hands with a number of university student unions to launch a crowd-funding campaign in order to provide a free bus service for young voters to return to their hometown. The "Go Home and Vote" project explicitly high-lighted the fact that there remained other ways to change politics than "camping on the asphalt road during the Sunflower Movement." The campaign initially set the target of 150,000 dollars (New Taiwan dollars), but it received 940,000 dollars in the end, six times more than the original plan.[8]

To sum up, the fact that the Sunflower leadership skillfully concluded the disruptive legislature occupation with a claim to victory in spite of the intransigence of the KMT incumbents gave a powerful boost to the subsequent activism. The Sunflower Movement has more or less become a synonym for youthful idealism and, therefore, political participation or even party politics was no longer negatively deemed as dirty and unworthy. As a result, many previously apolitical citizens joined these political campaigns. An example from the Appendectomy Project suffices here to understand the extent of interest aroused in public participation. In order to collect the signatures to re-call a KMT lawmaker, more than 3,000 volunteers responded to on-line recruitment to manage street booths throughout the Neihu and Nankang districts of Taipei City in one day. And the great majority of them were "amateur" (*sujen suren*), or first-timers in political activity.[9] Clearly the ability to tap into such new human resources demonstrated the positive legacy of the Sunflower Movement.

The 2014 local elections

The above-mentioned flurry of reform movements signified the institutional turn of Sunflower activists, since they eagerly explored the more conventional avenues to continue their commitment. The transition occurred smoothly as there was practically no voiced objection to this electoral turn from the movement participants. The "Nine-in-One" local election scheduled on November 29, 2014, taking place less than eight months after the termination of the legislature occupation, came as a window of opportunity that could absorb the energy of post-Sunflower political activism. In addition to the close timing, the local election amounted to the largest in scale because the Taiwanese electorate would jointly decide on the distribution of more than 11,000 public offices, which included the executive ones (autonomous cities, cities/counties, townships/indigenous districts, and wards/villages) and the representative ones (councillors for autonomous cities, cities/counties, and representatives for townships/indigenous districts). With so many elective positions opened up for competition, it appeared natural that young activists would make use of this political channel, and many of them joined as candidates or campaign staff.

Because of the huge scale of the 2014 election, it is better to focus on the intermediate-level positions where the activists were more likely to make a meaningful difference. Mayoralties of autonomous cities, cities, and counties traditionally remained the reserved areas for seasoned politicians, not an ideal arena to launch one's political career. While there were Sunflower activists who chose to take part in the grassroots-level elections for ward/village heads and township representatives and some of them even succeeded in their attempt, these efforts mostly stayed under the radar for the general public. Moreover, the election of local executives proceeded under the single-member district design, which often gave rise to bipartisan rivalry and thus minimized the winning chances of young participants. Therefore, the nation-wide election of councillors in autonomous cities, cities, and counties (with 907 seats in total), which became the battleground for young activists, provides the best viewpoint to gauge the extent of the post-Sunflower electioneering.

Since only very few Sunflower activists decided to join the councillor election individually or without any partisan membership, it is better to review their electoral participation by parties or political grouping.[10]

1 Taiwan Green Party (TGP)

The TGP rose in 1996 as Taiwan's anti-nuclear movement underwent a high tide of mobilization. It demonstrated a promising start in that year by winning one seat in the National Assembly (Fell 2012: 103); however, consecutive setbacks in the subsequent years cast doubt on its electoral viability and the TGP entered a period of dormancy in the early 2000s. The TGP resumed its electoral participation in 2008, and the rising curve of social protests evidentially helped to make the appeal of environmental protection more popular. In the 2012 legislative election, the TGP received 1.74 percent in the party vote.

The outbreak of the Sunflower Movement created an opportunity for the TGP to expand. A youth department led by Sunflower activists came into being and boasted nearly 40 active members.[11] The TGP also established four regional offices and party membership grew from 300 to 500, with newcomers mostly from the younger generation.[12] Inspired by the Sunflower Movement, the TGP adopted the slogan "citizens occupy politics" and nominated nine candidates. Two TGP members were elected as councillors in Taoyuan City and Hsinchu County, marking their first electoral success since 1996.

2 The Trees Party

The TGP could have performed better if there had been no split prior to the election, which gave rise to a new Trees Party, which nominated eight candidates for the councillor election. The Trees Party was led by a Taipei-based activist, who had participated in many environmental protests over the years. One of the Trees Party candidates was elected as mayor of Chichi Township in central Taiwan (population 11,356) and another was elected as a councillor in rural Ilan County.

3 "The Wing of Radical Politics"

"The Wing of Radical Politics" (*chichin ts'e i jijin ceyi*) hailed from a group of young pro-independence activists, first organized in 2012, who attempted to steer the Sunflower Movement onto a more radical course to no avail. Afterwards, they recruited more members and fielded five candidates, who were all under 30 years old. Although the Wing of Radical Politics was not formally registered as a political party, its candidates campaigned with a coordination office and a common platform. In the 2016 legislative election, this new organization worked with Taiwan Solidarity Union, symbolizing the confluence of younger and older streams of pro-independence activism.

4 People's Democratic Front

The People's Democratic Front (*jenmin minchu chenhsien renmin minzhu zhenxian*) originated from a labor movement organization that started to step into electoral politics in 2008. In the wake of the Sunflower Movement, it fielded 14 candidates.

All the above-mentioned political parties and groups played some role in the Sunflower Movement. As such, this flurry of electioneering represented one facet of subsequent political participation. As summarized in Table 5.1, the result might appear disappointing in that these self-professed Sunflower activists merely obtained two (or three, if one ex-Trees Party member is included)

Table 5.1 Sunflower activists in the 2014 local councillor election

Party	Candidate number	Elected candidate number	Candidates' average age	Total votes	Average vote share (%)
TGP	9	2	37	54,059	4.8
Trees Party	8	0	40	38,110	2.6
Wings of Radical Politics	5	0	26	31,222	4.7
People's Democratic Front	14	0	45	15,196	1.0

Notes
1 The average vote share is district-based, not nation-wide.
2 The data comes from the Central Election Commission's website (http://db.cec.gov.tw/, accessed February 28, 2015).

seats out of the total of 907 local councillors. Nevertheless, the 2014 election represented a high tide of Taiwanese social movement activists' political participation for the following reasons: (1) candidates in Taiwan's local election typically competed on their service, rather than ideology; hence it was difficult to canvass on the high politics issues of China factor or free trade; and (2) in terms of the total votes (138,587), these four parties and groups surpassed the previous record of the 1996 election for national assembly representatives (118,282 votes).

In short, regardless of its modest achievement, the 2014 local election witnessed the institutional incorporation of the youthful energy released in the Sunflower Movement. Most of the spotlight was cast on the election of mayors of autonomous cities and cities/counties, in which the DPP not only successfully defended its control of six local administrative areas, but also gained the executive positions of two autonomous cities (Taichung and Taoyuan) and four other cities/counties. The DPP-friendly Ko Wen-je won the mayoralty of Taipei City, terminating the 16-year KMT rule. Incidentally, Ko Wen-je's innovative and dynamic campaign also enlisted some activists in his team, and Ko later frankly acknowledged that he would not have become Taipei City Mayor were it not for the Sunflower Movement.[13] Since the KMT represented the arch-rival of the Sunflower Movement, its decisive defeat further elevated the morale among its supporters.

The 2016 general election

On January 16, 2016, Taiwanese voters chose the next president and 113 seats in the national legislature. Although the national-level lawmaker position represented a more difficult challenge for movement activists, the spectacular defeat of the ruling party in the preceding local elections became an inspiration showing that real change was possible. Again, Sunflower activists participated as campaign staff, who did not enjoy the limelight cast upon the candidates. In spite of the frustratingly low rate of success in the previous elections, the competition for the legislative seats in 2016 gave rise to an unprecedented wave of electoral participation among movement activists and formation of new parties (which were dubbed as the "Third Force" in the media), including the New Power Party (NPP), who obtained five seats in the legislature to become the third largest party in Taiwan's new political landscape.

The KMT's larger-than-expected defeat in the 2014 election also planted the seed of schism in the aforementioned Taiwan Citizen Union, a new movement-oriented party in the attempt to channel the rising social protests into electoral politics, originally proposed in the summer of 2013 and established shortly before the eruption of the Sunflower Movement. During the 2014 election, the Taiwan Citizen Union played a secondary role by concentrating on the "Go Home and Vote" campaign. Afterwards, Taiwan Citizen Union activists stepped up their preparations for the upcoming legislative election, and ironically, their intensified organizing activities exacerbated the growing divide of the two existing tendencies. Some organizers decided to set up the NPP in January 2015, and two months later a Social Democratic Party (SDP) was established, thus leaving the originally planned Taiwan Citizen Union an unfulfilled project.[14]

The NPP/SDP split, in part, reflected the ideological diversity of the Sunflower Movement in that both Taiwanese nationalists and social movement activists on a number of reform issues happened to oppose the same threat.[15] Once the legislature occupation ended, there remained few reasons for these two tendencies to collaborate under the same roof. On the whole, the NPP appeared more independence-leaning, while the SDP prioritized social reforms and wealth redistribution. Aside from the difference in worldviews, the tactical question whether to negotiate with the DPP became a bone of contention. Since the election of 73 district legislator seats proceeded in the first-past-the-post manner, the opposition camp incurred the risk of disastrous internecine warfare in the absence of prior coordination. While both new parties chose to target the KMT-dominant electoral districts, the NPP made explicit its willingness to coordinate with the DPP for the goal of fielding only one candidate in a district, whereas the SDP insisted on its independence by rejecting any party-to-party negotiation. The NPP positioned itself as a DPP ally by openly endorsing Tsai Ing-wen's bid for the presidency and welcomed the support by DPP politicians. The SDP, by contrast, drew its strength from Taiwan's movement NGOs and academic intellectuals, and it adopted a more or less neutral stance concerning the presidential election. In the end, the SDP opted to team up with the TGP to form a joint TGP-SDP ticket to join the foray for proportionate seats, while both parties operated their district election separately.

The TGP represented another approach of movement politics. Unlike the two splitter parties from the Taiwan Citizen Union, the TGP placed more emphasis on its autonomy because of its longer history as well as the recent progress in the preceding local election. Although the TGP expressed its willingness to cooperate with two new parties in early 2015,[16] the NPP leadership's unilateral decision to pursue a pro-DPP course ultimately ruled out the possibility of a grand triple collaboration. Since all three parties were empowered by the wave of political participation released by the Sunflower Movement, the constellation of the NPP, the SDP, and the TGP, in a sense represented three graded differences in terms of: (1) whether outvoting the KMT was a strategic goal; and (2) whether the assertion of Taiwan's national identity took precedence over social reforms. Clearly, the NPP embraced a pragmatic strategy to maximize its chances of winning, and the TGP took an idealistic approach to highlight its movement commitment, while the SDP tried to navigate a more balanced course. Table 5.2 summarizes the electoral result of these three parties.

The electoral result seems to vindicate the NPP's strategic choice of a pro-DPP stance in that its three district nominees, Huang Kuo-chang, Freddy Lim, and Hung Tzu-yung, succeeded in ousting the KMT veteran incumbents. The NPP successfully struck a delicate balance between the need to mobilize the DPP votes for its district candidates and the imperative of competing with the DPP for the proportionate seats in the second vote by the distinction between "main candidates" and "task candidates." With its two proportionate seats

Table 5.2 The NPP, the SDP, and the TGP in the 2016 district legislative election

Parties	Candidate number	Elected candidate number	DPP-endorsed candidate number	Candidates competing against the DPP nominees	Average votes	Average vote share (%)
NPP	12	3	3	8	29,270	16.9
NPP (Main candidates)	4	3	3	1	73,230	42.9
NPP (Task candidates)	8	0	0	7	7,291	3.9
SDP	6	0	1	1	24,231	14.1
TGP	5	0	0	4	11,655	6.1

Notes

1 Taiwan's electoral law required at least ten nominations in district election in order to qualify for the proportionate seats, which was decided by the party vote. The NPP nominated eight "task candidates" in order to meet that requirement with the promise that they would not set up individual campaign office or hold rallies in order not to create trouble for the DPP candidates in the same district. Hence, the NPP nominees were subdivided into main candidates and nominal candidates.

2 The data comes from the Central Election Commission's website (http://db.cec.gov.tw/, accessed March 10, 2016) and is arranged by the author.

(6.1 percent in party vote), the NPP emerged as the third largest party in Taiwan. On the other hand, the TGP-SDP ticket (2.5 percent) failed to clear the 5 percent threshold. The apparent failure of the SDP and the TGP both in district and proportionate elections also seems to indicate the virtue of pragmatism or the futility of sectarianism to insist on movement commitment without regard to the political reality. Only one out of six SDP candidates competed against the DPP one, while four out of five TGP candidates did so. Consequently the SDP candidates (14.1 percent) received higher vote shares on average than the TGP ones (6.1 percent).

The NPP's success does not necessarily imply that movement activists need to maintain a DPP-friendly gesture and emphasize their pro-independence commitment in order to win the election. First, all the successful NPP district candidates had long ago become charismatic celebrities, particularly popular among young voters before they decided to join the election, while most of the SDP and the TGP candidates struggled to receive media attention. Second, with the exception of Hung Tzu-yung, who incidentally stepped into the arena of politics and movement activism following the tragedy of her brother's death in 2013, which gave rise to the White-shirt Army protest, both Freddy Lim and Kuo-chang Huang were seasoned activists long before their electoral participation. Lim, a hard rock singer, worked as campaign staff in the DPP's presidential election in 2008 and later led the Taiwan chapter of Amnesty International, while Huang had been a student activist, leading the National Taiwan University Student Union in 1993–1994 before becoming an accomplished legal scholar. In other words, Lim and Huang had accumulated considerable personal experiences prior to their political career. Finally, my interview sources indicated that the NPP appeared financially stronger than the SDP and the TGP. All three successful NPP candidates ran on a budget of more than ten million New Taiwan dollars, whereas the top spenders in the SDP and the TGP only used five million and two million dollars respectively. There was evidence showing that the NPP possessed greater financial resources than other movement candidates. The Taiwan March, one of the post-Sunflower organizations that later evolved into one of the NPP's core constituents, enjoyed donations from businesspersons – an unusual advantage that was denied to other movement organizations.[17] According to their declaration to the government, three successful NPP candidates received 33 million, 28 million, and 13 million dollars in donations respectively, which actually surpassed the amount for many DPP candidates.[18] In short, aside from its more popular ideological positioning, the NPP's triumph, in part, derived from its better endowment of human and financial resources.

In addition, there were other constituent groups in the Sunflower Movement that also joined the legislative election. The pro-independence Taiwan Solidarity Union (TSU) had possessed three seats since 2012, and was threatened by the NPP's rise, it nominated a leader of Wing of Radical Politics as the number one candidate in its national ticket. In spite of the attempt to attract younger voters, the TSU ended by receiving 2.5 percent in the second vote, failing to obtain a seat in the legislature. The Alliance of Referendum for Taiwan, a pro-independence organization that played a facilitating role during the legislature occupation, launched a Free Taiwan Party, which received 0.4 percent in the second vote. The Trees Party also fielded 11 district candidates who received 2.9 percent of the vote on average and 0.6 percent in the party vote.

That the participants in the Sunflower Movement spread into different parties or coalitions to continue their activism should not come as a surprise. The anti-CSSTA protest drew strength from a variety of tendencies and groups, which were temporarily united for the opposition to the free trade deal with China in spite of their ideological differences. Once their moment of movement mobilization ended, it was difficult to build an inclusive political organization to incorporate these highly diversified activists. In hindsight, the NPP's electoral success helped the Sunflower Movement to secure a solid footing in the new legislature in spite of the criticisms that the NPP seemed to have stolen the thunder of the movement for its own political advantage. As the NPP entered the legislature with the Sunflower Movement's halo effect, its lawmakers' subsequent performances would be continuously measured by the demands and the spirit of that movement. The smooth transformation of illegal legislature occupiers to legitimate legislators with electoral mandate testified to the resilience of Taiwan's democratic institutions.

The DPP's coping strategy

The DPP emerged as the biggest winner in the legislative election by taking 68 out of 113 seats, which marked the first time for a DPP-dominant parliament. The larger-than-expected victory freed the DPP from the reliance on other friendly parties to form a coalition majority, which was actually the stated preference for the NPP[19] as well as the SDP.[20] Nevertheless, the DPP's success in part derived from its skillful crisis management during the Sunflower Movement as well as the adaptive strategy to cope with post-Sunflower forces.

Prior to the outbreak of legislature occupation, the DPP appeared to have fashioned out a more or less coherent strategy in dealing with social protests. As early as 2009, the DPP re-established a Department of Social Movements in its national headquarters for better liaison with NGOs. In order to make a political comeback, the opposition elites perceived the need to reconnect civil society organizations, which felt alienated and frustrated during the first DPP government (2000–2008). The rising wave of social protests certainly created political troubles for the KMT incumbents, but the opposition party weighed up all the pros and cons before offering its endorsement. For example, the student-led anti-media monopoly movement (2012–2013) opposed a pro-Beijing media tycoon's merger attempt. DPP lawmakers actively cooperated with movement activists in drafting and proposing the new regulation bill (Wang 2015: 148). On the other hand, in the case of the movement against the Koukuang Petrochemical project (2005–2011), which was initially proposed by the DPP during its incumbency, the DPP decided to stay neutral until the opposition movement had clearly won the mainstream public opinion (Ho 2016). The revival of an anti-nuclear promise following the Fukushima Incident of 2011 represented a more delicate issue. After the disastrous failure to terminate the fourth nuclear power plant in 2000–2001, the DPP leaders had practically shelved the anti-nuclear commitment, and their silence continued even after being voted out of office in 2008. Seeing the reawakened anti-nuclear protests after 2011, the DPP attempted to gain control over the movement leadership, which, however, incurred criticisms of opportunism. Thereafter, the DPP decided to take a back seat by offering its political support to the environmentalists' leadership (Ho 2014b). In other words, the opposition party practiced a *realpolitik* policy toward social movements. The DPP was willing to change its attitude only insofar as movements had gained sufficient momentum, or when a supportive stance appeared to bring about political advantages. In fact, it applied the same approach toward the controversial CSSTA. Previously its official policy was to insist on article-by-article review without expressly indicating its preference. Yet, once the students had successfully occupied the legislature, the DPP swerved to endorse the movement demand to withdraw the CSSTA.

In addition to adopting a well-calculated attitude toward social movements, the DPP also attempted to incorporate or even recruit new movement participants. Tsai Ing-wen's Thinking Taiwan Foundation, established in 2012, employed a number of student activists. In May 2014, as Tsai resumed the DPP's leadership, some Sunflower Movement activists were appointed to the executive positions in the party's national headquarters. Immediately before the 2016 election, as many as 11 core activists in the Sunflower Movement were working in the executive or secretarial positions in the national headquarters and Tsai's campaign office.[21] With this influx of new blood, the DPP not only enlisted a new generation of would-be politicians, but also established a better working relationship with the movement activists.

The same realism underpinned its coping strategy during the election. In the 2014 election, since most of the Sunflower activists concentrated their effort on local councillor seats, which were mostly selected by multiple-member districts, there remained little room for the intervention from the opposition party. Instead, the DPP launched a Democracy Grass (*minchu hsiaots'ao minzhu xiaocao*) project by sponsoring young first-timers to take part in the election for ward/village heads.[22] In the end, 37 candidates had signed up for that program and nine of them were successfully elected. Particularly noteworthy, the project did not require all participants to register under the DPP's name.

In the 2016 legislative election, the DPP practiced similar pragmatism in dealing with the challenge of the so-called "Third Force."[23] In early 2015, the DPP suspended the nomination in the districts where it had received less than 42.5 percent vote share in the last legislative election.[24] Consequently 30 out of the 73 districts were deliberately kept open as a gesture of good-will towards the friendly forces. Later, seeing that the NPP, the SDP and the TGP were unable to field strong candidates in the challenging districts, the DPP decided to proceed with the goal of maximizing its seats by nominating 60 district candidates and leaving only 13 districts vacant. Except for Mazu, the DPP eventually endorsed

12 candidates in these districts, including six nonpartisan (five of them were ex-KMT members), three NPP, one SDP, one TSU, and one People First Party candidates. A close look reveals the absence of favorable treatment toward the Third Force in spite of the fact that its Sunflower Movement origin appeared ideologically closer. The fact that the DPP encouraged its supporters to vote for ex-KMT or People First Party candidates who were competing against the Third Force ones clearly demonstrates its strategic calculation. For the DPP leaders, fielding its own candidates clearly remained the top priority; in the districts without strong contenders, minimizing the KMT seats took precedence over sponsoring the "friendly" forces. Moreover, one week before the election date, the DPP launched a campaign to urge its supporters to concentrate their party vote to fend off the surging NPP. Consequently the DPP was able to secure 18 out of 34 proportionate representation seats, whereas the NPP ended up with less seats than had originally been expected.[25]

Although the DPP played a hard-nosed game with the Third Force, there remained the need to present a pro-reform image. Its list of proportionate representation amounted to an impressive snapshot of contemporary social movements in Taiwan in that leaders in environmentalism, human rights, feminism, rural preservation, disability, and social enterprises were nominated. Two ex-TGP members, including one former party chair, now served as DPP lawmakers. The DPP's success in the general election gave it more wherewithal to incorporate the new political generation. In the new legislature after February 2016, at least more than ten Sunflower Movement activists worked as aides to the DPP lawmakers. Additionally, two SDP former candidates now worked as aides to the DPP lawmakers, while one SDP and one TGP candidates later joined Ko Wen-je's Taipei City government. The power turnover enabled the DPP to incorporate more activists into its governing team. One TGP-SDP candidate in the list of proportionate representation became the Vice-minister of the Environmental Protection Administration, while one of the NPP co-presidents was appointed as the Advisor of the National Security Council.[26]

In short, the DPP's attempted to reconcile a number of conflicting imperatives: (1) to enlarge its parliamentary seats to obtain a majority; (2) to present a pro-reform image to the voters; and (3) to replenish its younger generation workforce. In hindsight, they managed this difficult task rather successfully. Not only did the DPP obtain a legislative majority, but also the DPP-friendly NPP emerged as the third largest party, outperforming other Third Force parties. While the DPP played hardball with the newly emergent political forces during the election, it was nevertheless able to enlist the contribution of these activists. In the end, the DPP had managed well to minimize the conflict with the post-Sunflower activisms during election and at the same time to recruit new talents from an enlarged pool.

Conclusion

This chapter began the survey of Taiwan's post-Sunflower activism with Krastev's pessimistic observation concerning the spread of global large-scale anti-government movements. Aided by state-of-the-art digital communication, social protests had become paradoxically more powerful and less effective at the same time. Massive and disruptive protests now could take place without pre-existing mass organizations, political parties, or even ideologies, and yet they became more and more incapable of generating meaningful changes because no incumbents were able to satisfy citizens' increasing demands. In a sense, Krastev's pessimistic analysis echoed the conservative analysis of the turbulent 1960s in the developed countries. The massive outpouring of political participation originated from "an excess of democracy," consequently eroding the authority of governmental institutions and precipitating a crisis of governability in the democracies (Crozier, Huntington, and Watanuki 1975).

Contrary to such a conservative diagnosis, Pizzorno (1981) identified the explosion of the protest movements of the 1960s as a symptom of the limitation of liberal pluralism which failed to incorporate new identities or categories. Elections produced governing majorities precisely because they effected a great reduction of complexities to a list of contending parties so that the eruption of extra-institutional activities actually demonstrated the constraint of the existing institutions.

Did the contemporary social protests indicate a hopelessly systematic failure of democracy or represent a genuine yearning to democratize the existing democracy? Or to put in the Taiwanese context, when students' sit-in protest shut down the functioning of national legislature for more than three weeks, how could we evaluate their criticisms of "black box" of the government's decision-making and the demand for more procedural transparency? Were these demands overtly excessive so that no incumbents could ever satisfy them? Or were they legitimate concerns that have been excluded by the mainstream parties?

Observing the evolution of post-Sunflower political and electoral activism in Taiwan, my conclusion is closer to the latter perspective. Citizens engaged in massive and spontaneous extra-institutional activities, not necessarily because of their ingrained distrust of any representative institutions, but rather because the existing institutions failed to represent their opinions. As such, if these dissatisfied citizens found feasible institutional accesses to change the status quo and there existed meaningful likelihood of success, chances were their activism would be rechanneled into more rule-conforming actions. After all, occupying a square aimed at changing the mind of those in power; if it turned out that obtaining power was no more difficult than battling the police, why would anyone bother to venture into law-breaking behavior?

Moreover, the willingness to adopt the electoral route was related to a particular characteristic of the Sunflower Movement, which occupied the legislature because the lawmakers had failed to abide by the proper procedure. Their principal demand consisted precisely in asking the lawmakers to do their job properly.[27] Jones and Yen (2015: 4–6) contended that the movement represented an act of "democratic disobedience" to ward off the imminent threats of China, social injustices of free trade, the imperial executive, and "winner-take-all" politics. That the Sunflower Movement urged more supervision and transparency on cross-Strait negotiation meant that the participants had sufficient faith in the genuine democratic procedures. Protestors occupied the legislature not because of their inherent distrust of representative democracy; on the contrary, they believed it would have to be better, which in part explains the seemingly effortless transition from protest to electioneering.

In this chapter, I have argued that the Sunflower Movement unleashed a number of political activisms that attempted to reform current political institutions, and that this new political energy flowed into the subsequent election as many activists believed winning a public office represented a further step in realizing their commitment to change the status quo. These observations illustrate that many Taiwanese have faith in the democratic principle in spite of the limits of their existing democratic institutions. Perhaps, the fact that many protest activists transformed themselves from legislature occupiers to legislative candidates speaks volumes for the abiding attraction of electoral democracy. As such, the Taiwanese case clearly constitutes a refutation of Krastev's dismal analysis. True, democracy can be temporarily disrupted by the surge of protest activities, but the in the long run, disfranchised and excluded protestors might find their way back to the representative system, which eventually augments the legitimacy of democracy.

Notes

1 For the full text of the statement, see http://goo.gl/QoLuno (accessed May 13, 2016).
2 Interview with a member of the Small Group to Improve Working Conditions of Medical Doctors, May 5, 2014.
3 Interview with a member of Taiwan Publishing Freedom Front, July 20, 2016.
4 See https://goo.gl/7MnG2p (accessed August 5, 2016).
5 See http://goo.gl/RYHwUm (accessed August 7, 2016).
6 See http://goo.gl/1wl7KA (accessed May 13, 2016).
7 See http://goo.gl/XgQH1T (accessed May 13, 2016).
8 See https://goo.gl/xMGTys (accessed May 13, 2016).
9 Interview with the spokesperson of the Appendectomy Project, May 19, 2016.
10 According to the Central Election Commission's sources, there was only one unaffiliated candidate in the 2014 local councillor election who mentioned his participation in the Sunflower Movement in the electoral gazette.
11 Interview with a TGP legislative candidate in 2016, May 11, 2016.
12 See http://goo.gl/tvQeyF (accessed December 31, 2014).
13 See https://goo.gl/osOVTi (accessed May 17, 2016).
14 See http://goo.gl/YCiIJg (accessed May 18, 2016).
15 Wu (2016: 8) contends that the Sunflower Movement was "none other than an outbreak of Taiwan's civic nationalism."
16 See https://goo.gl/VRr7aw (accessed May 18, 2016).
17 See http://goo.gl/NE9jna (May 20, 2016).
18 See http://goo.gl/cFJViy (August 7, 2016).
19 See http://goo.gl/by49yH (accessed May 20, 2016).

20 See http://goo.gl/3oqyNp (accessed May 20, 2016).
21 Field note, January 15, 2016.
22 See www.storm.mg/article/33432 (May 21, 20160.
23 Taiwan's media imprecisely used the term "the third force" to refer chiefly the new political parties or candidates emanating from the Sunflower Movement, such as the NPP and the SDP. Sometimes the term is also applied to the non-partisan candidates or other newer parties that were not related to the movement. Understanding the term's ambiguity, I use the term to refer to the NPP, the SDP, and the TGP in this chapter.
24 See http://goo.gl/fq0WZz (accessed May 22, 2016).
25 One NPP leader estimated the DPP's last-minute offensive had cost two seats for the NPP. Interview with one NPP's co-president, April 12, 2016.
26 Moreover, the DPP appointed movement activists to the position of Vice-ministers of Ministry of Labor, Ministry of the Interior, and Council of Agriculture.
27 The author thanks François Mengin for this suggestion.

References

Calhoun, C. (2013) Occupy Wall Street in Perspective. *British Journal of Sociology* 64(1): 26–38.
Castells, M. (2012). *Networks of Outrage and Hope: Social Movements in the Internet Age*. Oxford: Polity Press.
Chu, Y. (2011). Old Constraints and Future Possibilities in the Development of Taiwan's Independent Labor Movement. *Capitalism Nature Socialism* 22(1): 58–75.
Crozier, M. J., Huntington, S. P., and Watanuki, J. (1975). *The Crisis of Democracy: On the Governability of Democracies*. New York: New York University Press.
Fell, D. (2012). *Government and Politics in Taiwan*. London: Routledge.
Fell, D. (ed.) (2017). *Taiwan's Social Movements under Ma Ying-jeou*. London: Routledge.
Gitlin, T. (2013). Occupy's Predicament: The Moment and the Prospects for the Movement. *British Journal of Sociology* 64(1): 3–25.
Graeber, D. (2012). *The Democracy Project: A History, A Crisis, A Movement*. New York: Random House.
Grano, S. A. (2015). *Environmental Governance in Taiwan: A New Generation of Activists and Stakeholders*. London: Routledge.
Green, J. K. (2016). Rising Powers and Regional Orders: China's Strategy and Cross-Strait Relations. *Globalizations* 13(2): 129–142.
Ho, M. S. (2005). Taiwan's State and Social Movements under the DPP Government (2000–2004). *Journal of East Asian Studies* 5(3): 401–425.
Ho, M. S. (2014a). The Resurgence of Social Movements under the Ma Ying-jeou Government: A Political Opportunity Structure Perspective. In Cabestan, J. P. and De Lisle, J. (eds.) *Political Changes in Taiwan Under Ma Ying-jeou: Partisan Conflict, Policy Choices, External Constraints and Security Challenges*, London: Routledge, pp. 100–119.
Ho, M. S. (2014b). The Fukushima Effect: Explaining the Recent Resurgence of the Anti-nuclear Movement in Taiwan. *Environmental Politics* 23(6): 965–983.
Ho, M. S. (2015). Occupy Congress in Taiwan: Political Opportunity, Threat and the Sunflower Movement. *Journal of East Asian Studies* 15(1): 69–97.
Ho, M. S. (2016). Making an Opportunity: Strategic Bipartisanship in Taiwan's Environmental Movement. *Sociological Perspectives* 59(3): 543–560.
Ho, M. S. (forthcoming). The Historical Breakthroughs of Taiwan's Anti-nuclear Movement: The Making of a Militant Citizen Movement. *Journal of Contemporary Asia*.

Hsiao, M. H. H. (1992). The Rise of Social Movements and Civil Protests. In Cheng, T. J. and Haggard, S. (eds.) *Political Change in Taiwan*, Boulder, CO: Lynne Rienner, pp. 57–72.

Hsiao, M. H. H. and Ku, C. H. (eds.) (2010). *Taiwan shehui yüntung tsaich'ufa Taiwan shehui yondong zaichufa* [Taiwan's Social Movements Get Restarted] Taipei: Chiuliu.

Huang, K. H. (2017). 'Culture Wars' in a Globalized East: How Taiwanese Conservative Christianity Turned Public during the Same-Sex Marriage Controversy and a Secularist Backlash. *Review of Religion and Chinese Society* 4: 108–136.

Jones, B. C. and Yen, T. S. (2015). Confrontational Contestation and Democratic Compromise: The Sunflower Movement and Its Aftermath. *Hong Kong Law Journal* 45: 1–12.

Krastev, I. (2014). *Democracy Disrupted: The Politics of Global Protest*. Philadelphia, PA: University of Pennsylvania Press.

Lee, C. (2017). Overcoming the Latecomer Dilemma: The Unintended Effect of Successful Strategies in the Community University Movement in Taiwan. *Social Movement Studies*, DOI:10.1080/14742837.2017.1319267 (accessed May 28, 2017).

Lee, M. C. (2015). Occupy on Air: Transparency and Surveillance in Taiwan's Sunflower Movement. *Anthropology Now* 7(3): 32–41.

Lin, Y. S. (2015). The Rise and Fall of the Reds: The Reiterated Dilemma-Solving Process and the Life Course of Social Movements. *Social Movement Studies* 14(3): 291–310.

Mason, P. (2012). *Why It's Kicking Off Everywhere: The New Global Revolutions*. London: Verso.

Noueihed, L. and Warren, A. (2012). *The Battle for the Arab Spring: Revolution, Counter-Revolution and the Making of a New Era*. New Haven, CT: Yale University Press.

Pizzorno, A. (1981). Interests and Parties in Pluralism. In Berger, S. (ed.) *Organizing Interests in Western Europe: Pluralism, Corporatism, and the Transformation of Politics*, Cambridge: Cambridge University Press. pp. 249–286.

Rowen, I. (2015). Inside Taiwan's Sunflower Movement: Twenty-Four Days in a Student-Occupied Parliament, and the Future of the Region. *Journal of Asian Studies* 74(1): 5–21.

Schubert, G. (ed.) (2016). *Taiwan and the "China Impact": Challenges and Opportunities*. London: Routledge.

Wang, J. (2015). Mobilizing Resources in Networked Social Movements: Cases in Hong Kong and Taiwan. PhD dissertation, Hong Kong Baptist University.

Wei, S. (2016). Recovery from "Betrayal": Local Anti-Nuclear Movements and Party Politics in Taiwan. *The Asia-Pacific Journal* 14(8): 1–21.

Wu, J. M., Tsai H. J. and Cheng, T. B. (eds.) (2017). *Tiaoteng li te chiumang: chungkuo yinsu tsoyungli yü fantsoyungli* [The Anaconda in the Chandelier: Forces and Reactions of the China Factor]. Taipei: Rive Gauche.

Wu, R. R. (2016). The Lilliputian Dreams: Preliminary Observations of Nationalism in Okinawa, Taiwan and Hong Kong. *Nations and Nationalism*, DOI: 10.1111/nana.12251 (accessed August 4, 2016).

6 The media in democratic Taiwan

*Jonathan Sullivan, Ming-yeh T. Rawnsley,
Chien-san Feng and James Smyth*

Introduction

Alongside a consolidated liberal democracy and dynamic civil society, Taiwan boasts one of Asia's most liberal and competitive media environments. With 236 newspaper publishers, 1,287 periodical and magazine publishers and 69 cable and satellite TV operators,[1] media liberalization in Taiwan is, like the democratization processes that facilitated and were subsequently solidified by it, a success story. Two waves of media reform in the democratic era, including the deregulation of the newspaper industry and the legalization of cable television, transformed an information environment previously dominated by the Chinese Nationalist Party's (國民黨, hereafter KMT) state-led authoritarian communications regime. A significant endorsement of Taiwan's progress in media freedom came in the form of the global non-profit organisation Reporters Without Borders announcing in April 2017 that it had chosen Taipei as the location for its first Asian bureau (Reporters, 2017a). Indeed, the media environment today is as free as at any time in Taiwan's history, and "communicative abundance" (Keane, 2013) is an inescapable feature of contemporary Taiwanese life. The vibrant appearance of Taiwan's democracy owes much to the trace data produced by the tools of this abundance: the all-news-all-the-time TV channels, politicians' constant presence on connected devices, student activists mobilizing via social media. Taiwanese citizens are by many standards engaged and politically active, not just turning out to vote in consistently large numbers, but also participating in diverse social movements. Yet for all the openness symbolized by the ubiquitous TV cameras and the politicians' social media status updates, the media and communications environments in Taiwan are a cause for concern in terms of the "quality" of their contribution to Taiwanese democracy. Long-standing regulatory and ownership issues remain unresolved, including political partisanship across the media-sphere. Like their counterparts in other democracies, Taiwanese media companies are grappling with the transition to digital and the challenge it represents to traditional business models in a highly media-saturated society. The pressures of intense commercial competition have problematized professional ethics and the effects of sensationalism. In this chapter, we outline the evolution and reform of Taiwan's media through three periods coinciding with the administrations of Lee Teng-hui (李登輝, 1988–2000), Chen Shui-bian (陳水扁, 2000–2008) and Ma Ying-jeou (馬英九, 2008–2016). We conclude by addressing the prospects for further advances under Tsai Ing-wen (蔡英文, 2016–) as the influence of the People's Republic of China (PRC) casts a growing shadow over media freedoms and highlights vulnerabilities caused by the stalled momentum to reform processes. The chapter demonstrates how the media in Taiwan have made a substantial positive contribution to democratization and consolidation processes, but argues that the prospects for further contributions in a new democratic era depend on enacting necessary reforms.

Taiwanese media 1987–2000: foundational reforms

Taiwan's media landscape was transformed during a first wave of reform that intersected with the democratization processes in the 1980s. Prior to the lifting of martial law in 1987, the Taiwanese media operated as part of a bureaucraticcommercial complex, with a small number of clientelist media companies enjoying profit-seeking opportunities under the authoritarian control of the KMT. Press freedoms were highly circumscribed and closely reflected the KMT's political agenda, to the extent that during the one-party era the media were a tightly controlled ideological apparatus confining the public sphere (Rawnsley and Rawnsley, 2004). Until deregulation and liberalization, the three terrestrial TV channels were owned by the government (Taiwan Television; TTV, 台視), the KMT (China Television; CTV, 中視) and the military (Chinese Television Service; CTS, 華視). These outlets prevented the spread of "alternative" viewpoints, particularly those related to national identity and pushing for political reform and social justice, and effectively locked the political opposition out of mainstream media. Government authorities granted a mere 31 newspaper licenses between 1960 and 1988, and most of these outlets were directly owned and managed by the party-state (Chen and Chu, 1987: 53–55, 91). The government also sought to co-opt private media owners, subsuming them into networks of "mutual interest". The two dominant newspapers during the authoritarian era, *China Times* (中國時報 established in 1950) and *United Daily News* (UDN; 聯合報 established in 1951), had intimate ties to the KMT via cross-representation on editorial boards and the party's Central Committee (Batto, 2004).

The KMT's response to pressures to reform from the underground opposition movement (黨外) and substantial sections of Taiwanese society, was incremental liberalization of multiple sectors, including the media, and expanded political participation through elections at the local and national level. The press ban was officially lifted in 1988, a year after Martial Law had been rescinded and two years after the formation of the Democratic Progressive Party (民進黨 DPP) added further pressure on the KMT to reform. Newspapers were deregulated, publication licenses granted and all manner of content and format restrictions lifted. The establishment of *Liberty Times* (自由時報) in September 1987, with close links to the DPP, signalled the end of near total dominance by the state, the military or party-owned media. Consciously targeting broad social constituencies (and DPP partisans) ignored by pro-KMT media, *Liberty Times* quickly established a substantial market share and became a significant space for the promotion of a specifically Taiwanese national identity (Hsu, 2014). A decade after its launch, *Liberty Times*, *China Times* and *UDN* constituted a clear triumvirate of the highest circulating newspapers. By 2000, the year the DPP candidate Chen Shui-bian won the Presidency, *Liberty Times* had surpassed *UDN* and *China Times* in terms of market share and advertising revenues (Lin, 2008: 198–200). Figure 6.1, setting out self-reported newspaper readership derived from the Taiwan Election and Democratization Surveys, shows how the dominance of the two pro-KMT newspapers was challenged by the pro-DPP *Liberty Times*. We discuss the rise of *Apple Daily* (蘋果日報), which is also shown in Figure 6.1, in the next section.

As liberalization gathered momentum, dozens of new radio stations received licences in 1992, cable TV was finally legalized in 1993 and a fourth terrestrial channel (Formosa Television; FTV, 民視) was established in 1997, with an ownership close to the DPP. FTV quickly established an audience share and financial security through the advertising-led business model that underpins all Taiwanese media. With the rise of FTV and increasing cable television penetration, the three traditionally pro-KMT terrestrial commercial television stations – TTV, CTV and CTS – lost their market dominance and began to experience financial losses for the first time in 2002 (Rawnsley and Rawnsley, 2012: 397). Figure 6.2, which sets out self-reported TV consumption, shows the extent to which the dominant terrestrial channels of the authoritarian era have declined over time. It also shows the immediate effect that FTV had in staking out one

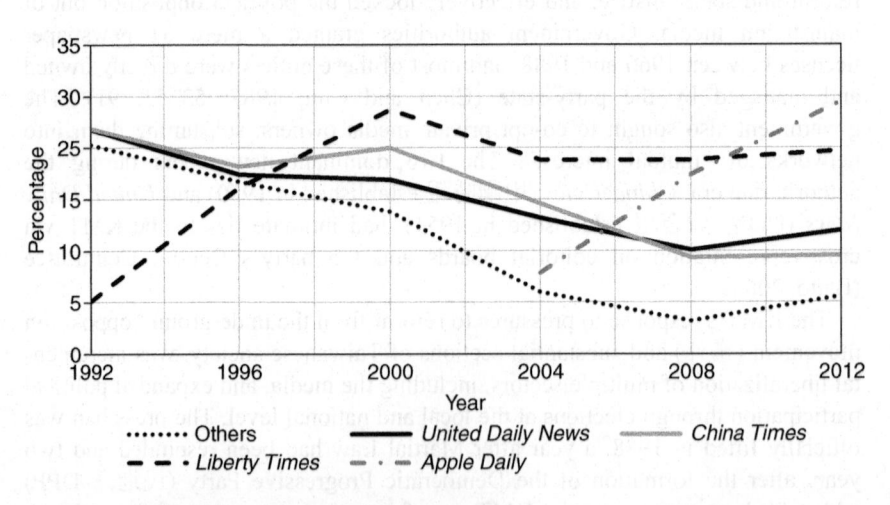

Figure 6.1 Self-reported newspaper readership (%).

Source: Taiwan Election and Democratization Survey.[1]

Note
1 We thank Dr Nathan Batto for generously sharing these survey data.

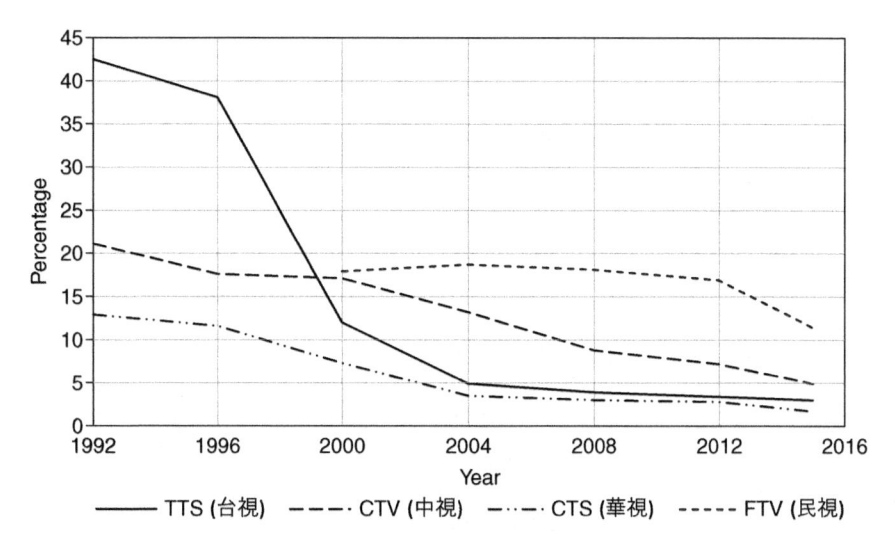

Figure 6.2 Self-reported consumption of terrestrial channels over time (% respondents).

Source: Taiwan Election and Democratization Surveys.

part of the audience, and the limits to growth that such targeting has. Indeed, since the emergence of other DPP-leaning channels, FTV's consistent 15–20 per cent audience share has also started to decline.

The legalization of cable TV in 1993 precipitated the expansion of local, national, regional and international TV programming. Operating illegally since the 1970s, unregulated cable TV was already widespread and "essentially run by the mafia" (Chin, 2003: 68). The Cable TV Act (有線電視法) legalized and brought regulation to the market. The first major entrant, in September 1993 was TVBS, owned by Hong Kong's TVB, which finally broke the three-terrestrial channel oligopoly (as suggested by the colloquial name for cable TV in Taiwan: "the fourth channel" 第四台). Over the remainder of the decade, the number of cable television channels increased dramatically (Chan-Olmstead and Chiu, 1999), and Taiwan became one of the most competitive pay-tv markets in the world, with a cable penetration rate of 93 per cent by 2000. The evident demand for news in Taiwan quickly led to the establishment of numerous 24-hour news channels, led by TVBS News in 1995, followed by FTV (民視) and ETTV (東森) in 1997, SET (三立) in 1998, CtiTV (中天) and ERA (年代) in 2000, and NextTV (壹電視) which joined ERA in 2013. These local all-news channels have become a characteristic part of Taiwan's media-scape, feeding off and nourishing high levels of political interest and knowledge. Figure 6.3 shows the increase in viewership for cable channels, using the self-reported media usage question in the Taiwan Election and Democratization Surveys.

As the media system transitioned from strong state control towards laissez-faire liberalization, Taiwan rapidly moved up the media freedom indexes

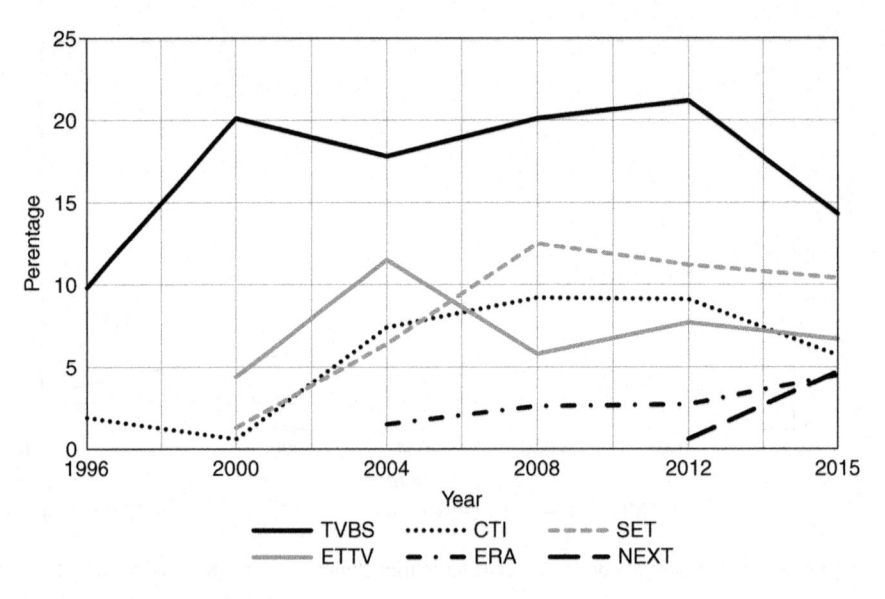

Figure 6.3 Self-reported consumption of cable news over time (%).
Source: Taiwan Election and Democratization Surveys.

compiled by Freedom House and Reporters Without Borders. In the 2017 Reporters Without Borders World Press Freedom Index, Taiwan was ranked 45th, the highest in Asia and just slightly below the United States. While this is an achievement of which Taiwanese are rightly proud, it is worth noting that conventional measures of press freedom are based on the extent to which the media can access and publish information without political interference. In other words, they are rooted in liberal norms that equate decreasing government intervention with normatively desirable "freedom" (Siebert, 1979). Since freedom by this definition is pursued through the elimination of government controls, it can be described as "negative" press freedom. Yet negative press freedom does not necessarily address issues of "media quality" suggested by investment in investigative journalism, pluralistic programming, professionalism and ethics. These "positive" press freedoms continue to be a cause for concern for Taiwanese scholars (e.g. Hung, 2006), who question public access to quality information in Taiwan despite its performance in press freedom indexes.

One area in which the tension between negative and positive press freedom is manifest are the political talk shows that first appeared in the mid-1990s. The first "call-in" show, *2100: All People Talk* (2100: 全民開講) aired on TVBS in 1994. Anchor Li Tao (李濤) introduced the issues of the day along with studio guests from politics, academia and the media and invited the public to have their say by calling-in to the show by telephone. An "infotainment" format reminiscent of pirate radio programmes during the one-party era, call-in quickly became a staple of primetime and late-night cable news schedules. Studio guests, including regulars on the punditry circuit known for their loquacious eloquence and sometimes pugnacity ("famous mouths" 名嘴), often responded with performative "political theatre" (Fell, 2007) and engaged in "saliva wars" (口水戰) with fellow guests (Chu, 2003). The increasing number of chat shows (reaching a peak of almost three dozen in 2004) established noise, partisanship and speculation as distinct features of Taiwanese TV political coverage. Over time the public participation element became increasingly problematic for producers to incorporate in a controlled way, and most shows have now changed to a studio format with discussion restricted to invited pundits from different political and professional backgrounds moderated by one or two journalist presenters. The change marks the victory of the self-contained "political talk show" (談話性政論節目) over the less predictable participatory "call-in" format. During the first wave of media reform, roughly between 1987 and 2000, the increasing number of media outlets expanded political coverage, creating a discursive public space for learning and participating in politics, as well as a new site for political competition between parties and other political actors. The contribution that media reform made to the diversification of Taiwan's information environment was substantial. However, liberalization and commercialization without appropriate regulatory responses led to sensationalism, superficiality and rowdiness that has reduced citizens' trust in the media and politicians. A common refrain among regular Taiwanese was that the media had become "too free".

Taiwan's media 2000–2008: a second wave of reforms

Following the DPP's victory in the 2000 and 2004 presidential elections, several reform initiatives were undertaken by the Chen administration. First, legislation was passed in 2003 to formalize the withdrawal of political parties, the state and military from direct media ownership stakes. By the end of 2005, the KMT had relinquished one-third of its shares in CTV, 97 per cent in the Broadcasting Corporation of China (BCC, 中廣), and half of its stake in the Central Motion Picture Corporation (CMPC, 中影). DPP legislator and party Standing Committee Member Chai Trong-rong (蔡同榮) was forced to resign from his position as chair of FTV and many other politicians were required to renounce their ownership or direct participation in media operations (Rawnsley and Rawnsley, 2012: 409). While largely successful in reducing direct political ownership, one of the unintended consequences of Chen's reform was the creation of opportunities for political influence by proxy. For instance, after 90 per cent of KMT-owned CTV shares were sold to the *China Times* media group in 2006, ownership fell into the hands of the pro-China Want group (旺旺集團) in a subsequent acquisition in 2008. The second of Chen's reforms, the establishment of the National Communications Commission (NCC, 國家通訊傳播委員會 or 通傳會) in 2006, was modelled on the American Federal Communications Commission (FCC). A neutral regulatory body under the Executive Yuan (行政院), the NCC was mandated to manage and supervise the commercial media sector, promoting competition, consumer protection and privacy rights. The third reform was the launch of a public service network, the Taiwan Broadcasting System (TBS, 台灣公共廣播電視集團 or 公廣集團), in 2006. TBS was formed through the consolidation of eight existing TV channels, including the Public Television System (PTS, 公視, launched in 1997), CTS (established in 1971), Hakka TV (客家電視台, founded in 2003 to serve Hakka communities) and Taiwan Macroview TV (宏觀電視, founded in 2000 to serve overseas Chinese). TBS' remit shared much in common with the Public Broadcasting Service (PBS) in the United States, in that it was expected to provide inclusive, diverse and educational programming. Despite becoming one of Taiwan's largest TV networks by number of channels, TBS struggled to make significant inroads against commercial competitors and investment remains limited.

The comprehensive commercialization of the Taiwanese newspaper market took a major step forward with the entry of the Hong Kong tabloid *Apple Daily* in May 2003, with its colour images, celebrity gossip and cut-throat price wars. An unapologetic purveyor of "popular journalism", it became known for its gruesome, and ethically questionable, front-page pictures of car crashes and salacious celebrity images captured by paparazzi. Paradoxically, *Apple Daily*'s political coverage was also relatively balanced and surprisingly nuanced, highlighting the partisanship of other newspapers. As Taiwanese politics became increasingly polarized during Chen's tenure (Sullivan and Lowe, 2010), the editorial stances of *Liberty Times* and *UDN* diverged to serve distinct partisan constituencies. Located between them on the political spectrum, readership of the *China Times* declined. The venerable newspaper continued to experience financial and operational difficulties and by 2008 it had been sold to Want Holdings, one of Taiwan's major food manufacturers. Want Want's extensive economic interests in China, the political preferences of its China-based CEO and Taiwan's richest man, Tsai Eng-meng (蔡衍明), and the company's aggressive attempts to acquire other media, have been a cause for concern, as we discuss below. Renamed *Want China Times* (旺旺中時), the paper adopted China-friendly coverage and a pro-China editorial stance. These changes failed to revive the paper's fortunes, and by 2013 its market share had fallen below 5 per cent, down from 17 per cent in 2000. The percentage market share for the top four newspapers in select years based on Nielsen media market data is set out in Figure 6.4.

The trends shown in Figure 6.4 suggests that one reason for the declining readership of the "Big3" was the arrival of *Apple Daily* in 2003. But, while the tabloid did indeed become the largest newspaper in Taiwan, newspaper readership has long been declining across the board. Declining newspaper readership is a global rather than a specifically Taiwanese phenomenon, and as in other contexts internet penetration rates have increased rapidly during the same period. By 2017, Taiwan had an internet penetration rate of 80 per cent of the population, placing it 34th globally (Miniwatts, 2017). Despite the declining fortunes of many newspapers, the performance of the all-news cable TV channels (and indeed online media) is testament to continuing high levels of interest in news

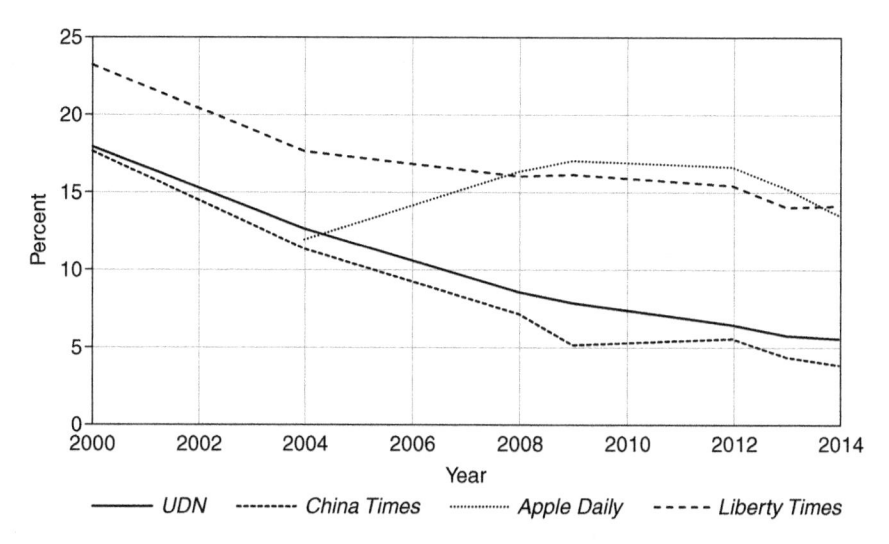

Figure 6.4 Market share of top four Taiwanese newspapers for select years (%).

Source: Nielsen Taiwan.

and politics. A further indication of this interest is the success of the local all-news cable TV channels. With a blend of news reporting, partisan political commentary and analysis, the news channels quickly established themselves among the most watched in Taiwan. The data set out in Figure 6.5 show the average audience share for programming on the all-news channels. Due to the huge number of cable channels available in Taiwan, competition is so intense that a programme is considered "a hit" if it can regularly reach a 1 per cent share, representing around 240,000 viewers. Although no single news channel reaches the 1 per cent threshold, the combined average ratings for six news channels is between 1.23 per cent and 2.46 per cent over the past 12 years. Furthermore, the combined average ratings for news is increasing year on year.

During Chen's first administration (2000–2004), the DPP proposed wide-ranging reviews of media policy frameworks. The Radio and Television Act (廣播電視法), the Cable Radio and Television Act (有線廣播電視法), and the Satellite Broadcasting Act (衛星廣播電視法) – known as the "Three Broadcasting Acts" (廣電三法) – had been established during the analogue era and were proving inadequate to regulate a media industry with an increasingly prominent digital component. However, like other policy areas during the four years of divided government, media reform became highly politicized and discussions within the Legislature failed to make headway. Taiwan's media industries were thus left in a state of under-regulation, at a time when Taiwanese media are facing many of the same structural challenges as their counterparts around the world. Increasing financial pressures due to the challenge of the internet to existing business models have led to layoffs, disinvestment in investigative

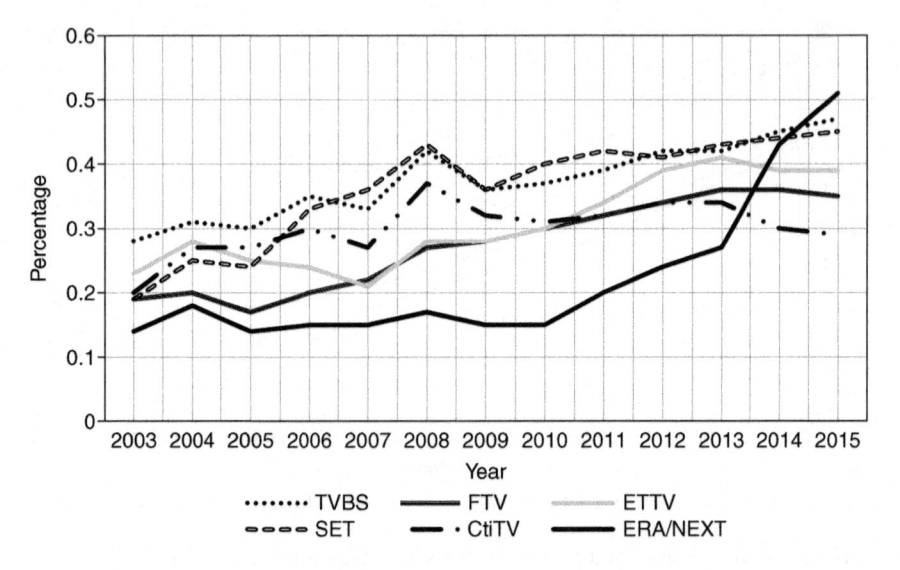

Figure 6.5 Average audience share for 24/7 news channels by year (%).

Sources: Individual TV company reports; Public Television System; ROC Advertising Yearbook.

journalism and the instrumental pursuit of advertising revenue streams. Commercial incentives are manifest in journalists receiving pressure from their employers to effectively act as salespeople by promoting sensational and outlandish views. Career progression through "sales performance" rather than journalistic ethics or professional conduct has become commonplace in the commercial media sector (P.H. Chen 2005). Product placement in news and other TV programming symbolizes the blurring of editorial and business considerations. The stalling of promising reforms under Chen prevented further advances in professionalism and the independence of the media even as Taiwan's press freedom index ranking continued to improve (Chuang, 2005).

Taiwan's media 2008–2016: ownership, activism and the growing "China factor"

Commercial competition within Taiwan's media has gradually led to the concentration of private ownership, with incomplete legal frameworks unable to provide proper regulation for dealing with mergers and acquisitions. Some of the vulnerabilities created by incomplete reforms were revealed by the expansion of media ownership and other forms of influence by actors close to or supportive of the PRC during the administrations of the KMT's Ma Ying-jeou. Launching a series of "China-friendly" initiatives seeking to revive the Taiwanese economy through closer cooperation with China (Sullivan, 2013), under Ma, the PRC became Taiwan's largest export market (2004) and trading partner (2005). Increasingly intense interactions across the Taiwan Strait accelerated economic interdependencies that have spilled over into the media sector. Among the substantial proportion of Taiwanese media firms seeking to expand their businesses overseas, the majority (90 per cent) invested in the Chinese market, to the tune of over 40 per cent of their total overseas business volume (P. Chen 2006: 57–68). In 2008, the long-time pro-KMT *UDN* secured permission from the Chinese government to access the huge Chinese market. For the first time, subscribers in nine Chinese cities could receive a Taiwanese newspaper the same or next day, while readers in another 30 specified cities could receive it within two days (Huang, 2012). The Chinese government subsequently relaxed the regulation of cross-Strait TV co-production to entice Taiwanese media enterprises. Many television stations, including traditionally pro-DPP companies like FTV and SET, seized the opportunity to diversify revenue streams by selling programming to the PRC, in some cases exercising self-censorship to avoid alienating Chinese media buyers. It has been reported that the SET news department reduced its coverage of issues deemed "sensitive" by the Chinese authorities, and shut down a popular pro-Taiwan independence political talk show, *Big Talk News* (*Da hua xinwen*, 大話新聞) in 2012, allegedly in response to pressures from the Chinese government (Zhong, 2012). The current ownership of major broadcast and print media is shown in Table 6.1, with the authors' assessment of each outlet's political orientation.

The potential vulnerabilities within the Taiwanese communications and media industries have been complicated by the emergence of a new type of owner. Entrepreneurs like Cher Wang (王雪紅) and Tsai Eng-meng, and the Fubon Corporation (富邦集團), have significantly different backgrounds and incentives than traditional media owners. They come from non-media sectors, are deeply embedded in globalized commercial networks, and have substantial investments in the Chinese market. Wang is a major player in the global digital industry through her chip manufacturing enterprise VIA Technologies and mobile brand HTC. In 2007, she launched the online gaming platform, CatchPlay (威望國際; Cao and Li, 2007) and in 2011 secured a 26 per cent share in Hong Kong's TVB. In 2015, she acquired a 53 per cent share in TVBS, which she soon increased with the approval of the NCC in 2016, giving her complete ownership of one of the most popular cable TV news channels in Taiwan (Chen and Zeng, 2016). Fubon, a real estate and financial services company, became one of the first Taiwanese companies to invest in the Chinese banking system and offer insurance services on the Chinese market in 2009 (Liu and Ouyang, 2009). Fubon entered the communications market in 2007 with the purchase of an 84 per cent share in Taiwan Fixed Network (TFN, 台灣固網), the second largest landline network, followed by a 35 per cent stake in Taiwan Mobile (TWM, 台灣大哥大), the second largest mobile telecommunications service (Fei, 2009). In 2010, Fubon acquired Kbro (凱擘), a cable system provider with a 20 per cent market share, becoming a major player in the telecommunications and cable TV industries. In addition to the acquisition of communications infrastructure, Fubon diversified into broadcasting with shopping and children's channels (Yu and Fei 2007), although the NCC rejected its application to create a news channel.

Table 6.1 Ownership and orientation of select TV news channels and newspapers

	Ownership	Political orientation
TTV News 台視新聞台	Feifan (Unique Satellite TV) Group	Neutral, pro-business
CTV News 中視新聞台	Want Want Holdings	Pro-China
CTS News Info 華視新聞資訊台	Taiwan Broadcasting System	Neutral
FTV News 民視新聞台	DPP	Pro-DPP
SET News 三立新聞	SET TV Group	Pro-DPP
ETTV News 東森新聞	US consortium (pending approval)	Pan-blue, pro-China
ETTV Financial 東森財經新聞台	US consortium (pending approval)	Pan-blue, pro-China
ERA News 年代新聞台	Mr Lian Tai-sheng (練台生)	Connection to local mafia
Next TV 壹電視新聞台	Mr Lian Tai-sheng (練台生)	Connection to local mafia
CtiTV News 中天新聞台	Want Want Holdings Ltd	Pro-China
TVBS News TVBS 新聞	HTC Corporation	Pan-blue, pro-business
Feifan News 非凡新聞台	Feifan (Unique Satellite TV) Group	Pro-business
Liberty Times 自由時報	Liberty Times Group	Pan-Green, pro-DPP
Apple Daily 蘋果日報	Next Media	Pan-Green, anti-establishment
United Daily News 聯合報	United Daily News Group	Pan-Blue, pro-KMT
China Times 中國時報	China Times Group	Pan-Blue, pro-China
Commercial Times 工商時報	China Times Group	Pan-Blue, pro-business
Economic Daily News 經濟日報	United Daily News Group	Pan-Blue, pro-business
Taipei Times 台北時報	Liberty Times Group	Pan-Green, pro-DPP, English
China Post 英文中國郵報	China Post Group	Pan-Blue, pro-KMT, English

Source: National Communications Commission. Political orientations per the chapter authors' assessment.

While Wang and Fubon's acquisitions largely flew under the radar, Want Group's attempt to expand capacity in Taiwan's print and cable sectors, and to expand operations as a content producer and service provider, provoked dramatic public opposition. The noted changes in the political orientation of the *China Times* following Want Want's acquisition in 2008 (Rawnsley and Feng 2014: 107–108) were followed by the launch of *Want Daily* (旺報) in 2009, a tabloid that promoted cross-Strait integration. Taiwan's Control Yuan (監察院)

also revealed that Want China Times Group received subsidies from several Chinese provincial and municipal governments and repeatedly embedded messages representing Chinese interests in news coverage and advertisements (ROC Control Yuan, 2010). Public discontent with these developments were exacerbated by Tsai's aggressive *modus operandi*, orchestrating media attacks on NCC commissioners during the review of the *China Times*, *Commercial Times*, CTV and CtiTV merger in 2009, and the threat of legal action against media scholars and journalists who questioned the conduct of Want China Times Group (Zhang *et al.*, 2009).

In October 2010, Tsai proposed to take over China Network System (CNS, 中嘉), a major cable TV provider, which would potentially "allow the Want conglomerate to secure 23 percent of Taiwan's cable subscribers and roughly one-third of the overall media market" (Freedom House, 2012). As the KMT intimated its support for Want Want's plans, the DPP voiced widely held concerns about the risk of Chinese influence on a company with most of its business in the PRC (L. Chen, 2010). Civic groups joined student-organized events under the aegis of the "Anti-Media Monster Youth Alliance" (反媒體巨獸青年聯盟), which would subsequently evolve into the Anti-Media Monopoly Movement (反媒體壟斷運動) when Tsai joined forces with China Trust (中信) and Formosa Plastic Corporation (台塑) to bid for Taiwan's Next Media (壹傳媒) in 2012 (Xu, 2012). Against a backdrop of huge public protests, the NCC prohibited both deals, while the prolonged dispute exposed several major weaknesses in the Taiwanese media system. There are insufficient regulations and a lack of coordination among regulators to prevent the creation of a media monopoly. Furthermore, politicians failed to demonstrate the capacity to examine the needs of media policy in a bipartisan and far-sighted way (Rawnsley and Feng, 2014: 115–116). Thus, while the civil society-led Anti-Media Monopoly Movement prompted the drafting of an Anti-Media Monopoly Act (反媒體壟斷法) in 2013, it stalled in the legislature like the amendments for the Three Broadcasting Acts before it. Reporters Without Borders describes Chinese influence as the main threat to media freedom in Taiwan (Reporters, 2017b).

The spectre of PRC leverage over Taiwanese media is not the only trend to solidify during the Ma era. Digital media matured during Ma's tenure, as evidenced by the Anti-Media Monopoly Movement itself, which began through organization via online networks. "The media" is no longer constituted by discrete entities like TV, radio and newspapers. With the popularization of WiFi and smartphones, "traditional" and "digital" media have converged and are accessible everywhere. The media-sphere is different than it once was, providing affordances and challenges to actors in the media, politics and civil society. The Ma era was replete with demonstrations, public protests and social movements characterized by activists' use of social media to circumvent traditional media gatekeepers and their perceived partisan filters. The students who occupied the Legislative Yuan for three weeks in spring 2014, which evolved into the Sunflower Movement (太陽花運動), relied on social media for internal and external communications (Chao, 2014; Rowen, 2015). Citizens, often anonymously, have used social media to break stories that were subsequently picked up by traditional media. The PTT Bulletin Board System (批踢踢實業坊) founded by National Taiwan University students in 1995, has facilitated a number of revelations, including a series of photographs of a purported Sinocentric new history textbook written after the Ma administration's controversial second round of curriculum revisions (Juo, 2014), the release of government documents indicating the Buddhist Compassion Relief Tzu Chi Foundation (慈濟) had acquired land within an environmentally sensitive area and then had its legal status changed to allow future development (Hsu and Chiang, 2015), and an accusation of sexual harassment against legislative candidate and Sunflower Movement and Anti-Media Monopoly leader Chen Wei-ting (陳為廷), which drove him to drop out of the race the day it went viral (Wu, 2014).

For Taiwan's media and political actors, the past decade has been a time of proliferating "disruptive" digital communications, a period of flux in which the political communications environment has been transformed, prompting evolving responses to new challenges, affordances and expectations. In the beginning, the responses of political actors were hesitant, partial and ad hoc. Although the DPP was an early adopter in terms of its digital election communications, notably Chen Shui-bian's presidential campaign in 2000, it did not represent a systematic attempt to adopt digital communications strategies. Other actors, notably the KMT with its greater reliance on ground-based factional mobilization, were left scrambling to respond. The hesitant responses of political parties and traditional media presented openings to non-traditional actors, bloggers and citizen journalists, but they have responded. Major media companies have adapted to the transition from offline to online media, running popular web platforms generating a high level of attention on social media (ROC Executive Yuan 2015: 234). New online-only news organizations such as *Storm Media* (風傳媒) and *The News Lens* (關鍵評論) have enriched Taiwan's news media environment, while elected officials and election candidates have found utility in social media for communicating with constituents and voters (Sullivan, 2010), which have enabled "insurgent" campaigns such as independent candidate and political neophyte Ko Wen-je's (柯文哲) successful bid for Taipei Mayor.

Conclusion: a third wave of media reform?

Despite the successes of media liberalization, Taiwan has struggled to find a balance between the interplay of state and market forces on the quality and independence of the media sector. During the martial law era, state power was dominant and press freedom was highly circumscribed, although the media industry was regulated by inadequate policies that were often expedient afterthoughts serving the interests of the KMT. For example, the three terrestrial channels established in 1962, 1967 and 1971 were legitimized after the fact by the Television Act of 1976, and regulations like the Publication Act (出版法) were deliberately vague to allow the authorities arbitrary power to interpret the guidelines in ways that best served them (Rawnsley and Rawnsley, 2001). After the rescinding of martial law in 1987 and a series of constitutional reforms undertaken in the 1990s that institutionalized societal pressures for democratic reforms, the first wave of media liberalization helped to shape the processes of democratization. The DPP administrations between 2000 and 2008 then initiated a second wave of reforms by passing long-needed Broadcasting and Television Acts, creating an independent media regulatory body, and expanding the public television sector. But these reforms were insufficient to catch up with the effects of national and international market forces and technological developments. Far from promoting pluralism and diversity of programming, market pressures have led to low-quality commercial programming, sensational tabloid journalism and the concentration of ownership in the hands of a few powerful private individuals and consortia that are accountable to shareholders rather than the public.

One way to reduce the impact of these problems is through appropriate legislation to boost investment in quality local programming and to curtail media monopolies. Unfortunately, Ma was reluctant to address the unfinished media reforms bequeathed by his predecessors, and for more than a decade the media sector, governments and audiences have demonstrated insufficient understanding or political will for any serious form of media regulation. The negative effects of market competition and the increasing power of private media owners whose interests may not be consistent with Taiwanese society have thus grown without constraint. The prospect of a third wave of media reforms increased with the transfer of presidential and legislative power to the DPP following the 16 January 2016 elections, but remains uncertain. As this chapter makes clear, Taiwan needs a third wave of reform for several reasons: (1) to guard against PRC influence via ownership or other commercial incentives; (2) to ensure the standard of media practices improves; and (3) to bring legislation up to date with technological developments. Reforms designed to maximize "positive" press freedom and minimize the "China factor" in Taiwan's media industry have emerged as higher priorities for progressive politicians like New Power Party (NPP, 時代力量) legislator Huang Kuo-chang (黃國昌), a prominent member of the Anti-Media Monopoly Movement. Huang, who experienced negative campaigning against him by Want China Times Group because of his stance during the Anti-Media Monopoly Movement, has proposed ambitious draft legislation aimed at preventing media monopolization (W. Chen 2016; Liu 2016). The proposed regulations include limits on ownership of multiple forms of media, restrictions on holding companies, banks, and insurance companies purchasing media operations, forced contributions to a "media pluralism fund" for companies with excessive programming produced outside Taiwan, and legally binding agreements on editorial autonomy between owners and employees. The NPP's history and membership, and as the de facto successor to the 2014 Sunflower Movement, lend it significant political capital on the issue.

During the first year of the Tsai administration, the NCC and the newly-formed Ill-gotten Party Assets Settlement Committee took the lead in media regulation. Merger proposals that have been scuttled under NCC scrutiny include DMG Entertainment's and Taiwan Optical Co.'s (TOC) separate bids for a 61 per cent stake in Eastern Broadcasting Co. (EBC) (Frater, 2016; Strong, 2017) as well as Far EasTone Telecommunications Co.'s (FET) bid for CNS (Wang and Shan, 2017). After months of scrutiny, the NCC did ultimately approve Asia Pacific Telecom's (APT) acquisition of Taiwan Broadband Communications. DMG's proposed acquisition of EBC, announced near the end of Ma's term, attracted concern because DMG Entertainment co-founder Peter Xiao, the chairman of the Beijing-based affiliate DMG Yinji, allegedly has family ties to the People's Liberation Army. DMG Entertainment chief executive Dan Mintz's argument that since he, not Xiao, signed the agreement, these questions were moot (Lin, 2015), failed to assuage concerns about greater Chinese influence over Taiwanese media. A major obstacle to both TOC's and FET's proposed acquisitions was that both companies included among their shareholders governmental or political groups, which are barred from direct media ownership. In addition, the NCC announced in June 2017 that it would soon unveil draft legislation to adapt anti-media monopolization legislation to the nation's contemporary circumstances, forecasting the Legislature would deliberate the bill in early 2018 (Shan, 2017a). In spring 2017, the NCC forced the BCC to close two frequencies the station had been requested to return to the government in 2007, so that these frequencies could be used by the government's Hakka and indigenous affairs councils, respectively (Shan, 2017b).

The Ill-gotten Party Assets Settlement Committee, which was formed to facilitate enforcement of new legislation regarding the divestment and disposal of assets illicitly acquired by political parties (namely, the KMT), has been probing the KMT's sales of CMPC, CTV, and BCC for below-market prices during the Chen administration. Given the political connections of some buyers, concerns include alleged failure to choose the highest bidders, difficulty in collecting payments, and possible illegal profiteering. Of note, the chairman of the KMT at the time of the sales was Ma Ying-jeou, but a subsequent probe by the Special Investigation Division (which was created by President Ma) did not include an interview with Ma because he was then president of Taiwan (Yang, 2017). The asset committee has also proposed breaking up BCC's media and real estate assets and returning the real estate to the national government (*Liberty Times*, 2017).

Meanwhile, the rise of "new media" and the downsizing of traditional print media has continued during Tsai's term. In May 2017, *The China Post* ceased production of print newspapers (ending a 65-year run) and became a fully digital news outlet. Moreover, in June 2017, reports circulated that *Apple Daily* was encouraging its reporters to give up full-time employment at the company and instead work for it as freelancers (Tong, 2017). New media has even begun to acquire old media: in April 2017, the digital platform *Storm Media* purchased the well-reputed print magazine *The Journalist* (新新聞) as well as the polling from Taiwan Indicators Survey Research. New digital news platforms to emerge in 2016–2017 included *Mirror Media* (鏡周刊) and *UP Media* (上報). As for the TV industry, local media have recently reported that China's Taiwan Affairs

Office has stepped up efforts to prevent certain Taiwanese TV networks, particularly those with pan-green ties, from selling programming in China (Liu, 2017). Meanwhile, SET-TV's chairman, a minor shareholder at FTV, reportedly intervened in the FTV's spring 2017 board election, possibly raising questions about the independence of the two stations.

Note

1 Statistical Yearbook of the Republic of China 2016 (Ed. 2017), p. 36. Available at: https://eng.dgbas.gov.tw/public/data/dgbas03/bs2/yearbook_eng/y020.pdf (accessed 15 May 2018).

References

Batto, P. (2004). "Democracy's impact on dailies", *China Perspectives* 51: 64–79.

Cao, Z.F. and Li, L.D. (2007). "VIA grabs the digital entertainment commercial potential (數位娛樂商機威盛插一腳)", *Economic Daily News*, 20 January: B3 (in Chinese).

Chan-Olmstead, S. and Chiu, P. (1999). "The impact of cable television on political campaigns in Taiwan", *International Communication Gazette* 61(6): 491–509.

Chao, V.Y. (2014). "How technology revolutionized Taiwan's Sunflower Movement", *The Diplomat*, 15 April. Available at: http://thediplomat.com/2014/04/how-technology-revolutionized-taiwans-sunflower-movement/ (accessed 24 May 2016).

Chen, K.X. and Chu, P. (1987). *The Evolution of the Press in Taiwan Over 40 Years* (台灣報業演進40年), Taipei: Independent Evening News (in Chinese).

Chen, L.R. (2010). "NCC withdrew four attachments to the merger of Want China Times Group (雙中董監事變更案, NCC四項附款遭撤銷)", *United Daily News*, 15 July: A8 (in Chinese).

Chen, P.H. (2005). "Exploring advertorials in television news: product placement vs. professionalism of news reporting (探討廣告商介入電視新聞產製之新聞廣告化現象：兼論置入性行銷與新聞專業自主)", *Chinese Journal of Communication Research* (中華傳播學刊) 8(December): 209–246 (in Chinese). Available at: http://cjc.nccu.edu.tw/issueArticle.asp?P_No=17&CA_ID=137 (accessed 24 March 2016).

Chen, P.H. (2006). "Market entry modes and determinants of Taiwanese media firms into mainland China (台灣媒體企業之中國大陸市場進入模式及其決策影響因素研究)", *Mass Communication Research* (新聞學研究) 89(October): 37–80 (in Chinese). Available at: http://mcr.nccu.edu.tw/word/22454292013.pdf (accessed 23 May 2016).

Chen, P.H. and Zeng, D.R. (2016). "NCC approved Cher Wang's acquisition of TVBS (王雪紅入主 TVBS, NCC 審核過了)", *Liberty Times*, 25 February: A5 (in Chinese).

Chen, W.H. (2016). "New Power Party proposal targets media monopolies", *Taipei Times*, 30 March. Available at: www.taipeitimes.com/News/taiwan/archives/2016/03/30/2003642776 (accessed 6 April 2016).

Chin, K. (2003). *Heijin: Organized Crime, Business and Politics in Taiwan*, Armonk NY: M. E. Sharpe.

Chu, A. (2003). "Political call-in shows in Taiwan: animating crisis discourse through reported speech", PhD thesis, University of Texas.

Chuang, J. (2005). "Taiwan improves ranking in press freedom index", *Taipei Times*, 21 October. Available at: www.international.ucla.edu/asia/article/32000 (accessed 24 March 2016).

Fei, J.Q. (2009). "Fubon plans to invest additional NTD 17 billion in TWM (富邦擬加碼台灣大170億)", *Economic Daily News*, 26 August: A15 (in Chinese).

Fell, D. (2007). "Putting on a show and electoral fortunes in Taiwan's multi-party elections", in J. Strauss and D.C. O'Brien (eds) *Staging Politics: Power and Performance in Asia and Africa*. London: I. B. Tauris.

Frater, P. (2016). "New bids emerge for Taiwan's Eastern Broadcasting after end of Dan Mintz offer", *Variety*, 17 October 2016. Available at: http://variety.com/2016/biz/asia/new-bids-for-taiwan-eastern-broadcasting-dan-mintz-1201890754/ (accessed 29 July 2017).

Freedom House (2012). "Taiwan: Freedom of the press 2012", *Freedom of the Press*. Available at: https://freedomhouse.org/report/freedom-press/2012/taiwan (accessed 24 May 2016).

Freedom House (2015). "Taiwan: Freedom of the press 2015", *Freedom of the Press*. Available at: https://freedomhouse.org/report/freedom-press/2015/taiwan (accessed 24 May 2016).

Hsu, C.J. (2014). *The Construction of National Identity in Taiwan's Media, 1896–2012*. Leiden: Brill.

Hsu, C.C. and Chiang, J.Y. (2015). "Taichung Tzu Chi park built atop environmental protection land and a faultline? Tzu Chi rebuts: Everything was legal (台中慈濟園區蓋在保育地斷層帶上? 慈濟駁: 通通合法)", *SET News*, 7 March (in Chinese). Available at: www.setn.com/news.aspx?newsid=64469 (accessed 6 April 2016).

Huang, X. (2012). "Taiwanese business people discuss UDN: Inferior quality (台商談聯合報: 品質不優)", *Commercial Times*, 17 November: A4 (in Chinese).

Hung, C.L. (2006). "Whose media? Whose freedom of speech? The right of access to media in post-martial law era", *Taiwan Democracy Quarterly* 3(4): 1–35.

Juo, F.Y. (2014). "Must brainwashing start from national public education? (心得洗腦要從國民教育做起?)", *PTT*, 5 May (in Chinese). Available at: http://disp.cc/b/163-7E3d (accessed 6 April 2016).

Keane, J. (2013). *Democracy and Media Decadence*. Cambridge: Cambridge University Press.

Li, M.H. (2017). "'The FTV storm is still burning': For this reason, SET-TV's chair is getting into it with Kuo Pei-hung (【民視風波延燒】就因這件事 三立海董就是要跟郭倍宏拚了)," *Mirror Media*, 27 May 2017, www.mirrormedia.mg/story/20170526fin012/ (accessed 30 June 2017).

Liberty Times (2017). "Party asset committee puts forward BCC breakup plan, with state as priority recipient of assets (黨產會擬推中廣分割案 資產先收歸國有)", 31 May 2017. Available at: http://news.ltn.com.tw/index.php/news/politics/paper/1106640 (accessed 30 June 2017).

Lin, E. (2015). "EMI shares up 10 percent on acquisition report", *The China Post*, 24 November 2015. Available at: www.chinapost.com.tw/taiwan/national/national-news/2015/11/24/451742/p1/emi-shares.htm (accessed 29 June 2017).

Lin, L.Y. (2008) "A historical experiment with deregulations: The changes and challenges of the press after the lifting of the press ban in Taiwan (變遷與挑戰: 解禁後的台灣報業)", *Mass Communication Research (*新聞學研究*)* 95(April): 183–211 (in Chinese).

Liu, C.H. (2017). "Resistance to Taiwan independence stations: Has the sword been pointed at FTV, SET-TV, PTS, and CTS? (抵制台獨台 劍指民視三立公視華視?)"

11 May 2017. Available at: www.new7.com.tw/coverStory/CoverView.aspx?NUM=15 74&i=TXT201705031754304MV (accessed 29 June 2017).

Liu, Y.Q. and Ouyang, S.L. (2009). "Interviewing Fubon CEO about the strategies for the Chinese market and a big financial future (獨家專訪富邦金董事長談中國布局, 蔡明忠 擘畫金融大未來)", *Business Today (今周刊)* 674 (19 November): 36–40 (in Chinese).

Liu, Y.S. (2016). "New Power Party drafts Anti-Media Monopoly Act, demands separation of media and finance (時代力量版反媒體壟斷法要求媒金分離)", *Storm Media*, 29 March Available online: www.storm.mg/article/95281 (accessed 6 April 2016) (in Chinese).

Media Palette (2013). "2012 media environment review and future projection (2012年媒 體環境回顧暨未來趨勢) (Industry Report)," Taipei: Media Palette (in Chinese).

Miniwatts Marketing Group (2017). "Internet world stats: Usage and population statistics", Miniwatts website, available at: www.internetworldstats.com/top25.htm (accessed 29 June 2017).

Rawnsley, G. and Rawnsley, M.Y.T. (2001). *Critical Security, Democratisation and Television in Taiwan.* London: Ashgate.

Rawnsley, G. and Rawnsley, M.Y.T. (2004). "Media reform since 1989", *China Perspectives* 56: 46–55.

Rawnsley, G. and Rawnsley, M.Y.T. (2012). "The media in democratic Taiwan", in D. Blundell (ed.), *Taiwan Since Martial Law: Society, Culture, Politics, Economy.* Berkeley, CA, and Taipei: University of California, Berkeley and National Taiwan University Press, pp. 395–417.

Rawnsley, M.Y.T. and Feng, C.S. (2014). "Anti-media-monopoly policies and further democratisation in Taiwan", *Journal of Current Chinese Affairs* 43(3): 105–128.

Reporters Without Borders (2017a). "Reporters Without Borders (RSF) opens its first Asia bureau in Taipei", RSF website, 6 April 2017 (updated 6 June 2017). Available at: https://rsf.org/en/news/reporters-without-borders-rsf-opens-its-first-asia-bureau-taipei (accessed 29 June 2017).

Reporters Without Borders (2017b). "Taiwan", RSF website. Available at: https://rsf.org/en/taiwan (accessed 29 June 2017).

Rickards, J. (2016). "Taiwan's changing media landscape", *Taiwan Business TOPICS*, 25 March. Available at: http://topics.amcham.com.tw/2016/03/taiwans-changing-media-landscape/ (accessed 22 May 2016).

ROC Bureau of Foreign Trade (2016). "Trade statistics #FSC3040: Ranking of total trade, exports and imports for Taiwan's trading partners (中華民國進出口貿易國家地 區名次表)", *ROC Bureau of Foreign Trade Website*, January (in Chinese). Available at: http://cus93.trade.gov.tw/FSCI/ (accessed 24 March 2016).

ROC Control Yuan (2010). "Correction case #099 jiaozheng 0022 (糾正案 099教正0022)", ROC *Control Yuan Website*, 11 November (in Chinese). Available at: www.cy.gov.tw/sp.asp?xdurl=./CyBsBox/CyBsR2.asp&ctNode=911 (accessed 24 March 2016).

ROC Executive Yuan (2015). *The Republic of China Yearbook 2015.* Taipei: Executive Yuan. Available at: https://issuu.com/eyroc/docs/the_republic_of_china_yearbook_ 2015 (accessed 24 May 2016).

Rowen, I. (2015). "Inside Taiwan's Sunflower Movement: Twenty-four days in a student-occupied parliament, and the future of the region", *The Journal of Asian Studies* 74(1): 5–21.

Shan, S. (2017a). "NCC to unveil revised bill to stem media monopolies", *Taipei Times*, 7 June 2017. Available at: www.taipeitimes.com/News/taiwan/archives/2017/06/07/ 2003672073 (accessed 29 June 2017).

Shan, S. (2017b). "Two BCC networks must go off the air: NCC", *Taipei Times*, 23 March 2017. Available at: www.taipeitimes.com/News/taiwan/archives/2017/03/23/2003667316 (accessed 30 June 2017).

Siebert, F.S. (1979). "The libertarian theory", in F.S. Siebert, T. Peterson and W. Schramm (eds), *Four Theories of the Press: The Authoritarian, Libertarian, Social Responsibility and Soviet Communist Concepts of What the Press Should Be and Do.* Champaign, IL: University of Illinois Press, pp. 39–72.

Strong, M. (2017). "NCC throws out Taiwan Optical bid for EBC TV Company", *Taiwan News*, 31 May 2017. Available at: www.taiwannews.com.tw/en/news/3176462 (accessed 29 June 2017).

Sullivan, J. (2010). "Legislators' blogs in Taiwan", *Parliamentary Affairs* 63(3): 471–485.

Sullivan, J. (2013). "Taiwan's 2012 presidential election", *Political Studies Review* 11(1): 65–74.

Sullivan, J. and Lowe, W. (2010). "Chen Shui-bian: On independence", *The China Quarterly* 203: 619–638.

Tong, E. (2017). "Apple Daily Taiwan encourages reporters to leave and become freelancers", 22 June 2017. Available at: www.hongkongfp.com/2017/06/22/apple-daily-taiwan-encourages-reporters-leave-become-freelancers/ (accessed 29 June 2017).

Wang, L. and Shan, S. (2017). "Far EasTone withdraws bid for CNS", *Taipei Times*, 9 February 2017. Available at: www.taipeitimes.com/News/front/archives/2017/02/09/2003664628 (accessed 29 June 2017).

Wu, J.M. (2014). "Attacked breast during high school? Chen Wei-ting cancels activities for a press conference (再爆高中就襲胸? 陳為廷活動取消將開記者會)", *Next Magazine*, 25 December (in Chinese). Available at: www.nextmag.com.tw/breaking-news/news/20141225/12298198 (accessed 24 May 2016).

Xu, C.F. (2012). "1 September Journalist Day ten thousand people marched anti-media monopoly (九一記者節萬人遊行反壟斷)", *Lih Pao*, 2 September (in Chinese). Available at: https://tw.news.yahoo.com/%E4%B9%9D-%E8%A8%98%E8%80%85%E7%AF%80-%E8%90%AC%E4%BA%BA%E9%81%8A%E8%A1%8C%E5%8F%8D%E5%A3%9F%E6%96%B7-134946801.html (accessed 24 May 2016).

Yang, C.H. (2017). "New evidence may see probe of KMT media sales resume", 10 April 2017. Available at: www.taipeitimes.com/News/front/archives/2017/04/10/2003668426 (accessed 30 June 2017).

Ye, X.H. (2010). "Fubon is allowed to acquire Kbro and becomes the new top dog in cable TV (富邦准併凱擘, 有線電視新龍頭)", *Economic Daily News*, 18 December: A5 (in Chinese).

Yu, L.Z. and Fei, J.Q. (2007). "Fubon spent NTD 70 million on buying QTV (富邦砸七千萬併緯來兒童台)", *Economic Daily News*, 18 January: A3 (in Chinese).

Zhang, L.D., Xu, Y.L. and Liu, Y.X. (2009). "149 scholars denounce *China Times* for being overly aggressive (中時捍權太暴力, 149學者聯名譴責)", *Apple Daily*, 17 June: A10 (in Chinese).

Zhong, N.H. (2012). *My Big Talk Life* (我的大話人生), Taipei: Qianwei Publishing (in Chinese).

7 Peace or war with Taiwan in China's foreign policy

Edward Friedman

Introduction

The professional consensus of analysts concerning PRC foreign policy, as President Tsai was inaugurated as the head of state of democratic Taiwan on May 20, 2016, was that CCP Supreme Leader Xi Jinping would sternly punish the people of Taiwan for not electing the KMT (China National Party) candidate because the prior KMT president of Taiwan had supposedly accommodated CCP interests and ideological claims. A subsequent decline in Chinese tourists going to Taiwan after Tsai's January landslide election was generally imagined as an indication of Xi's displeasure with the Taiwanese. CCP Supreme Leader Xi surely had no interest in being helpful to the newly elected Taiwan president.

The CCP, it was assumed by most international analysts, wanted to punish the now ruling Democratic Progressive Party (DPP), a Taiwan-identified party, for its unwillingness to embrace the so-called "1992 consensus" in which Taiwan and China supposedly agreed that there was only one China, but, under a one-China rubric by which the government in Beijing and the authorities in Taipei (the CCP would not describe the leaders voted into power in Taiwan as a government) each could interpret the consensus in its own way. The KMT could, as international observers saw it, take "one-China" to mean the Republic of China (ROC) founded after the 1911 republican revolution toppled the Manchu Qing monarchy, imagining the ROC on Taiwan as continuing the history of one China, the ROC. Actually this KMT understanding of one-China was never approved by the CCP.

In expecting China to wish to really hurt Taiwan, international observers assumed that CCP leaders imagined Taiwan as a top priority for Chinese ruling groups because Taiwan was felt to be, since time immemorial, sacred Chinese territory whose loss was deeply painful to all Chinese patriots. In this view, the 1949 civil war defeat of the ROC by the CCP armies and the KMT government's subsequent retreat to Taiwan had kept the CCP from ending China's civil war by conquering, at long last, the final redoubt of the prior Chiang Kai-shek ROC regime.

But does the historical record of PRC policy behavior support the notion that making Taiwan a part of the PRC has been, from the time the CCP conquered state power on October 1, 1949 up until Tsai Ing-wen was elected president in 2016, such a sensitive matter among Chinese that, unless the CCP soon annexed Taiwan, the CCP would lose its patriotic legitimacy? Was Taiwan really the top CCP priority? Actually, the evidence establishes that it was not then and is not now.

Analysts who have assumed the centrality to CCP legitimacy of ending Taiwan's independent existence as a country predicted that the PRC would, upon President Tsai's election, immediately pressure the governments with diplomatic relations with the ROC to end formal diplomatic relations with Taiwan and recognize the PRC as the one and only China in the family of nations. One African government cut diplomatic relations with Taiwan after President Tsai rejected a blackmail bid for more "aid." But there is no evidence that Beijing pressured all of Taiwan's diplomatic partners to make such a switch.

For those expecting China to become strongly anti-Taipei, Beijing would swiftly block Taiwan's participation in the WHA (World Health Assembly) as part of a general policy of taking the air out of Taiwan's international space. CCP Supreme Leader Xi Jinping indeed did block any further extension of Taiwan's international space. And tourism from China did decline by double digits in 2016. But such acts of displeasure by the Chinese side have little in common with the dire predictions about Taiwan–China relations which found Taiwan to be a top priority for China.

As evidence for the forecast that the CCP would immediately punish Taiwan harshly for choosing the DPP's Tsai Ing-wen as president, commentators pointed to PRC insistence that the "one-China" of the 1992 Consensus could not refer to the Republic of China, as the KMT believed it did, but, instead, "one-China" suddenly meant, and only meant, as never previously, the CCP's "one-China principle" under which the authorities on Taiwan accepted that Taiwan belonged to China and indeed was a local government of China's.

This indeed was a new and harsher CCP policy toward Taiwan. The PRC criticized President Tsai for not embracing the CCP's "one-China principle" in her May 2016 inauguration address, although the Beijing demand that the government in Taipei declare that it was a local government of the authoritarian, Han CCP state was a non-starter on democratic, multi-cultural Taiwan. Even former KMT President Ma had never embraced the CCP's "one-China principle." Given this CCP escalation of pressure on Taiwan's most recently elected president, commentators had some basis for forecasting that the CCP meant to penalize President Tsai's DPP-ruled Taiwan. But did Beijing seek to destabilize Taipei?

Tsai's Taiwan delegation to the WHA was immediately seated without incident. Analysts then found that the CCP noted that Taiwan President Tsai was committed to not provoking PRC Supreme Leader Xi, that she actually intended to strive to build on the positive achievements of former President Ma in improving China–Taiwan relations. Taiwan President Tsai definitely would not be looking for ways to challenge or provoke the CCP Supreme Leader, Xi. Yet Xi's political interests in the CCP made it imperative that Xi not seem to his colleagues soft on President Tsai.

According to rapporteur T.J. Pempel, a quadrilateral dialogue on May 26, 2016, among participants from China, Japan, South Korea, and the USA found that

> whether or not she [Taiwan President Tsai, a "practical" leader "dealing with China in highly pragmatic ways"] has a receptive partner on the other side of the Strait will determine whether this area reverts to being one of the region's more dangerous or not.

That is, war or peace depended on the balance of political forces in Zhongnanhai and not on purportedly deep and broadly shared Chinese passions about Taiwan as sacred Chinese territory, passions that are supposedly provoked by a continuation of Taiwan's de facto independence. War or peace between China and Taiwan "depends to a significant degree on the strategic choices and priorities of the leadership of the Chinese Communist Party," not on Taiwan's President Tsai. War or peace was not a problem brought on by long-held Chinese passions about Taiwan but was instead a problem inside of a chauvinistic Chinese politics. It was, however, true that these war-prone forces in the PRC were stronger than in prior CCP administrations. The real danger flows from changes in CCP politics.

Clearly, the presupposition of a continuing Chinese view of Taiwan as lost sacred territory, a view that led analysts to forecast a strong, negative CCP policy toward the new DPP government was not fully accurate. After all, ever since Mao's PRC backed a North Korean June 1950 invasion of the Republic of Korea in the south, the US government has partnered with Taiwan, reimagined as a Cold War partner in the camp opposed to Soviet-led expansionism, no longer merely the losing side of a Chinese civil war. China thereby lost the ability to seize Taiwan without American opposition. Since mid-1950, China has consistently chosen not to risk war with America over Taiwan. Many other matters were far more important to CCP ruling groups than trying to annex the island of Taiwan. The independence of Taiwan has not been a passionate and explosive issue for the CCP. In 2017, Beijing responded more harshly to South Korea seeking missiles to defend against North Korean threats than it did to Taiwan's President Tsai.

While I do not believe it is possible to predict what the CCP's future Taiwan policy will be, it is not a trivial factor that China, since 1950, has never tried to capture Taiwan. This reality suggests that there is something not quite right with the assumption that the leaders of the CCP have always imagined Taiwan as sacred Chinese territory that must be seized for PRC rulers to appear as legitimate patriots. What needs explaining, therefore, is why seizing Taiwan has in fact not been a passionate patriotic priority for the CCP, apart from neo-Maoist hawks who do talk more about China incorporating Taiwan. This newly risen force could yet opt to risk war with America and use the PRC's military to attack Taiwan under President Tsai. But such CCP aggression would reflect a major post-Mao, post-Deng, war-prone rupture in CCP attitudes and policy. Mao never tried to invade Taiwan after the invasion of South Korea by North Korea backed by Mao had turned Taiwan into an American ally. Mao prioritized avoiding war with the USA over annexing Taiwan.

Post-Mao policies

On December 15, 1978, Deng Xiaoping was concluding negotiations with America's Carter Administration on full normalization of USA-PRC relations. The Chinese side had been refusing to sign until America dropped a claimed right to sell defensive arms to the KMT government on the island of Taiwan. Carter, however, was adamant. Then, suddenly, Beijing dropped the Taiwan issue. Once again, for Deng, as previously for Supreme Leader Mao, something else was far more important to the CCP leadership than was Taiwan.

Author Zhang Xiaoming finds that the CCP state prioritized its regional and global interests. The Chinese military saw Vietnam trying to establish itself as the hegemon of Indo-China, with Vietnamese regional ambitions aided by a military treaty with the USSR. To the CCP, Vietnam had joined Soviet Russia's attempt to encircle China. In response to this imagined security threat, the PRC military urged a war against Vietnam. The Chinese military armed the mass-murdering Khmer Rouge regime of Pol Pot which carried out savage cross-border raids from Cambodia into parts of Vietnam that were once Khmer.

To contain and punish Vietnam, the Chinese military launched cross-border raids into northern Vietnam. The PRC military leaders wanted to destroy the purported threat from Vietnam. The PLA contended that the threat from Vietnam required an invasion of Vietnam to force the Hanoi government to abandon its policy goal of regional hegemony aided by its Soviet Russian military ally. The Chinese military would weaken Vietnam so it could not be helpful to a Soviet encirclement of China.

Soon after becoming the CCP's Supreme Leader in mid-1977, Deng Xiaoping agreed to an invasion of Vietnam. He then dropped China's opposition to US arms sales to Taiwan because China's military no longer opposed Deng's reform economics and Deng prioritized his power and his policies and China's security. He therefore did not want to invade Vietnam without first cementing entente with America. A need to respond to Vietnam and be safe from Soviet retaliation militarily were higher priorities to Deng than was Taiwan. If Deng kept pressing the matter of U.S. arms sales to Taiwan, and if China then invaded Vietnam without PRC–USA entente, Deng believed Soviet Russia would be far more likely to come to the military aid of its ally, Vietnam. Indeed, if Deng delayed entente with America because of Taiwan, Vietnam might first normalize relations with the USA, leaving China more isolated and vulnerable. For China to prioritize Taiwan would risk China having to pay a high price for its planned invasion of Vietnam, everything from losing American support for China's modernization to a need to defer modernization while dealing with the Soviet military.

With regional and global strategic concerns still privileged, as was the case in the Mao era, Deng normalized relations with the US, conceding on the issue of

US arms sales to Taiwan, camouflaged by President Carter agreeing to a one-year moratorium, which the US military undermined. Taiwan's independence not only did not threaten CCP legitimacy, Taiwan, in fact, continued to be a rather tertiary concern for the CCP. Even Vietnam was far more important.

Another view, one which does not contradict Professor Zhang's persuasive data and logic, is that, as with Mao, so in the Deng era and the post-Deng era, China's domestic politics and regional and global interests were and still are in command in Beijing, not a preoccupation with Taiwan. Deng, who had been side-lined by Mao, returned to the center of power in mid-1977 after Mao's death in 1976. At the end of 1978, Deng won agreement from ruling groups to reform China's Stalinist command economy into a world market-regarding economy. But left conservatives in the party's military and other institutions were not happy with Deng's new direction. They claimed that reform undermined the party and the nation, the CCP and the PRC. By agreeing to the Chinese military's urging of an invasion of Vietnam, Deng won the Chinese military to back his reform agenda. Narrow political and large international concerns, not a supposed fragile nationalist legitimacy tied to an alleged pressing patriotic imperative of incorporating Taiwan, preoccupied CCP leaders.

With China a life-and-death issue for Vietnam, Vietnamese leader Le Duan found, after carefully examining PRC aims, that, in contrast to Mao, Deng was not fixated on the USSR as China's enemy number one. Indeed, by 1981, Deng had committed the PRC to an independent foreign policy. That is, Beijing would court Moscow so as not to be overly dependent on Washington. Deng was well aware of how Mao's fixation on opposing Soviet socialist revisionism, with the CPSU regime understood as a continuation of Tsarist imperialism, had hurt China. Deng saw the leftist hawks in the CCP "exaggerating the Soviet threat" (Zhang 2015: 54).

Deng also hoped that a Cold War America that took the USSR as enemy number one, on seeing China humiliate Vietnam, a Soviet ally, would, in return, do more to help China rapidly modernize, a Deng-era priority. Deng courted America so China could become wealthy and strong. That was a top Chinese nationalist priority, not Taiwan.

Deng also hoped that the Chinese invasion of Vietnam would reveal that the Maoist doctrine of people's war had produced a military unsuited to modern warfare. With the military resisting reform, the PLA's subsequent "dismal performance … confirmed Deng's belief in the need for sweeping changes in the military" (ibid.: 58). Whether one is persuaded by Professor Zhang's shrewd analysis that the CCP state privileged China's place in a global strategic calculus or my view on how domestic matters were privileged in the PRC or perhaps that the two concerns, international and domestic, were reinforcing, CCP policies in 1978 reveal that Taiwan's de facto independence was not a threatening humiliation to Chinese patriots that could delegitimize the CCP and topple its leader. Manifestly, Taiwan was a lesser priority for the CCP and long had been.

This does not mean that Chinese military hawks did not press to use military means to establish the PRC's regional predominance. In 1974, the Chinese military used force to seize the Paracel Islands in the South China Sea which had been occupied by South Vietnamese forces. In 1975, left chauvinists in Fujian are rumored to have been planning an attack on Taiwan. But the central government, of which Deng was a key part, squashed the invasion effort.

Still, the left chauvinist conservatives continued to work against liberal reformers. The hawks were not happy with 1981 Deng overtures to Taiwan for trade and investments, a new policy which included dropping the vacuous 1958 slogan "we must definitely liberate Taiwan." To Deng, it was better for China to benefit from plugging in to the dynamic Taiwanese economy, benefitting from the rapidly rising East Asian neo-mercantilist economies centered on Japan, than it was for China to try to annex Taiwan through military power and risk losing helpful economic ties with East Asia and America that could make China wealthy and powerful.

By 1988, after the 1985 ousting of liberal reform leader Hu Yaobang, conservative hawks among CCP ruling groups were in the ascendancy. All sorts of reforms were rolled back, from an opening of access to Party archives to a reduction in repression against Lama Buddhist Tibetans. Rumors in Beijing about the marginalizing of CCP liberal reformers led to democracy salons discussing how liberals should respond to the rise of neo-Maoist chauvinists. The hawks won approval for the Chinese military attacking and seizing Vietnam's Spratly Islands. Bloody battles followed in 1988. The Central Military Commission also approved, in 1988, a plan to build infrastructure across from Taiwan that, within three years, could be equipped with missiles that could reach Taiwan (Stokes and Tsai 2016: 21).

Who wins the political struggle in Beijing is decisive for Chinese policy toward Taiwan. By the end of the 1980s, CCP hawks presented a military alternative to Deng's economic reform policy of China's modernization project benefiting from Taiwan's successful economic development. Deng, while far from all-powerful, remained the Supreme Leader.

But this CCP hawk policy of building offensive weaponry to confront Taiwan, a CCP policy reorientation toward more Chinese assertiveness in maritime Asia, including Taiwan, won. Yet, the Nixon policy, expressed in the 1972 Shanghai Communique, and re-stated by Reagan in 1982 was that the US commitment to reducing weapons sales to Taiwan was dependent on CCP policies in which tensions in the West Pacific kept diminishing. The rise of Chinese hawks and their policies in the 1980s, however, meant that China would increase tensions in the region and act on expansionist territorial ambitions in maritime Asia. The PRC focus, though, was the region, not Taiwan. China acted as a global power with global ambitions, starting with regional predominance, supposedly learning from US history in which a Monroe Doctrine of dominating the region of Latin America was a preclude to America's global power.

Offensive Chinese missiles, which were promised in 1988, were not put in place across from Taiwan until 1994, three years after originally scheduled. Perhaps one reason for the delay was a Deng decision, after the OECD nations in 1989 agreed to respond to Deng's June 4, 1989 bloody repression of pro-democracy protests by instituting economic sanctions on the PRC, which pushed Deng to act in a conciliatory way towards regional neighbors, to get the sanctions lifted so that the CCP could again unleash policies of rapid growth premised on FDI, joint ventures and industrial exports to Japan, the US and the EU. The Deng era priority was making the CCP state wealthy and powerful. Ending the sanctions had priority, not Taiwan.

In 1992, American President George H. W. Bush sold F-16 jets to Taiwan, hoping to create jobs and votes in a battleground state contested by Democratic candidate Bill Clinton. Since the sale violated America's promise to China to only sell defensive weapons to Taiwan, Bush explained his political need to Deng. Bush still wanted cooperative relations with Deng. But surging Chinese hard-liners wanted Deng to respond strongly to Bush's provocative act. Supreme Leader Deng, however, vetoed that policy proposal. Making the Chinese state wealthy and strong, a project which required economic cooperation with the USA, was far more important to Supreme Leader Deng than was military posturing over Taiwan.

But it is a fact that the Chinese military was urging the CCP to use the PRC's military against Taiwan. Hawks had become strong enough and chauvinism had become nasty and pervasive enough among the ruling groups in the PRC in the era after the 1991 implosion of the Soviet Union that the new PRC supreme leader, Jiang Zemin, had subsequently to respond to the hawk pressure. But Jiang, like Mao and Deng, was definitely not seeking to risk a military clash with the USA over Taiwan.

By 1993, the CCP leadership seems to have regained its confidence that openness to the world market would help its state become strong and prosperous, gaining the wherewithal to act as a global power. Yet, conservative hawks continued to push for more budget and military action against Taiwan. What seems decisive for war or peace in the Indo-Pacific then is not a so-called "Taiwan problem," but the changing balance of forces among China's ruling groups, at times pitting impatient chauvinist hawks who seek to use the Chinese military regionally, against patient reformist patriots who have confidence that in the long run China can rise peacefully toward world leadership through economic, cultural, and diplomatic strengths backed by a bullying, powerful military that would make a larger war unnecessary.

This issue of how to respond to a democratic Taiwan whose President, Lee Teng-hui was seeking international dignity and international space for Taiwan was fought out in the mid-1990s as conservative hawks pressed Supreme Leader Jiang Zemin to use military force against Taiwan. Although Taiwan spent less and less of its GDP on defense, the Chinese military used the invention of a supposed Taiwan threat in order to win budget and policy centrality. But Supreme Leader Deng's position had been that China needed to be conciliatory in order to get the June 4 OECD sanctions on China lifted.

Supreme Leader Jiang also wanted China not to be locked in to low-value manufacture. He therefore welcomed Taiwanese IT FDI to China. The government on Taiwan lobbied the US to end sanctions against a China with which

Taiwan wanted to do more business. Jiang, who embraced Deng's prioritizing of China's economic rise, therefore had no interest in a military effort to annex Taiwan that could undercut China's economic rise and wound USA-PRC economic relations, which would limit the prospects for China's economic growth and global influence. Supreme Leader Jiang needed the support of American President Bill Clinton to get the PRC into the WTO so that barriers to Chinese exports would fall and so that China would not be locked into low-end production.

In January 1992, Deng defeated the left conservative chauvinists who had blocked a further Chinese opening to the world market. New Supreme Leader Jiang Zemin vetoed provocative weapon requests from the Chinese military. But with the liberal reformers purged and left conservative chauvinist military discourse ever more influential among CCP ruling groups, it became difficult for Jiang simply to say no to the PLA on everything. Jiang got US President Clinton to guarantee that Taiwan President Lee, who was using various pretexts to visit South-east Asian nations and leaders, would not be allowed to visit the USA. Actually, America's one-China policy required that the US government avoid official relations with the Taiwan president.

But Clinton was soon concerned about his impeachment by the US Congress. He then gave in to Congressional pressure to welcome a visit by Lee Teng-hui, the president of a new democracy. Taiwan's Lee was to be treated just as America welcomed Mandela, the new democratic president of South Africa. Jiang looked bad to Chinese leaders when Clinton agreed to a visit by Lee. Jiang looked like he had been taken in by the Americans.

Jiang then got the Clinton administration to get Lee to agree that Taiwan's president would not deliver a political address while in America. Jiang could then assure conservative hawks that Jiang had the Lee visit to Lee's alma mater, Cornell, under control. Again America assured Jiang. But Lee actually gave a very political address at Cornell.

Jiang then looked so bad to CCP leaders that he was compelled to offer a self-criticism to the leadership. Jiang had seemingly facilitated America's undermining of a one-China policy by allowing Taiwan President Lee into the USA. Jiang then had to compensate for his errors by standing up strongly against the USA. But Jiang, as he saw it, had to do so without threatening China's future access to the world market, China's path to world power status, which required American cooperation. Jiang therefore was compelled to act tough, but not too tough, both toward Taiwan and toward the USA. He considered unleashing anti-American demonstrators against the US Embassy in Beijing to protest America's welcome of Taiwan President Lee in order to enhance Jiang's patriotic credentials and domestic political standing. As with Mao and Deng, Jiang too had no interest in trying to forcefully annex Taiwan.

But, since demonstrators in Beijing, only recently, in 1989, had turned against the CCP dictatorship, Jiang would not risk unleashing demonstrators in 1995 since they too might turn against the party-state. Instead, Jiang approved missile exercises off the coast of Taiwan's two great international ports. But he insisted that the missiles not be armed. Jiang was not looking for a military clash with the USA over Taiwan. No Chinese leader had.

Meanwhile, Jiang wanted to court Taiwan IT firms into China to help guarantee that China would not be locked in to low-value production. The great IT Chinese multinational Alibaba is built on Taiwanese talent trained in Silicon Valley. Jiang also needed to court the US government to allow China's entry into the new WTO so that trade barriers against China would fall so that China could export industrial goods and amass foreign exchange to be used to modernize and grow strong ever more rapidly. Here too Jiang was opposed by Chinese New Leftists who argued, in a most irrational way, that the PRC joining the WTO meant China being subordinated to and enslaved by imperialist American exploitation. In his own calculation, Jiang made the most minimal possible concessions to Chinese hawks on military action against Taiwan in 1995 and 1996 so as to limit damaging American-China relations and to avoid hurting China's rise toward becoming a major world power.

But the Clinton administration responded to the missile exercises Jiang agreed to off the Taiwan coast. China's missile launches had unleashed panic and anxiety in Taiwan and East and South-east Asia. By sending aircraft carrier battle groups to the Taiwan region, Clinton would reassure Taiwanese and others in Asia who were worried by the threat to them of the PRC's modern military force in their region of maritime Asia. They sought and won American reassurance. The Clinton administration pivoted to Asia to deter China. America increased its naval presence in friendly Asian ports, forward positioning military material in Guam, and greatly improving coordination with the Taiwan military.

> In the mid-1990s ... the Clinton administration and allies across Asia grew concerned ... as Chinese power and influence expanded. U.S. balancing efforts ... focused primarily on shoring up relations with key maritime allies and partners ... ensuring that states within the region are not easily intimidated by ... Chinese power.
>
> (Green and Wu 2014: 206)

Like Mao's military action in the Taiwan Strait region in 1958, so too Jiang's missile exercises in 1996 unintentionally unleashed concerns about a Chinese use of military force in the Asia-Pacific, an anxiety that produced reactions which were not helpful to Chinese security. PRC behavior provoked what could be called America's first pivot to Asia out of concern for Chinese military expansionism.

As one Chinese strategic analyst put it, China's maritime neighbors were challenged by "the emergence of China as a leading actor." This China insisted on "securing international space" in the region "for China to become a genuine world power." The CCP goal was "Asia for the Asians," which meant taking "China as the center," not the USA. Given the prior unhappy history of these nations with expansionist Chinese empires, China's neighbors did not recognize the CCP official story of a "long history of close ties." Instead, governments in maritime Asia concluded that they had to hedge against China's expansion. After all, "as a major power, China's rapid development will naturally cause anxiety and suspicion at least on a regional scale" (Ye 2011: 179–183). These regional governments sought an American pivot to Asia by 1996.

The strong American response to the fears of nations in the region about Chinese military expansionism unleashed a security dilemma, forcing Jiang to concede to yet more budget for the Chinese military to counter the enhanced American military presence meant to deter further Chinese military adventurism. Jiang tried to pacify the situation and win American support for China entering the WTO by agreeing to an exchange of visits with Clinton during which Clinton, while in China, would publicly repeat the "3 no's" pledged by Kissinger/Nixon in 1971–1972, a pledge that Washington would not promote *de jure* independence for Taiwan, although understanding that de facto Taiwan was already an independent state. Jiang, not looking for a military clash with America over Taiwan, actually sought to improve Beijing-Washington relations, not intensify tensions over Taiwan. Clinton shared Jiang's policy priority. The two presidents exchanged visits in 1997–1998. But events beyond Jiang's control again strengthened the Chinese hawks.

Taiwan President Lee, fearful that China–American conciliation would lead to collusion against Taiwan, forced Jiang to end Beijing-Taipei talks. Lee, in July 1999, insisted that China–Taiwan relations were "a special kind of state-to-state relation," a seeming step, as understood by ruling groups in the PRC, toward *de jure* independence for Taiwan. Hawks in China then pressed Jiang to do more against Taiwan. They argued in a geo-political way that China could not be a great power unless it incorporated Taiwan and stopped supposedly being suffocated by a so-called First Island Chain in the Western Pacific Ocean that included Taiwan. By 2001, China was insisting that it would have to use military force against Taiwan if Taiwan did not soon negotiate its unification with China. This was as close as China ever came to contemplating using military force against Taiwan. Chinese hawks seemed to hold the initiative on Chinese policy toward Taiwan at the end of the twentieth century. Former ambassador and China specialist, Chas. Freeman (2012), believed the Chinese hawks would win on policy toward Taiwan at that time. He therefore argued that America's choice was to allow China to annex Taiwan or to have to fight a war with China.

And then, suddenly, the seeming Chinese military threat to Taiwan disappeared. In fact, despite the 2000 election of a non-KMT Taiwan president, a member of the opposition party, the DPP, a person who was so deeply identified with Taiwan that he insisted on China recognizing that there were separate political entities on each side of the Taiwan Strait, previously imagined by the CCP as a step toward Taiwan's *de jure* independence, Supreme Leader Jiang and his 2002–2003 successor, Hu Jintao, rather than delivering on prior military threats toward Taiwan, instead welcomed American President George W. Bush interfering in China–Taiwan relations, warning Taiwan's new president, Chen Shui-bian, against provoking China.

Bush demanded that Chen stop talking provocatively about independence. Again, China was not seeking a clash over Taiwan. The PRC instead abandoned its policy of affirming that Taiwan was a domestic issue in which no foreign interference was allowed. CCP ruling groups welcomed American interference in Taiwan, a policy which would help Jiang tamp down hawk pressure for military action against Taiwan. Threats to Taiwan actually ended while the purportedly provocative Chen Shui-bian was president of Taiwan. China–Taiwan economic ties in fact grew substantially during Chen's presidency.

Despite the mainstream view that China–Taiwan relations crashed during the Taiwan-identified Chen Shui-bian presidency, in fact, China, in the Chen years, treated Taiwan in terms of the PRC's post-1998 regional Good Neighbor Policy. China's regional Good Neighbor Policy trumped Chinese hawk views on the island of Taiwan. The larger interest was China's economic rise to become an economic superpower. Taiwan investment in China soared in the Chen era. The PRC conceded that cross-Strait flights need not be considered international or domestic.

That is, China welcomed good relations with Taiwan. The Hu Jintao administration (2002–2012), as with all its predecessors, was not fixated on Taiwan as a traitorous threat that needed to be squashed. No CCP administration ever treated Taiwan as a threat that had to be defeated militarily. In the 1998–2008 era of PRC regional conciliation in the Indo-Pacific region, the CCP was even prepared to look into a peace accord with Taiwan that would be flexible on the interpretation of one-China (Stokes and Tsai 2016: 28–29).

In sum, changes in China's regional or global calculations of its vital interests and not some imagined uniquely patriotic Chinese passions about Taiwan, have driven the CCP's policy toward Taiwan. After 1998 (until 2008), the CCP, in the Indo-Pacific, practiced a Good Neighbor Policy, one of courting neighbors, what some call a charm offensive. The policy was also applied to Taiwan.

Clearly, something had happened inside CCP politics which defused the growing forces favoring war against Taiwan that were rising in 1988. Finding nothing in the literature explaining the defeat of Chinese hawks in the PRC between 1998 and 2001, I will speculate a bit further on this policy change which has so far kept the Chinese hawks contained and brought a continuation of peace in Taiwan–China relations.

With China entering the WTO in 2001, Chinese ruling groups agreed that the PRC could largely use economic means to win their global political objectives. Time was on China's side. The pressing for immediate military action by hawks now seemed self-defeating. The CCP would promote an economic charm offensive to court peoples in Asia, from ASEAN governments to farmers in southern Taiwan, who had seemed the political base of the DPP forces in Taiwan, the Taiwanese most committed to a politics in harmony with their Taiwan identity. CCP ruling groups had confidence that a world power of China's economic magnanimity could persuade Taiwan and other neighbors to subordinate themselves to the international interests of a beneficent China. It was best to win a "war" without having to fight a battle, as an old Chinese adage held.

In addition, as the Chinese economy went global around 2000, the Chinese military also went global. Budget for the military suddenly was not about stopping the US military from keeping China's military from annexing Taiwan. China's military was now needed to protect the Sea Lanes of Communication (SLOCs) carrying oil from the petro-states in the Middle East to keep the fast-growing Chinese economy going. China's focus was ever more global, ever less Taiwan. The PRC sought to build a blue-water navy. The island of Taiwan did not seem central to China's goals of predominance in East and South-east Asia and matching the American military in the Indo-Pacific. Taiwan was small, isolated, and nonthreatening and ever more dependent on the Chinese economy. Why would the CCP allow a marginalized Taiwan, no bigger or richer than the PRC's Fujian Province, to detract China, a world power which was central to international politics, from policies promoting China's rise to become a global power center? Chinese self-confidence soared.

By 2008, CCP ruling groups concluded that China's rise to global centrality was unstoppable. The PRC was certain to become the world's largest economy. This consensus on China's glorious future negated the hawk contention that time was not on China's side and that therefore it was in China's interest to act militarily to annex Taiwan, the sooner, the better, whatever the risks of war with America. Given the CCP's vision of China as a global force, the island of Taiwan, in 2008, the end of the era of Taiwan-identified President Chen, as throughout PRC history, has never much mattered in CCP politics.

Since the founding of the PRC, when General Su Yu was given the task of invading Taiwan in 1949, the CCP goal was not to recapture Taiwan as sacred Chinese land lost to the Meiji empire by the Qing empire in 1895. The goal in 1949–1950 was to win a civil war which the CCP imagined as a revolutionary struggle. The goal of so-called revolutionaries was to defeat the supposedly counter-revolutionary forces led by Chiang Kai-shek whose reactionary regime supposedly was already collapsing. Taiwan was not sacred Chinese territory for Mao's generation of CCP leaders who came of age in an era when the Japanese colony of Taiwan was not imagined by Chinese patriots as a sacred nationalist cause. The CCP target of Mao's revolutionaries was the reactionary Chinese, not Taiwan. By the twenty-first century, once again, CCP ambitions did not make Taiwan a high priority target. The 1988–2001 rise of forces in the CCP seeking military action against Taiwan had been, at least temporarily, contained.

Confident Chinese in state and society are sure that time is on China's side. The leadership of Supreme Leader Xi does not accept the notion that people who live in Taiwan deeply identify with Taiwanese-ness. The CCP position rather is that the ruling authorities on Taiwan have had the wherewithal to socialize Taiwanese to a Taiwanese identity. Once Taiwan has returned to being part of China, a Chinese government will succeed in socializing Taiwanese to identify as Han Chinese, since, to the Han CCP, Taiwanese share Chinese blood, whatever that racialist notion signifies. That Taiwanization actually intensified during the 2008–2016 presidency of the Chinese KMT's Ma Ying-jeou, who was opposed to de-Sinification, does not impress CCP ruling groups. Yet it is significant that Taiwanese became more Taiwanese even in the era of a KMT president promoting Sinification. Nonetheless, CCP leaders still believe in the power of the CCP to Sinicize anyone with so-called Chinese blood.

Chinese analysts I have talked to about Taiwan agree with their CCP rulers. They find Taiwan more culturally Chinese than the PRC. Saved from the Mao-era policies of annihilating so-called feudal culture in China, Taiwan was not de-Sinified. Chinese visitors in Taiwan tend to see the difference of the PRC with Taiwan as purely political. Receiving a warm reception from Taiwanese who evince no anti-China sentiments, the Chinese expect Taiwan to want to be part of their motherland, once China fixes its political system. Given China's rise toward dominating the Asia-Pacific and given a feeling that, at some point, the corrupt system of crony capitalist vested interests in the PRC will end, because otherwise China will stagnate or decline, many urban educated Chinese believe that time is on China's side, that inevitably, peacefully, Taiwan will become part of a politically reformed China. War against Taiwan is not needed to make Taiwan part of China. There is no popular cry in China for war with Taiwan. War could even create unnecessary impediments to China's rise to global centrality and glory.

Prospects

None of this is to suggest that Taiwan's democratic autonomy is secure. All this chapter establishes is that it is erroneous to assume: (1) that the CCP, since June 1950, has prioritized using force to incorporate the Republic of China on Taiwan into the PRC; or that (2) CCP leadership legitimacy depends on annexing Taiwan by force to achieve the goal of unifying China in order for the CCP to remain in good standing with patriots and therefore hold on to power.

In addition, the issue of ending Taiwan's political autonomy through military means seems a far less likely CCP policy choice in the twenty-first century than most observers have claimed since the founding of the PRC in 1949. According to Tsinghua University's international relations specialist Yan Xuetong, who, as a child of the 1958–1981 CCP propaganda about China's need to "liberate" Taiwan, used to urge the CCP to employ military means to annex Taiwan, it is now obvious that "there would be a danger of war between China and the US if China were to unite with Taiwan through military force" (Yan 2016: 19). From the days of Mao as supreme leader on, no Chinese leader has sought war with America. But that could change.

This chapter does not claim to know the future of China's policy toward an autonomous, democratic Taiwan, which is situated at the northern end of the South China Sea and the southern end of the East China Sea. Since 2013, PRC Supreme Leader Xi has been pursuing a policy of using China's economic clout to achieve the CCP's international goals. The PRC has succeeded in keeping most countries from agreeing to mutually beneficial economic deals with Taiwan, so-called Free or Preferential Trade Agreements. Less able to compete in South-east Asia because of CCP pressure on the nations of the Indo-Pacific,

Taiwan's economy has weakened. It has become more economically dependent on China, a dependency which has intensified inequality and societal contradictions within Taiwan. China is also making itself ever less dependent on Taiwanese IT. Taiwan President Tsai is aware of all of this and promises to address Taiwan's economic problems which have, to a not insignificant degree, been created or deepened by China. This will not be easy for President Tsai. Taiwan's international economic room for maneuver is seriously constrained by China.

The future of Taiwan's autonomous democracy is far from secure and the imperative of Taiwanese foreign policy must be state survival. Nothing short of a political deal between Taipei and Beijing can win a safe future for democratic autonomy on Taiwan. Chinese ruling groups expect to be able, however, to use China's economic leverage to achieve China's political goals and expect their comprehensive national power to grow so that Taiwan will inevitably surrender the one national interest that, in fact, Taiwan cannot surrender: Taiwanese self-rule. This is the insoluble contradiction in PRC policy to Taiwan. So far, the Chinese solution to this conundrum of demanding from Taiwan the one thing that no government of Taiwan can concede has been to define or re-define Chinese interests so that incorporating an autonomous Taiwan into China is a lesser priority for the PRC. Indeed, it long has been this way. None of this, however, is an absolute guarantee of a peaceful future in an era in which the CCP imagines itself as becoming the dominant power in maritime Asia, given Taiwan's location at the heart of maritime Asia.

What then will be the impact of the PRC pushing ahead on an agenda of regional hegemony? An opponent of strong responses to China's ever more militarily assertive rise, Alastair Iain Johnston (2013), nonetheless, found that "in 2009 and 2010 China's military and paramilitary presence in the South China Sea was more active." The CCP regime's "diplomatic rhetoric and practice … shift[ed] fairly sharply in a more hard-line direction." The regime began "to assert the extent of China's [territorial] claims." Changes in the balance of forces in Chinese politics made it impossible for PRC diplomats to appear "too soft on territorial issues." In the CCP's reconfigured political space, "PLA hard-liners were able to take more initiatives." There was more space for "nationalistic and militaristic voices." Beijing acted "with repeated and increasingly tough demands." Its "language became tougher, escalating …" New thinking on alternatives to war for China was ever more constrained.

In particular, according to another opponent of strong responses to deter further PRC expansionism, Michael Swaine, "China's current efforts to challenge directly Japan's long-standing administrative authority over the [Senkaku] islands through a fairly regular pattern of incursions" (2013: 12), backed by a chauvinistic "intensity of elite and public emotions," "significantly increase the likelihood of a serious crisis occurring, and perhaps escalating out of control …" China has been acting in an "inflammatory," "reckless and irresponsible" way, taking an "assertive, self-righteous and absolutist stance" (ibid.: 16).

All around Asia, from India to Japan, "apprehensive neighbors" of the PRC are confronted by an expansionary China which has large territorial ambitions.

According to Freeman (2012: 14), "for China, the [territorial] claims of others awaken angry memories [*sic*] of Chinese impotence ..." As a result, it may be difficult, as Susan Shirk has suggested in her (2008) book, *China: Fragile Superpower*, for ruling groups in Beijing, super-patriots all, to forever reject the policy proposals of Chinese hawks to seize what, in their recently imagined construction of Chinese history, which made even Genghis Khan Chinese, should always have been Chinese. Accordingly, to Freeman (2012: 15), "Armed clashes between China and any of these countries could pull America into the conflict." Indeed they "could well provoke China to cross the nuclear threshold into nuclear war" (ibid.: 16). The continuing militarization of CCP ambitions is creating war dangers. The problem of war sits inside PRC politics and could reach outside to Taiwan as elsewhere in the Indo-Pacific.

Indeed, if left chauvinists in China continue to grow in power in the CCP ruling coalition, they could make Taiwan a pretext for military action, but not because Taiwan under the leadership of President Tsai did anything provocative. Tsai continues to try to mollify the CCP state, for example, by declaring that Taiwan–China trade is not international trade. The question of war or peace, however, will be answered in Chinese politics, not Taiwanese. Taiwan is a democracy, after all. And it is a high priority for the authoritarian CCP to make the world safe for the ever more repressive, cruel Chinese dictatorship.

This is most obvious in China–North Korea relations. Since the CCP wishes its PRC to be the dominant military power and the only nuclear power in northeast Asia, it is irate at North Korea for its policy of going nuclear and building missiles capable of carrying nuclear weapons against Japan or America, since such policies make it more likely that other governments in the region, most importantly, Japan, might some day, for their own security, decide to go nuclear. Japan and South Korea now both welcome American missiles which can shoot down Chinese or North Korean missiles. The CCP will support forces opposed to missiles and nuclear weapons in Japan and South Korea.

A nightmare scenario for the CCP, one which trumps Chinese concerns about the regional consequences of North Korean WMD, is the Pyongyang regime collapsing, and then becoming part of a united Korea, which is both democratic and a military ally of the USA. The CCP does not wish to be even somewhat encircled by anything close to a ring of democracies from Myanmar to Mongolia. If Chinese rulers imagine such an outcome as threatening to the dictatorship of the CCP (not to the PRC), those hard-line Chinese chauvinists could then imagine a democratic Taiwan as part of this purportedly subversive encirclement of China by Asian democracies, from Abe's Japan to Modi's India. Taiwan would have done nothing provocative. But Taiwan could still become imagined among hawkish, somewhat paranoid Chinese ruling groups as an ultimate enemy. China–Korea relations can impact the larger region.

In this perspective, President Tsai's seeking to become less dependent on the PRC and seeking deeper economic ties with other nations in Asia as part of an attempt to balance against Chinese domination, could also lead Chinese hawk chauvinists to feel isolated, encircled, and endangered. The threat to peace in the

Western Pacific lies in the strength, worldview, and interests of war-prone forces among Chinese ruling groups. Taiwan, however peaceful, is not in full control of its destiny.

Chinese military hard-liners have been promoting PRC expansionism. They wish to see a Great Power China incorporating ever more territory from imagined threats to that territory or to grab opportunities to make China great globally or themselves more powerful and significant. As with the December 2008 CCP switch to hard-line assertiveness by the administration of Supreme Leader Hu Jintao, events outside of China (e.g. the 2008 US financial crash) and Chinese patriots outraged by global human rights supporters treating Tibetan rioters. who burned Chinese to death as somehow victims of a purportedly guilty China, could combine with an ever weightier hawkish force in the CCP to push more PRC military assertiveness. The threat of war in the Taiwan Strait region does not lie on the Taiwanese side of the Strait. Chinese nationalism may becoming more war-prone.

A CCP leadership which has presided over rapid economic growth and the accumulation of advanced offensive weaponry can persuade itself that the United States has no right to come to the defense of governments in the Indo-Pacific which will not surrender and submit to CCP territorial expansion and regional dominance, imagined by CCP ruling groups as China's natural and historical position in the world, no matter how much its neighbors resist subordination to China. Hawk chauvinists in the PRC can grow more powerful and seem more persuasive among ruling groups. As Steve Chan (2015: 8–9) puts it:

> If there is a Sino-American confrontation over Taiwan [initiated by the PRC], it is not because Beijing wants to challenge Washington ... but rather because [Beijing] has failed to persuade the latter to stay out of what it [Beijing] perceives to be its internal affairs, something now defined as China's regional dominance.

For the aggressive forces within the CCP, Chinese leaders who imagine an expansionist and militarist China as somehow defensive and a victim, America would be to blame for China invading Taiwan since Taiwan should have surrendered its autonomy when China "rightfully" insisted on peaceful unification. Indeed, the CCP expects all of China's neighbors to respect China's interests by accommodating China's territorial demands.

Domestic political changes in the PRC therefore are more powerful in deciding CCP policy to Taiwan than the long historical record of China since Mao rejecting war over Taiwan which this chapter recounts. History is not destiny. Politics is a most contingent arena. There is no way to accurately forecast the political future.

China's claim to Taiwan may turn out to be central to the CCP's effort to change the legitimizing norms of international society, which at present includes rigid borders. The move of legitimate territory from vague and mutable frontiers, in an age of empire where might is right, to a system of nation states with strong boundaries opposes CCP ambitions, imagined as a return of China to imperial glory. The CCP presents China as the benign center of a global hierarchy. The huge territories conquered by the Manchu imperial Aisingioro lineage of the Manchu Qing Khanate, whose military went far beyond the reaches of a Sinified Ming China, are regularly treated by the CCP as the boundaries of the PRC.

This means that the Aisingioro's early incorporation of south Tibet holds precedence for Beijing over India's Arunachal Pradesh controlled by the Indian government, despite the fact that that province is a normal participator in the constitutional system of India. There is also a future question of Mongolia's independence and one of Russian territory once controlled by the Qing, as was Mongolia – and Taiwan, also conquered by the Buddhist Manchu military empire. Imagining temporary Qing military power in East Asia as if it were eternally integral to China's natural and global centrality – a myth, not a fact – is a threat to the peace in maritime Asia and the Indo-Pacific region which includes Taiwan. A new blood nationalism has been constructed in China which imagines all Manchu conquests as incorporating communities which are supposedly blood Chinese since ancient times. This narrative construction which legitimates Chinese expansionism potentially includes the Taiwanese.

China, contesting the legitimacy of a Westphalian international system of nation states with fixed borders, in the minds of many CCP leaders, is China contesting an anti-China Western construction which unfairly contains China. Supreme Leader Xi Jinping imagines a glorious return to a China-centered world, something similar to an idealized version of the ancient tributary system, imagined in a Chinese nationalistic fantasy as having been peaceful, and mutually beneficial for ages. This China-centered hierarchy would compel its Indo-Pacific neighbors and others in Asia to accept the CCP's extraordinarily expansive and racist notion of what is Chinese. Many politically informed people in Mongolia and Russia fear that the CCP notion of Chinese territorial borders is far from settled. As China's power grows, these people fear the consequences of new, maximalist Chinese ambitions. The appetite of an ever heftier China would grow with the eating. In short, the history presented in this chapter of China's lesser interest in Taiwan is not the official story which will inform future PRC decisions on policy toward Taiwan. Historical facts are weak reeds again the typhoon-like force of chauvinist mythology which seems a useful instrument to ruling groups.

While contestation continues over CCP claims to Mongolia, Russia, Arunachal Pradesh, Taiwan, and maritime Asia, none of us knows for sure how these issues will play out in the future of CCP politics. But it is certainly obvious that there are ever more powerful forces inside the CCP state which are maximalists on territory and on racist amalgamation and on making the world safe for Chinese authoritarianism. These forces are not sources of peace. These ruling groups and their post-Mao political agenda could destabilize the Indo-Pacific or, instead, lose out in their expansionist struggle to get the nations of the region to accept a maximalist version of Chinese history and its territorial claims as new international legitimating norms. Imperial over-reach could destabilize the

Chinese regime itself. Or risk-adverse CCP leaders could abjure the maximalist agenda and continue to take economic cooperation with America as needed for China's continuing rise. This chapter does not forecast an inevitable worst case outcome.

The future is open. It is also unpredictable. Global ruptures could have large and unforeseeable impacts.

What this chapter merely finds is that the history of PRC foreign policy has so far often been dominated by the risk-adverse attitudes, especially with regard to Taiwan. Therefore, China–Taiwan relations have been peaceful. But this risk aversion is centered on a domestic politics of an unsettled but powerful Chinese nationalism in which ruling groups, albeit often minimalist in behavior, for the most part, never abandoned, for the domestic audience, a maximalist possibility. The post-Mao rise of a nationalism tied to an expansionist and racist construction of Chinese history rather than to leading world communism to a "city on the hill" true communism, as promoted by Mao, has strengthened the persuasive force of the arguments of territorial maximalists inside PRC ruling groups. This means that the possibility of the PRC using force to incorporate an autonomous, democratic island of Taiwan into an authoritarian Chinese neo-empire may yet win out. The CCP's constructed version of Qing Dynasty history in particular and Chinese imperial history in general are being used as a basis for legitimizing the PRC's maximalist territorial claims and global ambition (Zhang 2015) The CCP is committed to expanding the territory it controls no matter what the peace-oriented and stability-oriented Taiwan President Tsai does.

But, of course, since the targeted states in the Indo-Pacific accept a notion of settled borders which rejects the CCP's expansionist and neo-imperial notion of territorial legitimacy, the future remains wide open to the foreign policy consequences of the vicissitudes of domestic politics in the CCP state. This is true for CCP views of Taiwan, as well as Korea, Mongolia, Russia, Japan, maritime Asia, and India. Chinese policy toward Taiwan will, in no small part, be a consequence of domestic political forces in the CCP and of the international ambitions of the CCP and of responses of the independent nations of the Indo-Pacific to those large, territorial Chinese ambitions.

The policies of Taiwan's President Tsai will not much impact these CCP territorial ambitions. But Taiwan's future will be greatly influenced by CCP territorial claims in maritime Asia which, ironically for the ROC on Taiwan, echo the expansionist and racist pre-1949 ROC/KMT construction of Chinese history and of Chinese blood nationalism. Chinese ambitions do not leave much room for maneuver by Taiwan's peace-oriented and stability-oriented President Tsai Ing-wen. The question of war and peace is not about a stability-oriented, pragmatic President Tsai focused on solving Taiwan's domestic problems, but about China's Supreme Leader and the nationalism and politics of the war-prone political forces within the Han CCP state.

References

Chan, S. (2015). On States, Status-Quo and Revisionist Dispositions, *Issues and Studies* 51(3).

Cheng, J. Y. (2015). *Japan's China Policy*. Singapore: World Scientific Pub. Co.

Christensen, T. (1996). *Useful Adversaries*. Princeton, NJ: Princeton University Press.

Freeman, C. J. (2012). *Interesting Times: China, America and the Shifting Balance of Prestige*. Charlottesville, VA: Just World Books.

Green, M. and Wu, X. (2014). Regional Security Roles and Challenges, in Hachigin, N. (ed.), *Debating China.* New York: Oxford University Press, pp. 198–221.

Johnston, A. A. (2013). How New and Assertive Is China's New Assertiveness? *International Security* 37(4): 7–48.

Ning, L. (1997). *The Dynamics of Foreign Policy-Making in China*. Boulder, COL Westview Press.

Stokes, M. and Tsai, S. (2016). *The United States and Future Policy Options in the Taiwan Strait*. Arlington, VA: Project 2049 Institute.

Shen, Z. (2012). *Mao, Stalin and the Korean War.* New York: Routledge.

Shen, Z. and Dahhui, L. (2011). *After Leaning to One Side: China and Its Allies in the Cold War*. Washington, DC: Woodrow Wilson Center Press.

Shirk, S. (2008). *China: Fragile Superpower*. New York: Oxford University Press.

Swaine, M. (2013). China's Views Regarding the Senkaku/Diaoyu Island Dispute, *China Leadership Monitor* 41.

Yan, X. (2016). Political Leadership and Power Redistribution, *China Journal of International Politics* 9(1): 1–26.

Ye, Z. (2011). *Inside China's Grand Strategy*. Lexington, KT: University of Kentucky Press.

Zhang, X. (2015). China and the Struggle for Legitimacy of a Rising Power, *Chinese Journal of International Politics* 8(3): 301–332.

8 Has China's Taiwan policy failed? And if so, what next?

Shelley Rigger

Taiwan's 2016 elections brought bad news for Beijing's Taiwan policy makers. They were prepared for a DPP victory in the presidential race – that was predicted a year in advance. But the extent of the DPP's success in the legislative elections surprised everyone, as did the KMT's implosion. These results could hardly have been more unwelcome in Beijing, and the fact that the PRC's Taiwan policy experts failed to anticipate them only makes the outcome worse. It is hard, in the face of these events, not to wonder: has China's Taiwan policy failed? If China's Taiwan policy is to make sure the KMT wins elections, it has failed. But if the policy is to prevent Taiwan from declaring independence, it clearly has not failed. Our first task, then, is to define the PRC's Taiwan policy. Only then can we grapple with the question of its success or failure. All too often, analyses of cross-Strait relations fail to differentiate among China's goals, policy, strategy, and tactics. Even if we disentangle these dimensions, it is difficult to draw firm conclusions, but I argue China's policy has not failed, yet. The strategies and tactics through which it is implementing that policy are failing in one sense – they are not advancing China's ultimate (sufficient) policy objective of unification – but they are succeeding in another – they are advancing an important interim (necessary) goal, which is to deter moves toward formal independence.

Goal: territorial integrity

The policy toward Taiwan that has been adopted by the decision-making apparatus and personnel of the People's Republic of China is animated by what appears, on the surface, to be a straightforward objective: unification[1] of the Chinese nation. If we scratch the surface, however, we find that this goal is not as clear as we might think. One source of confusion is the difficulty of defining what is meant by "China" – in the PRC, in Taiwan, and in the rest of the world. The absence of a shared understanding of what constitutes "China" was the key driver of conflict in the Taiwan Strait for many decades. Even today, when the once-dominant discourse of Taiwan as the (temporary) refuge of the Republic of China has virtually disappeared, the question of Taiwan's relationship to a cultural or civilizational China is still being debated in Taiwan. Nor is the problem of defining "China" limited to Taiwan. Even within the PRC, the parameters of the "China" that needs to be unified are disputed. The 1993 *White Paper on the Taiwan Question and the Reunification of China* opens with a section entitled "Taiwan – an inalienable part of China" which states, "Taiwan has belonged to China since ancient times." This claim to antiquity is offered in defense of other territorial claims as well (some of which – such as "outer" Mongolia – have been abandoned), yet the implication that there is an uncomplicated, linear record of continuous "Chinese" possession of Taiwan is impossible to substantiate. Indeed, even the Chinese heartland cannot be said to have an uncomplicated, linear record of "Chinese" possession. What it means for Taiwan to be part of "China" rests on an understanding of "China" that is neither fixed, universal, nor uncontested.

If the definition of "China" is ambiguous, the concept of "unification" is even more so. Mountains of paper and barrels of ink have been devoted to debating this topic. At the moment, many conversations center on the question of whether "unification" means that Taiwan must be absorbed into the PRC, or that the two sides – Taiwan and the mainland – might merge into a new entity that is not embodied by any currently existing state. Nearly all Taiwanese oppose absorption into the PRC, but there are some who are willing to consider the second option. PRC officials occasionally have played with ideas that lean in the direction of a merger-of-equals, but they have rejected concrete proposals and formulas along those lines, including the European Union model and various forms of commonwealth and confederation.[2] They also have so far proved unable to communicate a sincere willingness to treat Taiwan as an equal, preferring, instead, familial metaphors and historical narratives that inevitably place Taiwan in a hierarchical relationship below the PRC.

Although it is impossible to say exactly what "unification of China" really means, the statements of PRC leaders, especially those directed to domestic audiences, suggest that their ultimate goal – their most preferred outcome – is for Taiwan to be incorporated into the PRC. Indeed, it is that version of the goal that is reflected most clearly in their stated policy. That said, however, PRC leaders also have a secondary, or interim goal: preventing Taiwan from becoming permanently separated from the mainland, either in the form of an independent Taiwan or in the guise of an alternative Chinese state existing in parallel to their own. Beijing has made preserving the possibility of unification a *sine qua non* for peace and progress in the Taiwan Strait. To sustain this possibility, Taiwan does not have to assert clearly and unequivocally that Taiwan *is* part of the same sovereign entity as the PRC, but it must not say clearly and unequivocally that it *is not* part of that entity.

Taiwan independence and "two Chinas" are unacceptable to the PRC for two reasons. First, both of these outcomes contradict the Chinese Communist Party's narrative that only one sovereign Chinese state *currently exists*, and Taiwan is part of that sovereign state. The existence of a state-like entity on Taiwan is a manageable, albeit highly inconvenient, threat to this narrative, but actually recognizing a state in Taiwan – whether Taiwanese or Chinese – would destroy the narrative completely. Second, even though there is no logical reason that an independent Taiwan or a "second China" could not, at some point, choose to unify with the mainland, the PRC government has convinced itself that the establishment of a separate sovereign state in Taiwan would permanently foreclose the possibility of unification. For that reason, preventing Taiwan from achieving independent sovereignty under any name (including "Republic of China") is a necessary, although not sufficient, condition for the PRC to achieve its goals in the Strait.

Policy: peaceful unification

Since its founding in 1921, the Chinese Communist Party has had three distinct declarative policies toward Taiwan and its residents. During the war against Japan, the CCP took the position that Taiwan was an external territory under Japanese occupation, equivalent to Korea, which should become an independent state after the defeat of the Japanese empire (Snow 1961 [1938]). As late as 1941, Zhou Enlai described the Taiwanese resistance to Japanese colonial rule as an "independence" movement, and in 1945 the CCP included "the Taiwanese" in a list of peoples whose national independence struggles it supported (Yang 1992). It was only after the ROC government relocated to the island in 1949, extending the civil war between the KMT and CCP to Taiwan, that the PRC abandoned this hands-off approach in favor of a new policy: liberation – if necessary, by force. That was its second Taiwan policy. The third declarative policy emerged gradually in the twilight years of the Mao era. Achieving rapprochement with the United States necessitated a less bellicose approach to Taiwan, so over the course of the 1970s, the language of "liberation" in CCP statements gave way to a new emphasis on "unification."

In 1979, China formally adopted a policy of "peaceful unification." During this same period, Beijing presented Taiwan with a series of unification proposals that emphasized continued autonomy for the island. Those proposals were ultimately bundled into a doctrine – one country, two systems – that was designed to serve as the institutional basis for the peaceful unification of Hong Kong and Macao as well as Taiwan. Deng Xiaoping first mentioned this formula to foreign guests in 1982, and in 1983 he explained to an American academic how one country, two systems would apply to Taiwan:

> After the reunification of the motherland, the Taiwan Special Administrative Region can have its own independence, practice a system different from that of the mainland, and its independent judiciary and right of final judgment need not reside in Beijing. Taiwan can retain its army so long as it does not constitute a threat to the mainland. The mainland will station neither troops nor administrative personnel in Taiwan. Taiwan's party, government and army departments are managed by Taiwan itself. The central government will reserve some seats for Taiwan.… The systems can be different, but only the People's Republic of China can represent China in international affairs.
>
> (Quoted in Wen 1984: n.p.)

In 1993, the PRC government published a White Paper entitled *The Taiwan Question and the Reunification of China* in which it detailed its Taiwan policy. According to the document, the "basic contents" of China's Taiwan policy are the One-China Principle ("There is only one China in the world, Taiwan is an inalienable part of China and the seat of China's central government is in Beijing.... 'Self-determination' of Taiwan is out of the question"), the coexistence of two systems ("socialism on the mainland and capitalism on Taiwan"), the promise of a high degree of autonomy for Taiwan after unification, and peace negotiations. The document also makes it clear that while attainment of its ultimate goal might rest on negotiations and peaceful measures, preventing the creation of a separate sovereignty for Taiwan is a non-negotiable feature: "Peaceful reunification is a set policy of the Chinese Government. However, any sovereign state is entitled to use any means it deems necessary, including military ones, to uphold its sovereignty and territorial integrity."

Another White Paper published in 2000 (*The One-China Principle and the Taiwan Issue*) reiterates many of these same themes:

> The One-China Principle is the foundation stone for the Chinese government's policy on Taiwan. On Comrade Deng Xiaoping's initiative, the Chinese government has, since 1979, adopted the policy of peaceful reunification and gradually evolved the scientific concept of "one country, two systems." On this basis, China established the basic principle of "peaceful reunification, and one country, two systems." The key points of this basic principle and the relevant policies are China will do its best to achieve peaceful reunification, but will not commit itself to ruling out the use of force; will actively promote people-to-people contacts and economic and cultural exchanges between the two sides of the Taiwan Straits, and start direct trade, postal, air and shipping services as soon as possible; achieve reunification through peaceful negotiations and, on the premise of the One-China Principle, any matter can be negotiated.

While the wording and emphasis differ across these two documents, the fundamentals of the policy are consistent, and they have not changed in the years since the second White Paper was published: China has a policy of peaceful unification under the "one country, two systems" formula, while reserving the option to use force to defend its claim that Taiwan does not and cannot possess sovereignty separate from the PRC.

Has this policy failed? It clearly has not succeeded, because China has not achieved its goal of unification under the one country, two systems model. But the policy has not exactly failed, either, for at least three reasons:

- Peaceful unification, as it is defined in China's policy documents, is not an end state, but a process. So long as the activities that constitute that process are underway, the policy cannot be said to have failed. Because those activities are continuing, the policy is ongoing today.

- Taiwan has made no progress toward the establishment of an independent sovereignty recognized by other nation-states. Based on the objective (de facto) situation in the Taiwan Strait – the existence of two separate state apparatuses which govern their respective territories without mutual inter-ference – it would seem that China's policy has not succeeded. But if we consider the discursive and legal (*de jure*) context China has fostered since the 1970s – a context which is accepted by all major countries in the world, and within which Taiwan conducts most of its external affairs – it is evident that China's Taiwan policy is succeeding. Taiwan participates in inter-national affairs at Beijing's pleasure; the PRC can, if it wishes, deny Taiwan access to every manifestation of international personhood to which it might aspire. Beijing's relentless policing of the language used in international communications has expunged "Taiwan" – both the word and the entity – from international documents, meetings, and organizations. In this discur-sive context, there is only one China, and Taiwan is defined within it, which constitutes a major success for Beijing's policy.
- Beijing has compelled Taiwan's leaders to back away from the pursuit of juridical independence. In the 1990s, President Lee Teng-hui asserted that Taiwan and China were two states that enjoyed a special relationship. In the early 2000s, President Chen Shui-bian observed that there were two states in the Strait, one on either side. Compared to these leaders, Taiwan's current president, Tsai Ing-wen, and her immediate predecessor Ma Ying-jeou have been far more cautious. In her inaugural address in May 2016, Tsai made reference to a 1992 law, the Act Governing Relations between the People of Taiwan Area and the Mainland Area. That law strongly affirms the ROC's identity as a Chinese entity with trans-Taiwan Strait claims. It is hard to avoid the conclusion that Tsai's decision to introduce this law at such a sensitive moment was aimed at reassuring Beijing that she will not pursue formal independence.

In sum, the PRC has succeeded in achieving its minimal goal – blocking Taiwan independence, and its "peaceful unification" process is still in operation, so its policy has not failed. However, progress toward its ultimate goal is not evident, so its policy hasn't succeeded, either. And that brings us to the question of strategy.

Strategy: peaceful development

In a 2016 article in the *Journal of Contemporary China*, Shanghai-based Taiwan specialist Lin Gang analyzes China's strategy toward Taiwan, the logic under-lying it, and its likely evolution in the near future. He writes, "Beijing's strategy of peaceful development of cross-Strait relations, first proposed in May 2004 and further endorsed by the party's national congresses in 2007 and 2012, aims to achieve its long-term goal of peaceful unification with Taiwan" (Lin 2016: 323). Although peaceful development was first proposed during the Chen Shui-bian administration, it was fully implemented only after Ma Ying-jeou assumed office. Ma's acceptance of the 1992 Consensus was sufficient, from Beijing's perspective, to bring Taiwan into minimal compliance with the prerequisite for this strategy, i.e., doing something Beijing can interpret as accepting the one-China principle.

As with most aspects of cross-Strait relations, "peaceful development" is subject to multiple interpretations. As Lin explains, Beijing understands the phrase to mean the peaceful development *of cross-Strait relations*, in the service of unification. Taipei, by contrast, "highlights peace *and* development of the *two sides* … while putting aside the issue of national unification" (ibid.: 323, emphasis original). Beijing pretends not to notice this difference so long as Taiwan is operating under the one-China principle, a condition China's leaders have decided is met by Ma's endorsement of the 1992 Consensus.

Lin's discussion of the peaceful development strategy emphasizes the friendly gestures Beijing made during the Ma era: opening direct transport links, inking economic agreements, approving tourist visits, even allowing contact between officials of the two governments. He reveals Beijing's ultimate hope at the beginning of Ma's presidency: that the two sides might sign a peace agreement during Ma's presidency. With the 1992 Consensus guaranteeing a *de jure* one China, Lin writes, "[China] is not eager to push for an instant unification by force against the free will of the majority of the Taiwanese people." Instead, it was on the lookout for opportunities to improve relations between the two sides (ibid.: 324).

Although Lin stresses the positive dimension of Beijing's strategy, he acknowledges that there is a negative side as well. Blocking moves toward independence continues to be a central task for Beijing's policy-makers. In fact, Lin's paper suggests the parameters of what is acceptable to Beijing may have diminished when he says the peaceful development strategy can continue, "as long as Taiwan does not declare independence *or openly challenge the one-China principle*, making it impossible for Beijing to reach its political goals someday …" (ibid.: 327, emphasis added). Lin further highlights China's two-sided approach when he writes, "This soft strategy, however, is intertwined with hard tactics of the anti-secession law" (ibid.: 323). The Anti-Secession Law (ASL) is, indeed, a tactic, but the decision to store sticks as well as carrots in its arsenal is part of Beijing's peaceful development strategy.

As Lin explains, the peaceful development strategy uses a wide variety of incentives and inducements to persuade Taiwan to enter into higher levels of engagement, ultimately leading to negotiations on the central question of unification. It includes some creative elements, including a promise to "pragmatically explore with Taiwan the nature of their political relations under the special circumstance prior to China's reunification," a formulation that comes closer than any other to acknowledging a separate status for Taiwan and implying that a new characterization of the nature of their relationship might be possible (ibid.: 324).

Lin makes no ruling on the success of the peaceful development strategy, but he does express disappointment at the progress made during the Ma administration. He says Beijing expected to reach a peace agreement during Ma's first term (some mainland commentators were so optimistic, Lin reports, that they recommended making the agreement "clearly oriented to unification"), but that was not to be (ibid.: 324). Nor did the economic agreements reached between the two sides glide smoothly through to implementation. Indeed, nothing was as easy as Beijing had hoped. Now, as Lin points out, the low-hanging fruits have been harvested, and the two sides are moving into "deep water" (ibid.: 324). The task in this deep-water phase is to address what Lin calls the "structural problem" in cross-Strait relations: the sovereignty issue. The fundamental problem at this end of the pool is the absence of a mutually acceptable formula to describe the relationship between the two sides – a necessary foundation for unification talks.

The Ma Ying-jeou administration made addressing the sovereignty issue slightly easier when he agreed to wear the fig leaf of the 1992 Consensus, but Tsai has so far refused to don that garment.[3] Based on Tsai's statements, including her inaugural address, the farthest her administration is likely to go is to affirm the status quo of Taiwan as ROC, complete with a one-China constitution and laws. On the one hand, this is far better than what might have happened, but it still falls far short of what Beijing has said it is willing to accept, because Beijing has declared two Chinas (one PRC, one ROC) just as much anathema as one China, one Taiwan.

Even if Taiwan were willing to go farther, however, it is hard to see how Beijing could find a formula acceptable *to itself* that would allow Taiwan to be represented in political negotiations. Says Lin:

> While mainland scholars are divided on whether Taiwan's authorities should be addressed as a political entity with separated governance or simply a regional government equivalent to mainland government under the same roof of *de jure* one China, they all agree that the two sides share the same sovereignty and territory of China.
>
> (Ibid.: 326)

But make no mistake: this does *not* mean Taiwan can call itself the ROC, because, Lin continues,

> It is inconceivable for the mainland to recognize the legitimacy of the Republic of China, as the latter is clearly related with the idea of statehood. Neither can the mainland accept the idea of two brother states (*xiongdi zhibang*) proposed by supporters of the DPP....
>
> (Ibid.: 326)

Evidently, the PRC is willing to talk to Taiwan only as a Chinese-identified, non-state entity seeking unification with an existing Chinese state (the PRC) – a set of requirements that constitute unconditional surrender from the Taiwanese (or ROC) point of view. Most Taiwanese have no desire to pursue unification; they are willing to talk about it in a desultory way in order to avoid worse outcomes. In a negotiating process it is customary to impose conditions in exchange for something one's partner desires, but Beijing's determination to impose such conditions in exchange for something its negotiating partner *doesn't want* is very hard to understand. Here again, Beijing's strategy is working in one sense – the availability of carrots and the threat of sticks increase Taiwanese citizens' and leaders' willingness to accommodate the PRC's bottom line (no independence) – but is failing in another sense, in that neither carrots nor sticks do much to advance the cause of unification.

Beijing's peaceful development strategy is based on the logic that, with the threat of force holding back independence, the Taiwanese will come to appreciate the benefits of unification and will be willing to engage in negotiations toward that goal. The problem with this logic is that it overestimates the attractiveness of unification, and it fails to offer a coherent notion of what it is the PRC is actually asking Taiwan to do. By allowing hocus pocus like the 1992 Consensus to substitute for genuine understanding and offering to negotiate while taking most of the content of potential negotiations off the table, Beijing gives Taiwanese no basis on which to choose engagement. In my view, PRC leaders' disappointment with this strategy is not so much proof of the strategy's failure as of mainland policy-makers' wishful thinking.

Tactics: carrots and sticks

The PRC has a small army of Taiwan specialists who are charged with designing tactics for implementing the strategy of peaceful development. They have a very difficult task: to simultaneously intimidate the Taiwanese into abandoning independence and seduce them into accepting unification. Of these tactics, the Anti-Secession Law has worked the best. The 1992 Consensus has had some success, and asymmetrical engagement has been a failure.

The Anti-Secession Law

As a matter of policy, Beijing has always reserved the option of using force to achieve its objectives in the Taiwan Strait. Chinese authorities have stated this on many occasions, including in both White Papers, while the PRC's military deployments, doctrines and exercise routines telegraph its preparations for armed conflict in the Strait. The strongest statement of military resolve is the Anti-Secession Law, which was passed in 2005 as part of the roll-out of the peaceful development strategy. Understandably, analysts focused most of their attention on Article 8:

> In the event that the "Taiwan independence" secessionist forces should act under any name or by any means to cause the fact of Taiwan's secession from China, or that major incidents entailing Taiwan's secession from China should occur, or that possibilities for a peaceful reunification should be completely exhausted, the state shall employ non-peaceful means and other necessary measures to protect China's sovereignty and territorial integrity.[4]

By authorizing – even mandating – the use of force under particular circumstances, Article 8 constitutes the strongest statement to date of China's resolve never to tolerate independence. However, the ASL is not just about sticks; it also enumerates and authorizes the carrots that are an equally important part of the peaceful development strategy. Article 6 lists measures aimed at promoting cross-Strait relations, including personnel exchanges, economic interactions, communications links and people-to-people ties. Article 7 spells out the various topics on which the two sides can negotiate.

The ASL sent important signals, both within China and externally. The bill was a message to hard-liners in the CCP and the Chinese military that the peaceful development strategy was not a naïve abandonment of military pressure, but a balanced strategy of carrots and sticks. The law was a strong message to Taiwan (and the rest of the world) that the PRC was serious about deterring independence and maintaining momentum toward unification.

Article 8 of the ASL has been a successful tactic. Codifying the military threat against Taiwan helped pacify domestic constituencies within the PRC that might otherwise have resisted peaceful development and the myriad forms of cross-Strait cooperation it entails. The law also got the attention of leaders in Taiwan and the US, inspiring them to be even more cautious and thoughtful about managing the cross-Strait issue. The ASL has been less effective in persuading ordinary Taiwanese to take Beijing's military bluster seriously, but given the minimal appetite among Taiwan's citizens to test the PRC's resolve, further reinforcement may not have been necessary.

Article 6 has also had many successes. The economies of the two sides were deeply intertwined even before the ASL was passed, but the measures enabled by the law – especially direct links and travel – pulled them even closer. One result is that many Taiwanese recognize that the island's economic prosperity depends on the mainland economy to an unprecedented extent; in 2012, concern about the possible consequences of losing access to the PRC economy was an important factor motivating Taiwanese to vote against the DPP's presidential and legislative candidates.

Nonetheless, the "carrots" in the ASL were not enough to persuade Taiwan's people to accept unification. In fact, by the middle of Ma's second term, many Taiwanese were beginning to question whether continuing to allow the PRC to play such an important role in their economy was prudent. Between 2012 and 2014, a series of social movements challenged the conventional wisdom that increases in cross-Strait economic interaction were unambiguously positive.

During Ma's presidency, Taiwan's economic growth slowed, wages stagnated, real estate prices increased, and wealth inequality skyrocketed. Most Taiwanese believed Ma's mainland-facing economic strategy was the cause of these woes. The same Sino-skeptical policies that had hurt Tsai Ing-wen's candidacy four years earlier were an asset to her in 2016. Meanwhile, increased contact with PRC people only reinforced the tendency of Taiwanese to feel themselves politically and even culturally distinct from the mainland. In sum,

Article 6 of the ASL had many positive effects, but it did not create the groundswell of support for unification that its designers had hoped. After eating carrots for eight years, Taiwanese were ready for a new dish.

The "1992 Consensus"

A second key tactic serving the peaceful development strategy is the "1992 Consensus." Peaceful development was unveiled early in Chen Shui-bian's second term of office, but its implementation required that Taiwan be in compliance with the "one China principle." Thus, as Lin puts it, the ASL "only maximized its flexibilities after the KMT came back to power in 2008" (2016: 323). It was the KMT's willingness to move forward under the framework of the "1992 Consensus," which the PRC had decided was an acceptable simulacrum of "one China," that enabled this result.

This was an especially important outcome, because the PRC's determination to be the sole Chinese sovereign in the world has made it much more difficult to achieve its goals. I submit that Beijing made a strategic – and possibly fatal – error when it decided that "two Chinas" was an unacceptable way station on the road to unification. In its zeal to exterminate the Republic of China, the PRC eliminated its most promising partner for unification.[5]

The ROC was an authoritative (and even authoritarian) counterpart that shared the PRC's desire to unify China. It is possible the ROC's leaders were bluffing, that they had no intention of unifying with the PRC under any circumstances. But we will never know, because instead of calling the ROC's bluff, Beijing refused to recognize its existence. With the ROC unavailable as a vehicle for the unification project, the PRC finds itself forced to deal with 23 million "Taiwan compatriots," about 21 million of whom have no interest in unification. This blunder helps explain how the "1992 Consensus" – a perfect example of an empty slogan – became a keystone of cross-Strait relations. Having backed itself into a corner by refusing to acknowledge a willing partner, the PRC was left with no choice but to accept a terribly imperfect substitute: Taiwan's agreement to continue being the ROC in exchange for Beijing's pretending not to notice.

The "1992 Consensus" is an example of working-level policy-makers' creativity and flexibility rescuing their bosses from a self-defeating policy. When representatives of SEF and ARATS began meeting in the early 1990s, they had an impossible mandate: find a way to negotiate a foundation for unification without acknowledging one another's existence. They managed to fulfil their mandate by agreeing that since both sides believed Taiwan was Chinese territory all was well; no further elaboration was required. This was world class smoke-and-mirrors, and it solved a lot of problems, at least in the short run. But the "1992 Consensus" is a very slender reed.

To begin with, it has no content. The words "1992 Consensus" are not short for something else that can be said – they are all there is. The two sides have never agreed on any content for the phrase. That actually makes it perfect for closing the gap between the CCP and the KMT – they came up with it, they have jointly made it a fetish ("an object of irrational reverence or obsessive devotion," according to Merriam-Webster) and they both have a way of deploying it that works for their domestic audiences.[6] Unfortunately, the words do not have the same power for the DPP that they have for the KMT and the CCP. The PRC cannot force the DPP to say the magic words; instead, Tsai Ing-wen has chosen what to Beijing must surely be an utterly infuriating approach: remaining stubbornly asymptotic to the "1992 Consensus" coming closer and closer but never uttering the precise words: *jiuer gongshi* (九二共識).

In response, Beijing has suggested that as long as she shows fidelity to the spirit, or core connotation, of the "1992 Consensus," Tsai needn't necessarily recite the words. But while this may seem like a concession, it doesn't really help. What is the spirit of the "1992 Consensus"? It is as empty as the words themselves. Presumably Beijing wants Tsai to embrace its interpretation of the spirit, which is, at its heart, a recognition that Taiwan is part of China. But if that is the standard, even the KMT is not really on board with the *spirit* of the "1992 Consensus."

The problem with the "1992 Consensus" is that the minute we try to pin down what it is, we are back where we started: the KMT believes Taiwan is part of China in the sense that China is part of the ROC – Taiwan's *Chineseness* is part and parcel of the ROC's statehood. But for the PRC, the ROC cannot have statehood, so Taiwan cannot be part of China by virtue of being (part of) the ROC. So the KMT's position is unacceptable.

Despite its limitations, the "1992 Consensus" does have value, because it has *utility*. It allows the two sides to set aside disagreements on fundamental issues and do useful things together. It is precisely tactical. Tsai is not interested in reciting the mantra, but she is willing and eager to do useful things. The problem is that the utility is activated by paying lip service to the "spirit," which defeats the purpose of tactical flexibility. We have seen this very clearly since Tsai took office: Beijing has reduced the space for cooperation between the two sides precisely in an attempt to compel Tsai to utter the magic phrase.

The problems with the "1992 Consensus" point to deep challenges for Beijing's Taiwan policy, most of which boil down to this: what Beijing wants and what the people of Taiwan want are incompatible. Both are willing to make adjustments in the short term to avoid a confrontation, but their long-term goals cannot be harmonized. This is the reason Beijing's policy-makers have become so attached to the "1992 Consensus." It is a mantra they can chant that allows them to levitate above the details, to visualize a gap between the two sides that is narrower than it really is, to occupy a mental space that is neither success nor failure.

Asymmetrical engagement

Yet another tactic the PRC uses to implement its peaceful development strategy – one which clearly *has* failed – is what Lin Gang calls "asymmetrical engagement" with Taiwan's major parties. CCP leaders are convinced that the KMT shares their core values (*unificationism* and Chinese nationalism), and that the DPP is committed to Taiwan independence and thus can never be trusted. This superficial view of Taiwanese politics created problems when the KMT was in power – Lin says "the swift but unsustainable developmental model over the past years has been attributable to Beijing's asymmetric engagement strategy" – but now that the DPP is in power and the KMT is in free fall, asymmetric engagement could undermine all the progress that has been made to date (Lin 2016: 330).

Prospects for cross-Strait relations

The PRC's Taiwan policy has not been a failure. It has avoided the worst-case scenario, which at one time seemed quite plausible. It has shifted the position of its least-preferred interlocutor in a direction that – while it is far from satisfactory – is less adverse to its desires than it once was. That said, it has not made progress toward its best-case scenario, and trends in Taiwan are not promising for such an outcome. If Beijing wants to move beyond its minimal requirement (blocking independence) toward its preferred outcome (unification), it needs to revisit its strategy and tactics. It needs to be more realistic about what is possible, given the state of Taiwan's public opinion. Wishful thinking only leads to disappointment and frustration – and risks activating nationalists within the PRC to make demands that cannot be met at an acceptable cost. Both Beijing and Taipei tend to make cross-Strait policy in processes that are far more sensitive and responsive to domestic factors than to the circumstances on the other side. It is not surprising that those policies often miss their targets.

PRC policy-makers need to rethink their strategy of asymmetric engagement. The KMT is staring down the barrel of a long and painful rebuilding process. Waiting for the KMT to come back and hoping for the DPP to fail are not strategic moves. The DPP is the authentic representative of the Taiwanese people's will, at least for now. Believing the KMT's propaganda has enabled wishful thinking on the mainland for too long. It has insulated Beijing's policy process from important realities, and has produced unrealistic expectations and hard disappointments. One useful step would be for the CCP to revisit its position on the ROC. While the CCP may never be able to refer to the Taiwan "authorities" as the Republic of China, the DPP would be hard-pressed to pass up an opportunity for genuine, open-ended negotiations (in contrast to take-or-leave-it package deals such as Ye Jianying's Nine Points and Jiang Zemin's Eight Points) that recognized the Taiwan government's stateness. The outcome of such negotiations might not look like one country, two systems, but they might look like a way forward. Waiting for Taiwan to decide it wants to be part of the PRC is not consistent with President Xi Jinping's statement that a political solution should not be postponed too long. Finally, insisting on the recitation of a mantra like the "1992 Consensus" puts too much power in Taipei's hands. It allows Taipei to control the pace at which relations unfold, and it makes the PRC look petty. If Beijing is committed to a policy of peaceful development, it needs to build on a solid foundation, not hide behind a fig leaf.

Notes

1 The PRC government uses an English-language term "reunification" to translate a Chinese term (統一) that does not contain the meaning conveyed by the prefix "re." That is, in Chinese, the word used to describe this goal means simply "unification." Beijing's ability to normalize the use of "reunification" in the English-speaking world is a good example of how, by controlling discourse, China has transformed its political preferences into presumptive "facts."

2 The first expression of the "marriage of equals" concept came in 2000 when vice premier Qian Qichen told a group of KMT legislators that the One-China Principle could be stated as "there is only one China in the world, both the mainland and Taiwan belong to that same one China, and China's sovereignty and territory cannot be divided." Qian repeated the formula few times in 2001. Nonetheless, when KMT chair Lien Chan put forward a unification plan structured around a "common roof" with "separate jurisdictions" that same year, Beijing rejected it out of hand.

3 There are many reasons for Tsai's reluctance to accept the 1992 Consensus. One of the most important is undoubtedly her conviction that she should make such a concession only if there is a counter-concession from the other side. Another reason, though, may be her past experience. In 2000, when Tsai was head of the Mainland Affairs Council under Chen Shui-bian, Chen mentioned that he would accept the 1992 Consensus. The backlash from DPP supporters was swift and severe, and Tsai was compelled to walk back her boss's statement.

4 The English language text of the Anti-Secessionism Law can be found at: http://news.xinhuanet.com/english/2005-03/14/content_2694180.htm.

5 Gunter Schubert points this out in his article, writing:

> For roughly a decade ... this [internal Taiwanese] consensus was flexible enough to integrate the idea of a Chinese nation, as long as Taiwan's sovereignty was not put into jeopardy. However, the PRC ignored this window of opportunity and, thus far, stuck to its own concept of a Chinese nation that tolerates no divided sovereignty of any kind under the roof of "one China" – although some form of divided sovereignty may be the key to unification in the future.
>
> (2004: 553)

6 What the Taipei government had in mind when it "agreed to" the 1992 Consensus is detailed in Gunter Schubert's excellent article on the national identity issue. Writes Schubert: "Through this mechanism [the 1992 Consensus], the KMT made clear that it would insist on Beijing's acknowledgement of Taiwan's (the Republic of China's) sovereignty before any final agreement on the definition of 'one China' could be achieved." Schubert also reminds us of Taiwan's 2004 White Paper which said the two sides "should coexist as two legal entities" and defined "China" as "the 'historical, geographical, cultural, and familial China' that both sides of the Taiwan Strait considered as their legacy" (ibid.: 540).

References

Lin, G. (2016). Beijing's New Strategies toward a Changing Taiwan. *Journal of Contemporary China* 25(99): 321–335.

Schubert, G. (2004). Taiwan's Political Parties and National Identity: The Rise of an Overarching Consensus, *Asian Survey* 44(4): 534–554.

Snow, E. (1961 [1938]). *Red Star Over China*, First Revised and Enlarged Edition. New York: Grove Press.

Taiwan Affairs Office of the State Council PRC (n.d.). The One-China Principle and the Taiwan Issue. Available at: www.gwytb.gov.cn/en/Special/WhitePapers/201103/t20110316_1789217.htm.

Wen, Q. (1984; updated 2009). One Country, Two Systems: The Best Way to Peaceful Reunification. *Beijing Review* (52). Available at: www.bjreview.com.cn/nation/txt/2009-05/26/content_197568.htm.

Yang, C. Y. (1992). One Country, Two Systems: Mainland China's Policy Toward Reunification with Taiwan 1979–89, PhD thesis, London School of Economics, University of London. Available at: http://etheses.lse.ac.uk/1319/1/U062759.pdf.

9 New directions in Taiwan's foreign policy

Saša Istenič

Taiwan's foreign policy in context

In her first remarks as president-elect of the Republic of China (ROC or Taiwan), Tsai Ing-wen (蔡英文) said: "Our democratic system, national identity and international space must be respected."[1] The sentiment was reiterated in her inauguration address on 20 May, 2016: "We will bring Taiwan closer to the world, and the world closer to Taiwan."[2] What have been the new directions for Taiwan on the world stage? Have we witnessed a significant redirection of foreign policy? To provide answers to these questions, this chapter assesses the main factors shaping the formulation of Taiwan's policy towards expanding its international space and critically evaluates Tsai's new foreign policy directions.

Like any other government's foreign policy apparatus, Taiwan's foreign policy decision-making is affected by a combination of both internal and external factors. Throughout the period of Chiang Kai-shek (蔣介石) and his ROC government's retreat to Taiwan, up to the present, Taiwan's foreign policies have been predominantly shaped by external variables such as the international system, and in particular by the influences of the People's Republic of China (PRC or China), the United States (the US), and its ally Japan, all striving to maximize their own national interests. In order to defy China's oppression and reinforce its security and international presence, Taiwan has endeavoured to cultivate stronger ties with the US and Japan as they both share an interest in maintaining the balance of power in the Taiwan Strait. Nevertheless, such a unique strategic framework among Taiwan, China, the US and Japan has made the relationship highly complex and extremely volatile. Internally, Taiwan's highly dynamic political and social environments have likewise greatly affected the government's foreign policy; the combination of democratization, institutional evolution, generational change, and economic progress has visibly shaped and limited the courses of action open to Taiwanese foreign policy decision-makers. Even more so, as the societal players, such as political parties, think tanks, the mass media and public opinion have become influential foreign policy actors. Nevertheless, the impact of China, which continues to contest Taiwan's sovereignty, remains the most formidable force that the Taiwanese leadership has to contemplate in its foreign policy implementation. Ever since its withdrawal from the United Nations (UN) in October 1971, the government of Taiwan has had to confront increasing international isolation and adopt several major redirections of foreign policy (Huang 2016: 465–481). While its primary long-term foreign policy goal has remained focused on gaining international recognition of its sovereignty and preventing China from using force to take Taiwan, the "one China" set-up imposed by Beijing has continued to weaken Taiwan's sovereign position and to confine its international manoeuvring space. Accordingly, Taipei has strived to strengthen both formal and informal relations with nations and increase Taiwan's global visibility in as many international organizations and venues as feasible. It has invested tremendous energies to finding alternative channels to advance national interests and prevent further diplomatic isolation.

Whether under the KMT or the DPP leaderships, the government in Taipei believes that maintaining a certain amount of diplomatic allies, regardless of their small size and economic conditions, is necessary to support the ROC's claim to sovereignty. Formal relations with these states bolster Taiwan's argument of being a sovereign entity separate from China and elevate the country's profile in the international community. Taiwanese allies have the power to speak on Taipei's behalf in important international organizations that deny Taiwan membership, such as the UN, and thereby support Taiwan's interests. Official visits to diplomatic allies are also enabling Taiwan's political leaders to obtain international publicity and media coverage. Moreover, they are also given an opportunity to make transit stops and make contact with influential politicians. However, in order to maintain the official diplomatic relationships, Taiwan had often utilized various economic instruments, including trade, aid, investment and bribery, which greatly tarnished Taiwan's national dignity (Rickards 2008). What is more, many times, economic diplomacy could not provide immunity from de-recognition. In the 1970s, President Chiang Ching-kuo (蔣經國) paved the way for the development of more substantive relations with nations that have switched diplomatic ties from Taiwan to China, while the major shift in Taiwan's foreign policy came in 1988 with President Lee Teng-hui (李登輝), who adopted a more practical and flexible diplomacy in order to sustain both official and unofficial relations with as many countries as possible. By accepting the principle of "dual recognition" and regarding Taiwan and mainland China as two equal political entities which should enjoy unrestricted international space individually, President Lee was hoping to manage external relations in a less provocative and a more reciprocal way. His pragmatic diplomacy succeeded in forging several new diplomatic relationships as well as in setting up and upgrading representative offices and foreign missions in Taiwan and abroad. In addition to promoting trade, economic and civil society exchanges, active dispersal of foreign aid became an integral part of Taiwan's foreign policy. Nevertheless, since material incentives had been employed to facilitate Taiwan's diplomatic needs, Taiwan's economic diplomacy was scorned as "chequebook diplomacy".

When the DPP was voted into power for the first time in 2000, it was an entirely new experience for all actors involved in Taiwan's foreign policy making. However, although President Chen Shui-bian (陳水扁) pledged the Four Noes and One Without (四不一沒有)[3] in his inaugural address and encouraged greater cross-Strait interaction, Beijing had no interest in negotiating with him. Since the Chinese government did not want to see the DPP maintain its leadership over the long term, it wasted no time in putting spokes in the Chen administration's wheels. After all, President Chen considered the promotion of Taiwan's independent sovereign status as one of Taiwan's most important foreign policy objectives and was extremely active in enhancing Taiwan's profile internationally. He determinedly promoted Taiwanese sovereignty and persistently rejected the existence of a "one-China principle", even in the form of "one China, different interpretations" or the so-called "1992 Consensus" (九二共識).[4] He hoped that shared international values of democracy, freedom, human rights and humanitarianism would give Taiwan's regime legitimacy in world politics and expand its international space. Accordingly, his administration endeavoured to build public and civil society actors' capacity in international affairs and enhance people's diplomacy so as to more effectively confront China's repression. Although President Chen harshly criticized "chequebook diplomacy", his handling of presidential funds used for diplomatic work overseas was heavily criticized. Among the damaging scandals was also the unfortunate disappearance of the US$30 million, a secret governmental financial inducement, which was supposed to help forge diplomatic relations between Taiwan and Papua New Guinea in 2006 (Rickards 2008). Most inopportunely, his more assertive foreign policy observed in a "name rectification movement for Taiwan", the UN full membership campaign, and in particular the initiation of a referendum in 2004, which was perceived by China as an exercise for an eventual vote on Taiwan independence, encountered strong opposition not only from Beijing but also from Washington (Huang 2016: 467). In spite of a very favourable approach towards Taiwan by the US government in the beginning of Chen's presidential term, Washington soon took a much more restrained tone. As a consequence of the turn in global politics caused by the 11 September, 2001 terrorist attacks on the US World Trade Center and the Pentagon, the US visibly tilted towards China to obtain its support in combating terrorism. Washington even used unusually harsh statements to criticize President Chen as it began to perceive his cross-Strait policy as provocative and against American national interests (AFP 2007). For this reason, many scholars have considered President Chen's diplomatic approaches as major destabilizing factors in Taiwan's relations with China and the US (Ross 2006: 443–458; Copper 2008; Su 2009: 161–258).

In 2008, the Ma Ying-jeou (馬英九) administration adopted a much less confrontational approach toward expanding Taiwan's international space. By accepting the controversial "1992 Consensus", the two governments in Taipei and Beijing tacitly agreed to a diplomatic truce (外交休兵) in the international arena. This verbal truce was regarded by the KMT as the most effective and successful foreign policy initiative that stopped the diplomatic battle with Beijing, who no longer opted to entice or pressure countries to break diplomatic relations with Taiwan. Indeed, in order to sustain a diplomatic détente with Taipei, Beijing had until 17 March, 2016 rejected any country's request to switch diplomatic recognition.[5] When the Gambian president unilaterally decided to cut off diplomatic ties with Taiwan in November 2013, Beijing did not opt to embrace Gambia immediately. Instead, it tactfully waited for the results of Taiwan's January 2016 elections and applied the recognition of Gambia as a warning to the incoming DPP government (Chen, Wen and Hsu 2016).

Undoubtedly, both external and internal constraints will continue to feature prominently in Taiwan's foreign policy-making and will continue to play a key role in restraining the current DPP government from adopting any radical policy measures in the new term of office. While the international setting has not substantially changed for Taiwan since 2008, its domestic political environment has. The DPP now for the first time in history controls the Presidential Office, the Executive Yuan (Cabinet) and the Legislative Yuan (Parliament). That means, that unlike during the Chen period (2000–2008), marked by the constant partisan political bickering between a DPP-led executive branch and a KMT-dominated legislature, President Tsai's legislation and policies are more likely to be endorsed. Furthermore, in line with the election promises for an era of "new politics", there have already been some positive signs towards seeking to establish the impartiality to ensure a more representative and professional Cabinet and Legislature. Nevertheless, as a number of deep-rooted systemic problems will continue to weigh down on political culture, it still remains to be proven whether a new coalition, will manage to promote greater understanding and pursue grander initiatives in foreign affairs. Taiwan's vibrant civil society has also reflected the new dynamic and revealed its political diversity. In the 2014 local elections, independent candidate Ko Wen-je (柯文哲) became the first ever non-partisan Taipei City mayor in Taiwanese history, while a record high number of political parties (18) competed in the 2016 legislative elections. Noteworthy, a significant portion of Taiwanese voters chose to cast their ballots for the freshly emerged parties (also referred to as the "Third Political Force"). The DPP has been very skilful in capitalizing on the growing popularity for the new parties and its decision to recruit many young social movement activists brought it a very strong public support. Owing to a palpable generational change, a large majority of the island's residents today consider themselves exclusively as Taiwanese, portraying their homeland and people as a nation distinct from China. They support the maintenance of the status quo regarding the country's future and want Taiwan to function as a sovereign state in the international community (Election Study Center 2016). Since the growing Taiwanese national identity forms an extremely important part of public opinion, it will undoubtedly increasingly affect the foreign policy decision making. In her victory speech, President Tsai assured Taiwanese citizens, that her administrative team will follow the public's will and abide by democratic principles.[6] Accordingly, public opinion will play an important role in the shaping of new policies whereas the strength of public support will significantly affect Tsai administration's foreign policy agenda.

Moreover, owing to a strong correlation between public opinion and media, the new communication and information technologies will additionally impact Taiwan's foreign policy-makers. A recent survey has shown that 80.9 per cent of Taiwanese use social media apps such as Line, Facebook, Twitter, WeChat and Instagram on a daily basis (Chung and Huang 2016). The extent of influence of these new social media in foreign relations was exposed very clearly in the 2014 Sunflower Movement, which handed former president Ma his toughest crisis. Taiwanese students have been very agile in deploying online communication tools and creating more innovative political practices. They voiced public concerns about government policies and thereby eroded support for both, President Ma and the KMT (Harrison 2016). Undeniably, the new social media (especially websites, blogs and online forums) will continue to flourish and present an increasingly important factor in shaping a voice of the Taiwanese people. Furthermore, since they provide an additional source of information to both domestic and international audiences, they are also co-shaping a new field for global public discourse. Accordingly, public diplomacy activities can now be extended to the popular social media platforms and can therefore provide the government with an alternative channel to communicate policy to international audiences and more effectively balance strong counter-narrative imposed by Beijing's "one-China policy" in the international media. To an internationally isolated Taiwan, this is surely of a special value as it offers Taiwanese citizens a new venue where they can be heard and better understood. Such new media environment, particularly apparent since the 2016 election campaign, might provide Tsai administration a much stronger basis (ibid.).

A year on after the period of diplomatic truce

All in all, judging from the vitality of Taiwan-related activities, engagement in international organizations as well as economic, cultural and travel exchanges between Taiwan and diplomatic allies and non-allied nations alike, Taiwan's presence in the international arena has been on the increase under the Ma administration (2008–2016). Two Taiwanese diplomatic allies, Kiribati and St. Lucia, set up embassies in Taipei in 2013 and 2015, respectively, and Myanmar and Papua New Guinea opened trade offices in Taipei in 2015. Taiwan has also established new representative offices in Chennai, India; Sapporo, Japan; and Surabaya, Indonesia (Her 2016). The number of countries and territories granting ROC passport holders visa waivers, landing visas or e-visa facilities has by 2017 increased to 165, making the power ranking of Taiwanese passports among the world's top 28 (*Taiwan Today* 2017a). This is certainly a remarkable diplomatic achievement since a passport still presents the most important and authoritative document that one has. Nevertheless, Taiwanese around the world, especially students, still complain about discrimination due to their unrecognized passports and their identification by foreign administration authorities as Chinese, i.e. PRC citizens. The frustration is so deep that some even prefer to be classified as "Stateless" instead of "Chinese" nationals when given such an option (Gerber 2016a). Moreover, any private citizen who carries a ROC passport could be regarded as a PRC national when abroad as observed in a series of recent deportations of Taiwanese fraud suspects to China and not their home country Taiwan (Newcomb 2017).[7]

On a similar note, the "one-China policy" continues to significantly limit Taiwan's global engagement. In spite of the hope that a more pragmatic approach under the Ma administration would nurture China's goodwill, Taiwan's membership of inter-governmental organizations (IGOs) has remained very limited. Even though Taiwan attempted to join UN-affiliated organizations as an observer seeking meaningful participation and no longer as a full member, China has continued to block Taipei's initiatives. As of March 2017, Taiwan has remained a member of 37 IGOs or their subsidiary bodies (MOFA 2017). In August 2015, the Japan-based North Pacific Fisheries Commission (NPFC) that regulates all deep-sea fishing activity in the northern Pacific Ocean became the latest IGO to welcome Taiwan's membership. Taiwan was accepted under the name *Chinese Taipei* as a "fishing entity", the compromised name under which Taiwan has already joined five other similar regional fishery organizations.[8] By the same token, as an "economy", Taiwan participates in the Asia-Pacific Economic Cooperation (APEC), in the World Trade Organization (WTO) as a "customs territory", and in the Asian Development Bank (ADB) as *Taipei, China*, a title most disliked by Taipei due to its implication that the government in Taipei is subordinate to China. In addition, Taiwan currently has observership or other status in less than 20 IGOs or their subsidiary bodies (ibid.). In 2009, Taiwan could finally enter the WTO's Government Procurement Agreement (GPA), join the World Health Organization's (WHO) International Health Regulations and attend the annual meeting of the World Health Assembly (WHA) as an observer under the name *Chinese Taipei*. However, due to Beijing's Memorandum of Understanding (MOU) imposed on the WHO, the organization's internal documents refer to Taiwan as a province of China. On the same note, Taiwan's ports on the International Health Regulations (IHR) Authorized Ports List are placed under the entry of *China*, while the Global Health Atlas refers to Taiwan as *China (Province of Taiwan)* (WHO 2016a, 2016b). In spite of the granted observer status in the WHA, the Taiwanese medical community is excluded from much of the highly important WHO's international health network. What is more, Taiwan's participation at the WHA is subject to annual renewal with China's consent. In May 2016, just prior to President Tsai's inauguration, the delayed letter of invitation from the WHO for Taiwan to attend the 2016 session of the WHA, for the first time since 2009 included the "UN Resolution 2758", "WHA Resolution 25.1" and the "one-China principle" as a basis for Taiwan's attendance. The UN Resolution 2758, which governs international organizations, recognized the PRC as the only lawful representative of China to the UN in 1971, whereas the WHA Resolution 25.1 expelled the ROC from the WHO in 1972. Therefore, China succeeded in imposing a unique provisional paragraph into the invitation letter, which sparked a heated debate over whether Taiwan's government should be sending representatives to the WHA meeting at all. The NPP and DPP legislators have attempted to pass a legislative resolution condemning the WHO's citation of the "one China principle", while some even suggested that Taiwan's delegation to the WHA should take mosquitos carrying the Zika and dengue fever viruses to the Geneva gathering to protest against Beijing subordinating Taiwan's sovereignty (Chen 2016; Gerber 2016b; Lin 2016a). Although pressured into a corner, the incoming government opted to accept the invitation and even upheld the "Chinese-centred" rhetoric during the WHA speech, completely avoiding any mention of "Taiwan" to prevent giving any incentives to Beijing to accuse the Tsai administration of distorting the "status quo". This was a clear signal that the Tsai government intends to keep a low profile approach and to follow her predecessor's convention on Taiwan's participation at the WHO in spite of the criticism and calls from the Taiwanese medical community for a more proactive approach (Chung and Chin 2017). Nevertheless, notwithstanding the Tsai administration's prudent reaction, China was no longer willing to allow the WHO to invite Taiwan to attend the 2017 WHA meeting and specifically linked WHA participation to Taipei's refusal to acknowledge the "1992 Consensus".

The International Civil Aviation Organization (ICAO) was the second UN specialized agency to invite Taiwan to participate in its triennial assembly during President Ma's term (in September 2013), however, not as an observer but merely in a capacity as "a guest". Since Taiwan is neither an official member nor an observer, it is not allowed to attend ICAO's technical meetings and its regional mechanisms, while similar to its attendance at the WHA, an official invitation is needed for it to be granted entry to assembly. To its great disappointment, Taipei did not receive an invitation letter to attend the latest 39th session in September 2016, even though the Tsai government was highly pragmatic and only sought to join the ICAO in a proper capacity and under a title acceptable to all. Beijing was not willing to forge any compromise, making it clear that adherence to the "one-China principle" and the "political basis" of the so-called "1992 Consensus" was a precondition for Taiwan's attendance. In this way, Beijing attempted to place the blame for Taiwan's exclusion on the Tsai administration. On the same note, Beijing has also opposed Taiwan's inclusion in the International Criminal Police Organization (INTERPOL), the world's largest transnational police association, even though this non-UN body has no prerequisite for an applicant to be recognized as a sovereign nation. Not even particularly strong support for Taiwan's attendance as an INTERPOL observer by the US government could outdo China's opposition at the latest 85th General Assembly held in November 2016.[9] Taipei has also long sought the international support for observer status at the UN Framework Convention on Climate Change (UNFCCC). However, so far, even apolitical nomenclature as an "emissions entity" did not grant Taiwan membership to this key global environmental apparatus. As a non-member state, Taiwan could only attend the UNFCCC's activities via its NGOs, listed as non-governmental observers and designated as belonging to "China" (UNFCCC

2016). At the latest UN climate conference held in Morocco in November 2016, Taiwan participated in the event in a same line as previously, through a 'technical approach'. It conducted talks with other nations via its NGOs' representatives (Industrial Technology Research Institute, Taiwan Power Company, CPC Corporation, Taiwan and China Steel Corporation), which it regarded as a 'realistic' participation. While the non-governmental observers were due to Chinese pressure unable to obtain approval for their applications to join the UNFCCC's side events, talks with other nations were free from Beijing's intervention (Tseng and Lee 2016). On the other hand, in a meeting of the UN Food and Agriculture Organization's (FAO) Committee on Fisheries (COFI) in July 2016, Taiwanese officials, registered as members of NGOs and not as government representatives, were still forced to leave this intergovernmental forum that examines major international fishery and aquaculture problems. It was the first time such an incident had occurred at a COFI meeting since 2003, when Taiwanese officials began participating as NGO members or experts (Chen and Yang 2016).

China's leverage over Taiwan's international economic relations has also not faded. In April 2016, for the first time since 2005, when Taiwan joined the Organisation for Economic Co-operation and Development (OECD) steel committee as an observer, its delegation was requested to leave an OECD conference in Brussels (Hsu and Hsiao 2016). Furthermore, China is also using its influence on global economic powers to prevent them from signing free-trade agreements (FTAs) with Taiwan. As the importance of regional and bilateral trade agreements has increased, it is vital for Taiwan to expand its cooperation network as broad as is feasible. In 2013, New Zealand and Singapore became Taiwan's first partners with whom Taiwan does not maintain diplomatic relations to sign the bilateral quasi-free trade agreements (FTAs). However, in spite of high expectations, the two FTAs did not pave the way to the wider market. From Taiwan's perspective, the most lucrative FTAs would be with the US, the EU and Japan, whereas joining the Trans-Pacific Partnership (TPP) (in spite of the recent withdrawal by the US, the remaining 11 member countries are still exploring different possibilities for regional integration), the Free Trade Area of the Asia-Pacific (FTAAP), and the Regional Comprehensive Economic Partnership (RCEP) would protect Taiwan from the threat of being marginalized by the rise of regionalism in global trade. Nevertheless, Taiwan is kept out of most of the region's important multilateral organizations even though its economy is far more advanced than that of many of the other member countries. Previous administrations believed that bilateral agreements with China, such as Economic Cooperation Framework Agreement (ECFA), would serve as a springboard for developing FTAs with other countries. However, up to now, signing of ECFA did not raise the value of Taiwan nor offered the anticipated spill-over effects. Furthermore, in 2015, Taiwan's attempt to join the China-led Asian Infrastructure Investment Bank (AIIB) as a founding member under the name *Chinese Taipei* was swiftly swept under the carpet (*Taipei Times* 2015). Although the Ma government reapplied to join the AIIB as a regular member, Beijing insisted that

Taiwan should be treated as a non-sovereign economic body and that its membership application could only be processed on behalf of the Chinese Ministry of Finance (*Taipei Times* 2016a). Since Beijing is the gatekeeper to Taiwan's RCEP and AIIB memberships, any progress on this front remains highly unlikely.

Furthermore, owing to China's increasing economic influence coupled by Beijing's intensified diplomatic pressure, Taiwan's aid diplomacy is no longer sufficient in preventing its allies from switching ties to the fiscally richer side. Gambia's surprising de-recognition of Taiwan in 2013, which was due to unfulfilled monetary demands made by the Gambian president, has prompted Taipei to forge a bi-partisan consensus regarding the need to stand up to the extortionist practices of Taiwan's aid recipients and pursue a more cautious foreign aid approach (Tubilewicz 2016). When in December 2016, São Tomé and Principe attempted to acquire a large sum of money from Taipei as an exchange for the continued maintenance of formal diplomatic relations with Taiwan, Taipei refused to pay heed. Consequently, São Tomé and Principe turned away from Taiwan and resumed diplomatic relations with China, who a year earlier already had offered the island a huge investment deal to develop a deep sea transhipment port (Strohecker 2015; Lee 2016). The two remaining African allies, Burkina Faso and Swaziland, have so far remained faithful to Taiwan, nevertheless, temptations to establish official ties with China have been getting stronger and stronger (Cabestan 2017). As China had begun to overshadow Taiwan as a commercial partner, Taiwanese allies are increasingly tempted to turn toward China's economic orbit, especially in Latin America and the Caribbean Community where Taiwan maintains the most diplomatic allies. To shore up support, President Tsai's first two overseas trips were to Latin America, reflecting the continued importance of diplomatic relationships for Taiwan (Malkin 2017). The question, how many allies Taiwan can afford to lose, remains, however, very difficult to answer.[10] Among the approximately 20 diplomatic allies only the Holy See – the government of the Vatican – bases its recognition on explicitly ideological grounds and does not need foreign aid and, most importantly, is the only ally that has a unique ability to exert soft power on global affairs. However, even the Holy See has been seriously considering the option to embrace the much bigger number of Catholics on the opposite side of the Taiwan Strait.[11] Nonetheless, while the diplomatic recognition of small powers certainly reinforces Taiwan's *de jure* statehood and bolsters Taiwan's geopolitical interests, it should not be viewed as being of an existential importance. After all, the main threat to Taiwan's security comes not from diplomatic recognition but from China. Furthermore, Taiwan's formal allies provide very limited economic and security benefits. Besides, almost NT$10 billion worth of financial assistance that Taipei offers its allies on a yearly basis is certainly not easy to justify to Taiwanese taxpayers, especially as even these allies often fail to speak firmly in support of Taiwan (*Taipei Times* 2016e; Yeh 2016). As the former Foreign Affairs Minister Francisco Ou (歐鴻鍊) reasoned, the greater crisis for Taiwan in the diplomatic arena would be the diminished international space rather than the loss of diplomatic allies as

Taiwan's substantial benefits all lie in the countries with which it does not maintain official ties (CNA 2016a). Developing substantive trade relations with these nations should thus be of higher importance than spending a great deal of effort and money on maintaining formal diplomatic links. Faced with harsh reality, Tsai's leadership has already started "preparing the ground" for the new era of diplomacy.

The new foreign policy agenda

The change in cross-Strait policy from the Ma Ying-jeou government to the Tsai Ing-wen government has undoubtedly been the most significant immediate impact on Taiwan's internal and external relations. In one of her interviews, President Tsai said that the biggest difference between the incoming and the outgoing government is the DPP's commitment to adhering to public opinion, respecting democratic principles, and guaranteeing the right of the Taiwanese people to determine their own future (*Taipei Times* 2016b). In order to consolidate public support, amass political power and maintain stability, the DPP has moved toward the centre of the political spectrum and adopted a more moderate and diverse policy stance over the issue of self-determination and independence. However, while the DPP's dominance has made policy implementation easier on the domestic front, the intensified external pressure has tightened up the manoeuvring space on the international front. Since Beijing perceives the Tsai administration's moves as challenging its "one-China policy", the level of pressure exerted by China has visibly increased. When Chen Shui-bian refused to accept the "one-China principle" as a precondition for cross-Strait talks in 2000, Taipei was left without institutional SEF-ARATS and MAC-TAO channels for managing cross-Strait interactions. This was also the reason that President Chen could not significantly expand Taiwan's international opportunities as Beijing resolutely obstructed any of his moves (Mainland Affairs Council 2005). The Ma administration hoped that improved relations with China would open doors for Taiwan in the international arena. However, Beijing's goodwill was very limited and in spite of some positive developments, it did not meet Taiwanese expectations. Consequently, many Taiwanese started to accuse the Ma administration of only serving Beijing's agenda and jeopardizing Taiwan's autonomy. The DPP in particular argued, that

> The conducting of foreign relations conditioned upon Chinese goodwill, and seeking international participation via negotiation with China, have all undermined Taiwan's sovereignty and the right of Taiwan's people to international space, relegating Taiwan's international participation to a subset of cross-Strait relations.
>
> (DPP 2014)

For that reason, despite the greater trust that the viable diplomacy in general managed to shore up, it has also raised much debate in Taiwan. Similar to Chen,

President Tsai has also refused to accept the "1992 Consensus" as a precondition for cross-Strait dialogue. Nevertheless, she has expressed respect for the "1992 historic fact" and the ROC constitutional framework and has so far remained highly moderate and pragmatic. Although it seemed at first that Beijing would offer some room for forging a consensus needed for cross-Strait dialogue, the annual sessions of the Chinese People's Political Consultative Conference (CPPCC) and the National People's Congress (NPC) in March 2016 revealed that Beijing was determined to insist on the "1992 Consensus" as its key political foundation (Xinhua Net 2016). Since then, Beijing has suspended official dialogue and communication channels with the Tsai government and repeatedly sent assertive messages, calling on Tsai to accept the "1992 Consensus" (*South China Morning Post* 2016). In addition to stripping Taiwan of its remaining diplomatic allies, blocking Taiwan from participating in international bodies, the Chinese oppression has increasingly been noted on many other occasions. For instance, a dispute over the Olympic emblem on Taiwanese athletes' uniforms at the Rio de Janeiro Paralympics in September 2016 (Cole 2016a); a ban by the Cambodian Prime Minister on raising Taiwan's flag in Cambodia (Soumy 2017); a controversial directive by the Emirates Airline asking Taiwanese cabin crew to remove their "Taiwanese flag pins" and replace them with Chinese flag pins (Shan 2017); exclusion from the 2017 Kimberly Process meeting (Munro 2017); and most alarmingly, an order by the Nigerian government to Taipei to curtail its trade office's "diplomatic privileges" and to move it out of its political capital, Abuja, to Lagos, the country's commercial hub in order to bring Abuja in full compliance with the "one-China policy" (Cole 2017; Scott, Shi and Ibukun 2017).

In view of the wider campaign of pressure by Beijing to isolate Taiwan, the Tsai government will have no choice but to invest even more energies into expanding Taiwan's international presence, raising its international profile, increasing people-to-people contacts and strengthening the level of support from the international community. Since only an economically strong and thriving Taiwan will lure nations to develop stronger substantial relations with it, the government will also need to work hard to revitalize Taiwan's flagging economy. Merging and streamlining of Taiwan's overseas representative offices seem to be a part of the new scheme towards maximizing the nation's limited resources (CNA 2016b). Widening Taiwan's global market and accelerating its multilateral and bilateral economic cooperation have also been given a fresh impetus. As the Tsai administration desires to diversify Taiwan's economy in order to alleviate Taiwan's asymmetrical economic dependence on China, priority focus has been set on expending trade exchanges with emerging economies in South and South-east Asia, as well as Australia and New Zealand. To facilitate the so-called "New Southbound Policy" (新南向政策), the government has already adopted several new measures to realign Taiwan's role in Asian development (New Southbound Policy Official Website 2017). These new strategic views are actually very close to those of former President Lee, whose "Southward Policy" (南向政策) similarly endeavoured to expand economic ties with South-east Asia in the early 1990s. The policy was further continued by President Chen, whereas the Ma administration has also maintained an upward trend in the trade exchanges between Taiwan and South and South-east Asian countries. Therefore, many have remained sceptical, doubting that the new policy can bear any fresh fruit (*China Post* 2016; Chung 2016). Undeniably, Beijing's "One Belt, One Road" (OBOR or also "Belt and Road Initiative," BRI), and the AIIB initiatives will only increase the Chinese presence and influence in the region. As the recent cases in Central Asia and Europe have shown, Chinese alluring transportation infrastructure deals and port investments have increased economic dependence on China and made local governments even more restrained and cautious.[12] Furthermore, Chinese officials have already accused Taiwan's new policy of being politically motivated and serving as a means to promote independence, what President Tsai has firmly denied (An 2017; Taiwan Affairs Office, 2017). Tensions that could additionally hinder the new policy might also arise from the sovereignty claims over the South China Sea. The ROC claims the Pratas Islands (Dongsha, 東沙), the Spratly Islands (Nansha 南沙), Xisha Islands (西沙), Macclesfield Bank (Zhongsha, 中沙) and their surrounding waters. In the aftermath of the UN Tribunal's verdict on the South China Sea arbitration case in July 2016, the Tsai government declared it does not accept it and reiterated that the South China Sea Islands are part of the territory of the ROC. By bolstering the ROC claims, President Tsai signalled she will continue her predecessor's policy and gave the priority consideration to a stable cross-Strait relationship. Nevertheless, since five other South-east Asian nations also claim parts of the sea, any serious maritime tension would hamper the progress made by the New Southbound Policy in these five countries.

Therefore, Taiwan might need to overcome even higher hurdles to reach its economic and political goals in the region. The Tsai administration believes, that since this time the emphasis of the Southbound Policy will be laid on the people and interaction of the grassroots – nurturing talent, developing a network of relationships and encouraging bilateral industrial, agricultural, trade, cultural, educational and tourism exchanges (i.e. by the means of visa entry privileges) – the policy will more likely translate into bigger success (*Taipei Times* 2016c). One year on, the official statistical data reflect the initiative is indeed bearing fruit. The Ministry of Finance statistics show exports to the 18 countries covered by the New Southbound Policy surged 20.1 per cent year on year to US$5.37 billion in December 2016. The statistics gathered by the Taiwan Tourism Bureau also shows that the number of visitors from the targeted countries increased 42.8 per cent year on year in January 2017 (*Taiwan Today* 2017b). The number is likely to continue growing, and is expected to make up for the reduced number of Chinese visitors to Taiwan (*Taiwan Today* 2017c). The Ministry of Education's financial investment for programmes to advance education ties under the new policy is also expected to bring an annual 20 per cent growth in the number of students from the 18 countries coming to Taiwan from 2017 until 2020, which is all very encouraging (Chen 2017).

Conclusion

Owing to Taiwan's precarious and ambiguous political status, a strong international presence has always been a high priority for the government in Taipei. Accordingly, Taiwan's foreign policy ends are unlikely to change upon any new shift in power. Nevertheless, the foreign policy means toward finding a solution for overcoming Taiwan's diplomatic challenges can change. Since major problems that Taiwan confronts in conducting foreign affairs are all related to China (its national security, its relationship with the US and Japan, its formal and informal ties with the global community, etc.), Beijing has the power to impose serious constraints in order to intimidate Taiwan and affect the status quo. In spite of the unprecedented détente in China–Taiwan relations since 2008, key facets of the relationship have remained unchanged. All of the deeply rooted problems and mistrust between Taipei and Beijing have not disappeared whereas incidents in cultural, academic, sports and other non-political international events in which both Taiwanese and Chinese participate have continued unabated. As the current status quo means that Taiwan cannot join international organizations as a nation, obtaining an observer status will continue to be an utmost achievement for the new government in Taipei. Accordingly, the new administration's diplomacy essentially does not differ much from the approaches applied in the past. The Tsai government has continued President Ma's approach of not pursuing a UN seat nor seeking full membership in UN-affiliated agencies, as witnessed at the 2016 and 2017 sessions of the UN General Assembly. Taipei reaffirmed it will only endeavour for "meaningful participation" in UN bodies. A highly cautious approach was also affirmed by the Tsai delegation's "Chinese Taipei" rhetoric during the 2016 WHA speech. Nevertheless, as Beijing's relentless opposition of Taiwan's attendance at, not just the WHA, but even mid-level functional organizations like ICAO or INTERPOL to date has shown, even the objective of meaningful participation will not be easy to achieve. Beijing made it clear that adherence to the "one-China policy" was a "prerequisite" for Taiwan to participate in any international activity (Hsu 2016). Therefore, raising the level of international support to offset China's pressure will be one of the most crucial tasks for the Tsai administration. Without stronger support from the global community, it is difficult to foresee any significant progress for the position of Taiwan. By the end of 2017, Xi Jinping (習近平), who is believed to be the most powerful leader in China since Mao Zedong (毛澤東) and Deng Xiaoping (鄧小平), will have begun his second term as China's president. As China continues to view unification with Taiwan as its core national objective, President Xi will do whatever it takes to prevent Taiwan taking any steps perceived to lead toward greater legal sovereignty and accomplish his goal to unify the country. Accordingly, the military and diplomatic pressure will continue to increase. Beijing has visibly intensified its moves to increase Taiwan's diplomatic isolation, while China's rising global influence and assertiveness have only heightened anxiety and intensified pressure on other governments to withhold support for Taiwan.

Due to escalating pressure, stronger ties between Taiwan and major non-diplomatic allies are now more important than ever. While the Ma administration significantly eased the cross-Strait tensions, the fast pace of interactions between Taiwan and China had also raised some eyebrows in both the US and Japan, Taiwan's two most important allies. A debate on whether or not the US should abandon Taiwan reoccurred among American experts (see Mearsheimer 2014), whereas Japan was visibly anxious when some politicians started to advocate that Beijing and Taipei should take joint actions to defend claims over the East China and South China Seas (Matsuda 2010). The Tsai administration considers relations with Japan as a diplomatic priority and in spite of their ongoing sovereignty dispute over the Senkaku/Diaoyutai Islands, the relations have palpably improved. In 2017, Japan officially changed the name of its de facto embassy from the "Interchange Association, Japan" to the "Japan–Taiwan Exchange Association", whereas Taiwan's Executive Yuan approved a change of name of its representative office from the Association of East Asian Relations to the Association of Taiwan–Japan Relations (Hsu 2017). In March 2017, a senior Japanese Cabinet member officially visited Taiwan, what was the highest-ranking Japanese government official visit to Taiwan since 1972, when Japan and Taiwan severed their diplomatic ties (*The Japan News* 2017). On the issue of Okinotori (沖ノ鳥) in the Philippine Sea, President Tsai, unlike her predecessor, opted not to seek a legal approach to refute Japan's claim that Okinotori is an island entitled to an EEZ and continental shelf, but instead resorted to negotiations with Tokyo to resolve differences over fishing rights.[13] Such an approach is enabling President Tsai to keep a low profile and is assuring Taiwan's relations with Japan would not be hampered. While it is still too early to foresee how relations between Taiwan and the US will evolve under the Donald Trump administration,[14] what is certain is, that for the Tsai administration, nurturing firm relations with the US will remain vital. The construction of a new compound of the American Institute in Taiwan (AIT), a representative office which will be protected by the US Marines, visibly demonstrates mutual commitment between the two allies (Yeh 2017).

To sum up, in its drive for global recognition, Taiwan will have to tread very carefully. The most realistic foreign policy goal for Taiwan is to uphold the current status quo in which Taiwan already enjoys autonomy and de facto independence. The new administration believes, that as long as the two sides avoid the issue over the interpretation of "one China", relations with Beijing will proceed on a regular pace, albeit more belligerently. Up to now, President Tsai has worked in low-key way and has given China little incentive to escalate pressure any further. Accordingly, pragmatic diplomacy will remain the cornerstone of Taipei's foreign policy and most likely there will not be any substantive changes in Taiwanese policy vis-à-vis international space. Hopefully, Beijing will recognize that coercion and suppression of Taiwan's presence on the world stage will only alienate Taiwanese further. Until this is not the case, the government in Taipei will need to invest a lot of energy into cultivating a robust internal and external support. Nevertheless, even though many nations, including the US, Germany, Japan and Australia, spoke up for Taiwan at the latest World Health Assemblies, Taiwan was still unable to attend them due to objections from Chinese authorities (Lee 2017). It is particularly bewildering, how despite the US substantial financial support of the key global IGOs, Washington had up to now no sufficient leverage to outmatch Chinese pressure and ensure Taiwan's participation (Stanton 2016). Hopefully, the international community will show stouter support and more creativity in forging greater space for Taiwan in the international arena. After all, issues of health, pollution, crime, terrorism and air-safety all transcend borders and should never be used for political leverage.

Notes

1 The full text of President Tsai's victory speech is available at: http://focustaiwan.tw/news/aipl/201601160053.aspx (accessed 16 January 2016).
2 The full text of President Tsai's inaugural address is available at: http://focustaiwan.tw/news/aipl/201605200008.aspx (accessed 20 May 2016).
3 President Chen pledged at his inaugural addresses on 20 May 2000 that, as long as the Chinese Communist Party regime has no intention to use military force against Taiwan, he would not declare independence, he would not change the national title, he would not include the doctrine of special state-to-state relations in the ROC Constitution, and he would not promote a referendum on independence or unification. In addition, he promised not to abolish the National Reunification Council or the National Reunification Guidelines (nevertheless, this promise was not kept because the former ceased to function and the latter ceased to apply in 2006).
4 The 1992 Consensus, a term the former Mainland Affairs Council chairman Su Chi (蘇起) admitted making up in 2000, refers to a tacit understanding between the KMT and the Chinese government that both sides of the Taiwan Strait acknowledge that there is "one China", with each side having its own interpretation of what "China" means.
5 According to a leaked US diplomatic cable, Beijing refused offers of diplomatic recognition from at least five of Taiwan's allies. Some have even claimed that 18 Taiwanese allies have been turning to Beijing's Foreign Ministry (Hsu 2015).
6 See note 1.
7 Since April 2016, almost 500 Taiwanese criminal suspects had been sent to China from countries including Malaysia, Cambodia, Vietnam and Armenia and most recently, a European Union member state, Spain.
8 The five organizations are: the Western and Central Pacific Fisheries Commission, the Inter-American Tropical Tuna Commission, the Commission for the Conservation of Southern Bluefin Tuna, the International Scientific Committee for Tuna and Tuna-like Species in the North Pacific Ocean, and the South Pacific Regional Fisheries Management Organization.
9 The 85th INTERPOL General Assembly was held in Indonesia on 7–10 November, 2016 and it was the first one since President Barack Obama signed a bill for the US government to help Taiwan gain observer status at Interpol, after Congress voted and approved it as Public Law 114–139 on March 18, 2016 (see Istenič 2016; *Taipei Times* 2016d).
10 See, among others, Jennings (2014); Huang (2016); Fulco (2016); Hsiao (2016); Jacobs (2016); Hickey (2016); and Matsumura (2016).
11 Recently, Beijing and the Vatican have started to discuss more actively toward resolving a core disagreement over who has the authority to select and ordain Catholic

bishops in China. Whether or not the discussions will pave the way to diplomatic relations is nevertheless, yet to be seen (Chiang 2017).

12 The Taiwan-based China Airlines (CAL) was forced to cancel 18 direct flights to Athens after Greek authorities refused to grant it a licence, presumably due to political considerations. Furthermore, some Polish journalists critical of China's human rights record were unable to receive proper accreditation to cover President Xi Jinping's visit to Poland. In Central Asia, Kyrgyz authorities had rejected Taiwan's NGO application to provide medical services this summer due to political interference by Beijing, as well as growing economic dependence on China (Cole 2016b, 2016c, 2016d).

13 The new government pledged it has no specific stance on Okinotori legally and will accordingly respect the ruling of the Commission on the Limits of the Continental Shelf (CLCS) under the UN on its legal status. Nevertheless, as the CLCS does not have jurisdiction to decide Okinotori's island/atoll status, issuing recommendation on Japan's claim has been indefinitely postponed (CNA 2016c; Lin 2016b).

14 President Trump managed to both raise and lower Taiwanese hopes as he broke decades-long US protocol by speaking with President Tsai directly, questioned the "one-China policy" dogmas but at the same time contributed to concerns that Taiwan might merely be a bargaining chip against China.

References

AFP (*Agence France Presse*) (2007). "U.S., China join forces to warn Taiwan over U.N. bid", 6 September.

An, D. (2017). "Wooing Southeast Asia: 'New Southbound Policy' meets 'Belt and Road Initiative'", *The Global Taiwan Brief*, 2 (22). Available at: http://globaltaiwan. org/2017/05/31-gtb-2-22/ (accessed 1 June 2017).

Cabestan, J. P. (2017). "Burkina Faso: Between Taiwan's active public diplomacy and China's business attractiveness", *South African Journal of International Affairs*, DOI: 10.1080/10220461.2016.1271746.

Chen, C. and Yang, S. M. (2016). "Taiwan officials forced out of UN fisheries meeting allegedly by China", *CNA*, 1 September. Available at: http://focustaiwan.tw/news/ aipl/201609210017.aspx (accessed 1 September 2016).

Chen, C. H., Wen, K. H. and Hsu, E. (2016). "Gambia case seen as warning to Taiwan's president-elect", *CNA*, 18 March. Available at: http://focustaiwan.tw/news/acs/201603 180011.aspx (accessed 10 May 2016).

Chen, W. H. (2016). "NPP takes aim at invite, three agencies", *Taipei Times*, 11 May Available at: www.taipeitimes.com/News/taiwan/archives/2016/05/11/2003646001 (accessed 17 May 2016).

Chen, W. H. (2017). "Luring students becoming more difficult: Cabinet", *Taipei Times*, 10 March. Available at: www.taipeitimes.com/News/taiwan/archives/2017/03/10/ 2003666489 (accessed 16 March 2017).

Chiang, H. C. (2017). "New view on issues of diplomacy", *Taipei Times*, 12 January. Available at: www.taipeitimes.com/News/editorials/archives/2017/01/12/2003662933 (accessed 16 March 2017).

China Post (2016). "New Southward Policy must go beyond chasing white elephants", *China Post*, 19 May. Available at: www.chinapost.com.tw/editorial/taiwan-issues/2016/ 05/19/466600/p2/New-Southward.htm (accessed 19 May 2016).

Chung, J. and Huang, F. (2016). "LINE tops other social media among Taiwanese smart-phone owners", *CNA*, 2 February. Available at: http://focustaiwan.tw/news/ast/ 201602020027.aspx (accessed 18 May 2016).

Chung, L. (2016). "Don't make us suffer even more, Taiwanese businessmen on Chinese mainland tell president-elect Tsai Ing-wen", *South China Morning Post*, 21 February. Available at: www.scmp.com/news/china/policies-politics/article/1915118/dont-make-us-suffer-even-more-taiwanese-businessmen (accessed 16 May 2016).

Chung, L. H. and Chin, J. (2017). "Apply for WHO membership: groups", *Taipei Times*, 8 March. Available at: www.taipeitimes.com/News/taiwan/archives/2017/03/08/2003666350 (accessed 8 March 2017).

CNA (2016a). "Former FM warns of potential crisis of Taiwan's international room", 20 March. Available at: http://focustaiwan.tw/news/aipl/201603200008.aspx (accessed 12 May 2016).

CNA (2016b). "Foreign minister-designate watching for diplomatic war with China", 16 May. Available at: http://focustaiwan.tw/news/aipl/201605160016.aspx (accessed 16 May 2016).

CNA (2016c). "New government's stance on Okinotori questioned", 24 May. Available at: http://focustaiwan.tw/news/aipl/201605240017.aspx (accessed 24 May 2016).

Cole, J. M. (2016a). "Taiwanese Paralympians forced to wear KMT emblem after China pressured officials", *The News Lens*, 20 September. Available at: https://international.thenewslens.com/article/49626 (accessed 20 September 2016).

Cole, J. M. (2016b). "Politics behind Athens' denial of license to China Airlines", *The News Lens*, 14 June. Available at: http://international.thenewslens.com/article/41927 (accessed 16 June 2016).

Cole, J. M. (2016c). "Polish journalists denied accreditation due to Chinese pressure", 1 July. Available at: http://international.thenewslens.com/article/43329 (accessed 1 July 2016).

Cole, J. M. (2016d). "Citing 'One China,' Kyrgyzstan bans all contact with Taiwan", *The News Lens*, 20 June. Available at: http://international.thenewslens.com/article/42360 (accessed 20 June 2016).

Cole, J. M. (2017). "Beijing leans on Nigeria to 'fully implement' 'One China' policy, avoid 'Two Chinas'", *Taiwan Sentinel*, 23 March. Available at: https://sentinel.tw/beijing-nigeria-one-china/ (accessed 23 March 2017).

Copper, J. F. (2008). "Taiwan's Failed President", *Asian Affairs* 34(4): 172–192.

DPP (2014). *2014 China Policy Review: Summary Report*, 9 January. Taipei: DPP China Affairs Department.

Election Study Center (2016). "Trends in core political attitudes among Taiwanese",' N.C.C.U., 24 August. Available at: http://esc.nccu.edu.tw/course/news.php?class=203 (accessed 23 March 2017).

Fulco, M. (2016). "Taiwan's diplomatic dilemma", *AmCham Taipei*, 17 February. Available at: http://topics.amcham.com.tw/2016/02/taiwans-diplomatic-dilemma-2 (accessed 16 March 2017).

Gerber, A. (2016a). "Student rails against 'stateless' ID", *Taipei Times*, 20 November. Available at: www.taipeitimes.com/News/front/archives/2016/11/20/2003659621 (accessed 16 March 2017).

Gerber, A. (2016b). "Efforts to condemn WHO letter fail", *Taipei Times*, 17 May. Available at: www.taipeitimes.com/News/taiwan/archives/2016/05/17/2003646459 (accessed 17 May 2016).

Harrison, M. (2016). "How the digital age changed Taiwan", *APPS Policy Forum*, 18 February. Available at: www.policyforum.net/how-the-digital-age-changed-taiwan/ (accessed 19 May 2016).

Her, K. (2016). "Viable approach to diplomacy", *Taiwan Today*, 1 April. Available at: http://taiwantoday.tw/ct.asp?xItem=243116&ctNode=2235&mp=9 (accessed 12 May 2016).

Hickey, D. (2016) "Taiwan's diplomatic partners in the global community: the big influence of small allies", paper delivered at the 2016 Annual Conference of the EATS, Czech Academy of Sciences, Prague, 30 March–1 April.

Hsiao, A. (2016) "Stop 'bickering,' Tsai urges KMT" *Taipei Times*, 2 January. Available at: www.taipeitimes.com/News/front/archives/2016/01/02/2003636227.

Hsiao, A. (2017). "Saint Lucia relationship 'under control': minister", *Taipei Times*, 8 March. Available at: www.taipeitimes.com/News/taiwan/archives/2017/03/08/2003666351 (accessed 8 March 2017).

Hsu, S. (2015). "Taiwan's allies fleeing to China: KMT", *Taipei Times*, 29 December. Available at: www.taipeitimes.com/News/taiwan/archives/2015/12/29/2003635936 (accessed 28 April 2016).

Hsu, S. (2016). "MAC urges China to show goodwill", *CNA*, 22 September. Available at: www.taipeitimes.com/News/taiwan/archives/2016/09/22/2003655684 (accessed 22 September 2016).

Hsu, S. (2017). "Taiwan–Japan relations are a priority: president", *Taipei Times*, 21 March. Available at: www.taipeitimes.com/News/taiwan/archives/2017/03/21/2003667178 (accessed 21 March 2017).

Hsu, S. and Hsiao, A. (2016). "Taiwan rejected from OECD meeting", *Taipei Times*, 20 April. Available at: www.taipeitimes.com/News/front/archives/2016/04/20/2003644360/2 (accessed 16 May 2016).

Huang, K. B. (2016). "Tsai's diplomatic dilemmas", *East Asia Forum*, 20 January. Available at: www.eastasiaforum.org/2016/01/20/tsais-diplomatic-dilemmas/ (accessed 22 September 2016).

Istenič, S. (2016). "Taiwan's exclusion from Interpol and implications for global security", paper presented at the 12th Annual Conference on The Taiwan Issue in China–Europe Relations, 21–22 September. SIIS: Shanghai.

Jacobs, B. "Leaders misunderstand global ties", *Taipei Times*, 8 January. Available at: www.taipeitimes.com/News/editorials/archives/2016/01/08/2003636675 (accessed 22 September 2016).

Jennings, R. (2014). "Taiwan can afford to lose more diplomatic allies", *Forbes*, 11 June. Available at: www.forbes.com/sites/ralphjennings/2014/06/11/taiwan-can-afford-to-lose-more-diplomatic-allies/#7cdd1a792086 (accessed 22 September 2016).

Lam, W. (2016). "Is 2049 Beijing's 'deadline' for taking over Taiwan?" *Global Taiwan Brief*, 1(1), 21 September. Available at: http://globaltaiwan.org/2016/09/21-gtb-1-1/#WillyLam092116 (accessed 21 September 2016).

Lee, W. (2016). "China resumes ties with São Tomé in blow to Taiwan", *Taiwan News*, 26 December. Available at: www.taiwannews.com.tw/en/news/3058228 (accessed 16 March 2017).

Lin, S. (2016a). "Ko says Beijing's pressure might provoke backlash", *Taipei Times*, 11 May. Available at: www.taipeitimes.com/News/taiwan/archives/2016/05/11/2003646003 (accessed 17 May 2016).

Lin, T. H. (2016b). "Okinotori: a new beginning for Taiwan–Japan maritime dialogue", *AMTI CSIS*, 17 June. Available at: https://amti.csis.org/okinotori-new-beginning-taiwan-japan-maritime-dialogue/ (accessed 17 June 2016).

Mainland Affairs Council (2005). "Taipei's olive branches". Available at: www.mac.gov.tw/public/MMO/RPIR/book388.pdf (accessed 16 May 2016).

Malkin, E. (2017). "Taiwan works to keep its Central America friends (among its few)", *New York Times*, 13 January. Available at: www.nytimes.com/2017/01/13/world/americas/taiwan-president-tsai-central-america-china.html?_r=0 (accessed 16 March 2017).

Matsuda, Y. (2010). "Improved cross-Strait relations confusing to the Japanese", *Asia Pacific Bulletin*, 47. Washington, DC: East-West Center.

Matsumura, M. (2016) "Losing allies but winning the 'war'", *Taipei Times*, 23 March. Available at: www.taipeitimes.com/News/editorials/archives/2016/03/23/2003642214.

Mearsheimer, J. J. (2014). "Taiwan's dire straits", *The National Interest*, 130 (March/April), pp. 29–39.

Ministry of Foreign Affairs, Republic of China (Taiwan) (2017). "國際組織參與現狀 *Guojizuzhi canyu xiankuang*". Available at: www.mofa.gov.tw/igo/cp.aspx?n=DED5DAB0D6C7BED6 (accessed 16 March 2017).

Munro, K. (2017). "'Disgusting' and 'extraordinary' scenes as Chinese delegation shouts down welcome ceremony", *Sydney Morning Herald*, 3 May. Available at: www.smh.com.au/federal-politics/political-news/disgusting-and-extraordinary-scenes-as-chinese-delegation-shouts-down-welcome-ceremony-20170502-gvxbou.html (accessed 3 May 2017).

Newcomb, M. (2017). "Deportations and Taiwan's threatened international space", *Global Taiwan Brief*, 2 (11).

New Southbound Policy Official Website (2017). www.newsouthboundpolicy.tw (accessed 16 March 2017).

Rickards, J. (2008). "$30 million lost in diplomatic scandal, Taiwan says", *Washington Post*, 4 May. Available at: www.washingtonpost.com/wp-dyn/content/article/2008/05/03/AR2008050301600.html (accessed 19 May 2016).

Ross, R. S. (2006). "Explaining Taiwan's revisionist diplomacy", *Journal of Contemporary China*, 15(48): 443–458.

Scott, B., Shi, T. and Ibukun, Y. (2017). "Nigeria snubs Taiwan as China pledges $40 billion investment", *Bloomberg*, 12 January. Available at: www.bloomberg.com/politics/articles/2017-01-12/nigeria-closes-taiwan-office-in-capital-abuja-china-says (accessed 16 March 2017).

Shan, S. (2017). "Emirates Airline retracts flag pin directive", *Taipei Times*, 1 June. Available at: www.taipeitimes.com/News/front/archives/2017/06/01/2003671679 (accessed 1 June 2017).

Soumy, P. (2017). "Hun Sen bans Taiwan flag from Cambodia", *Cambodia Daily*, 6 February. Available at: www.cambodiadaily.com/news/hun-sen-bans-taiwan-flag-from-cambodia-124609/ (accessed 16 March 2017).

South China Morning Post (2016). "Beijing threatens to suspend talks with Taipei until Tsai Ing-wen acknowledges '1992 Consensus'", 21 May. Available at: www.scmp.com/news/china/policies-politics/article/1949425/beijing-threatens-suspend-talks-taipei-until-tsai-ing (accessed 21 May 2016).

Stanton, W. (2016). "What should US policy toward Taiwan be under the Trump Administration?", *Global Taiwan Brief* 1(11). Available at: http://globaltaiwan.org/2016/11/30-gtb-1-11/#WilliamStanton113016 (accessed 16 March 2017).

Strohecker K. (2015). "São Tomé signs memorandum with China on deep-sea port", *Reuters*, 12 October. Available at: http://af.reuters.com/article/saoTomeNews/idAFL8N12B12220151012 (accessed 16 March 2017).

Su, C. (2009). *Taiwan's Relations with Mainland China: A Tail Wagging Two Dogs*, New York: Routledge.

Taipei Times (2015). "Taiwan will join China-led AIIB under Chinese Taipei name or not at all: Ma", 5 July. Available at: www.taipeitimes.com/News/taiwan/archives/2015/07/05/2003622312 (accessed 16 May 2016).

Taipei Times (2016a). "Government gives up AIIB application for 'dignity'", 13 April. Available at: www.taipeitimes.com/News/front/archives/2016/04/13/2003643828 (accessed 16 May 2016).

Taipei Times (2016b). "INTERVIEW: Tsai's cross-strait policy to rest on democratic will", 22 January. Available at: www.taipeitimes.com/News/front/archives/2016/01/22/2003637766 (accessed 16 May 2016).

Taipei Times (2016c). "Ex-minister touts southbound policy", 18 May. Available at: www.taipeitimes.com/News/taiwan/print/2016/05/18/2003646534 (accessed 18 May 2016).

Taipei Times (2016d). "Obama inks bill supporting Interpol bid", 20 March. Available at: www.taipeitimes.com/News/front/archives/2016/03/20/2003641989 (accessed 16 May 2016).

Taipei Times (2016e). "EDITORIAL: Shutting overseas offices unwise", 23 September. Available at: www.taipeitimes.com/News/editorials/archives/2016/09/23/2003655733 (accessed 23 September 2016).

Taiwan Affairs Office (國臺辦), (2017). "維護一個中國原則有利于臺灣參與區域經濟合作 [Safeguarding One China Principle benefits Taiwan's regional economic cooperation]", 25 May. Available at: www.gwytb.gov.cn/wyly/201605/t20160525_11466770.htm (accessed 25 May 2017).

Taiwan Today (2017a). "ROC passport secures 28th place in global ranking", 17 January. Available at: http://taiwantoday.tw/news.php?post=110442&unit=10 (accessed 16 March 2017).

Taiwan Today (2017b). "New Southbound Policy pays handsome trade, education dividends", 17 January. Available at: http://taiwantoday.tw/news.php?post=110410&unit=6 (accessed 16 March 2017).

Taiwan Today (2017c). "New Southbound Policy boosts tourist numbers", 16 March. Available at: http://taiwantoday.tw/news.php?post=112677&unit=6 (accessed 16 March 2017).

The Japan News (2017). "Senior Cabinet member pays official visit to Taiwan", 25 March. Available at: http://the-japan-news.com/news/article/0003600328 (accessed 26 March 2017).

Tseng, E. and Lee, H. Y. (2016). "Taiwan achieves realistic participation in U.N. climate conference: EPA", CNA. Available at: http://focustaiwan.tw/search/201611200004.aspx?q=cop22 (accessed March 2017).

Tubilewicz, C. (2016). "State transformation and the domestic politics of foreign aid in Taiwan", *The Pacific Review*, 29(1): 45–66.

UNFCCC (2016). http://unfccc.int/parties_and_observers/ngo/items/9411.php (accessed 16 May 2016).

WHO (2016a). "WHO, IHR List of Authorized ports to issue Ship Sanitation Certificates". Available at: www.who.int/ihr/ports_airports/ihr_authorized_ports_list.pdf (accessed 12 May 2016).

WHO (2016b). *Global Health Atlas*, http://apps.who.int/globalatlas/dataQuery/default.asp (accessed 12 May 2016).

Xinhua Net (2016). "President Xi warns against 'Taiwan independence' in any form", 5 March. Available at: http://news.xinhuanet.com/english/2016-03/05/c_135159249.htm (accessed 16 May 2016).

Yeh, J. (2016). "MOFA 'respects' the silence of allies at UN assembly", *The China Post*, 29 September. Available at: www.chinapost.com.tw/taiwan/foreign-affairs/2016/09/29/479681/MOFA-respects.htm (accessed 29 September 2016).

Yeh, J. (2017). "US Marines to be stationed at new AIT building in Taipei: former director", *The China Post*, 17 February. Available at: www.chinapost.com.tw/taiwan/intl-community/2017/02/17/491791/US-Marines.htm (accessed 16 March 2017).

Index

Page numbers in **bold** denote tables, those in *italics* denote figures.